AF704744

PROGRAMMING YOUR OWN ADVENTURE GAMES IN PASCAL

No. 1768
$19.95

PROGRAMMING YOUR OWN ADVENTURE GAMES IN PASCAL

BY RICHARD C. VILE, JR.

TAB TAB BOOKS Inc.
BLUE RIDGE SUMMIT, PA. 17214

FIRST EDITION

FIRST PRINTING

Copyright© 1984 by TAB BOOKS Inc.
Printed in the United States of America

Reproduction or publication of the content in any manner, without express permission of the publisher, is prohibited. No liability is assumed with respect to the use of the information herein.

Library of Congress Cataloging in Publication Data

Vile, Richard C., 1943-
Programming your own adventure games in Pascal
Includes index.
1. Computer games. 2. PASCAL (Computer program language) I. Title.
GV1469.2.V55 1984 794.8′2 84-8577
ISBN 0-8306-0768-4
ISBN 0-8306-1768-X (pbk.)

Cover illustration by Larry Selman

Contents

Introduction viii

1 **The Elements of Adventure Games** 1
Rooms or Locations—Objects and Treasures—Beings and Monsters—Problems

2 **Notations for Describing Adventures** 5
Rooms or Locations—Travel Indicators—Problems—Objects—Beings and Monsters—Embellishing the Map—Map Layout and Organization—Examples

3 **Adventures and Problem Solving** 8
Clues to Problem Solutions—Problem Difficulty: From the Obvious to the Obscure—Repeatability—Logic—Surprise

4 **UCSD Pascal Review** 12
What You Should Know about Pascal—What Is the UCSD System?

5 **Preview of Adventure 1** 15
Preview Chapters—Preview of Adventure 1—Chapter Previews

6 **Pascal Adventure 1** 23
Listing 6-1. Pascal Miniadventure

7 **Representing the Map** 54
Representing the Adventure Map—Enumerated Types in Pascal

8 **Controlling the Play** 59
Case Statements in Pascal—Controlling the Adventure Game

9 **Mazes in the Middle** 63
Local Declarations—Local Procedures and Functions

10 **Other Techniques Used in Adventure 1** 66

11 **Preview of Adventure 2** 68
Maps, Diagrams, and Code Outlines—Chapter Previews

12 **Pascal Adventure 2** 78

13 **Command Processing in Adventure 2** 115
An Overview of the Command Handling Code—Command Processing in Detail

14 **Carry and Drop: Pascal Sets** 125
What Are Sets and How Can They Be Used?

15 **Problems in Adventure 2** 130
Events—Boolean Expressions and Events—Problems in Adventure 2

16 **Other Techniques Used in Adventure 2** 135
Counting Turns—Displaying the Contents of a Set—Simplification of Travel—The Use of File Variables—Scoring Your Adventures—The Help Command—The Lamp and the Light Command—The Dig Command—The Eat Command—The Ogre

17 **UCSD Pascal Development Techniques** 139
Managing Your Files Effectively—UCSD System Tricks and Pitfalls

18 **Preview of MAKEDESC and BROWSE** 145
Database Concepts—Previews of Chapters 19 through 24

19 **MAKEDESC and BROWSE** 147
Listing 19-1. Make80 Database Generator—Listing 19-2. Browse80 Database Snooper

20 **Creating a Database of Descriptions** 166
MAKEDESC: The Descriptions Generator—How to Use MAKEDESC Instruction Lines—Ditto Lines—Continuation File Lines—Running MAKEDESC

21 **Random Access Files in UCSD Pascal** 173
What Are Random and Sequential Files?—The File Creating Program—The File Reading Program—Random Access—The BROWSE Program—Using Descriptions Databases in Your Adventures

22 **The Structure of Adventure Databases** 177
Index Files and the Descriptions Index—Using the Descriptions Databases in Adventure Games—The BROWSE Program for Previewing Databases

23 **Programming Techniques Used in MAKEDESC** 182
Symbol Tables—Lookup Techniques: The Linear Search—Hashing: A More Efficient Search Technique—The Hash Table Lookup Technique

24 **What Else Can You Put on Disk?** 190
Other Descriptions—Putting the Whole Program on Disk: Adventure Interpreters

25 **Preview of Adventure 3** 192
Outlines, Diagrams, and Maps—Chapter Previews

26 **The Listings of Adventure 3** 203
Listing 26-1. Adventure 3 Main Program—Listing 26-2. Location Procedure Unit—Listing 26-3. Commands 1 Unit—Listing 26-4. Commands 2 Unit—Listing 26-5. Commands 3 Unit—Listing 26-6. Problems Unit—Listing 26-7. Adventure 3 Data

27 **Larger Programs: Using UCSD Units** 239
Why Units?—The Units in Adventure 3—Units: Syntax and Semantics—Linking Programs that Have Units—Maintaining a Program Written with Units

28 **Problems in Adventure 3** 245
The Probs Unit—The Problems in Adventure 3—Implementing Adventure 3 Problems

29 **Other Techniques Used in Adventure 3** 250
Putting More into the Database—Coding Techniques to Get Around UCSD Limitations—Trickery in Showgoodies

30 **Writing Your Own Adventures** 254
Extending Adventure 3—Using a Skeleton Adventure—A Systematic Approach to Writing Adventures—Farewell

Appendix A Skeleton Adventure Program 261

Appendix B The Adventure 2 Database 286

Appendix C The Adventure 3 Database 292

Index 304

Introduction

Welcome to the world of adventure games and Pascal. The purpose of this book is to teach you how to use the Pascal programming language to create adventure games on your home computer. I shall cover topics related both to the design and creation of the games themselves and to the style and use of the Pascal language. I shall concentrate on the style of adventure game referred to as a *text adventure.* I shall use the UCSD implementation of Pascal, which is widely available on microcomputers.

ADVENTURE GAMES

Adventure originated in the 1970s. The first adventure was a game written by Don Woods and Willie Crowther. The language used was FORTRAN and the computer used was a PDP-10, a mainframe computer common in universities and research laboratories. The game was an exercise in problem solving, artificial intelligence, and simulation. The main goal of the original adventure was to be a problem-solving exercise.

The original adventure found its way onto many different computer installations. Since it was written in FORTRAN, people moved it to other computers besides the PDP-10. It was rewritten in other FORTRAN dialects and in other languages as well. In the early 1980s, it first became available for microcomputers. Microsoft, Inc. as well as other software companies adapted the game for use on personal microcomputers such as the Apple II and the TRS-80.

Since the advent of adventure on microcomputers, an entire subindustry of adventure game software producers has been created. Many companies created and sold adventures in the spirit of the original adventure. Most notable of these is probably the series of games known as Zork. Zork was also originally written on a large computer. The authors, several M.I.T. students, created a company called Infocom and began marketing Zork and its descendants.

A programmer from Stromberg-Carlson in Florida, Scott Adams, created a system for writing adventure games on the TRS-80. He published an article in *Creative Computing* magazine describing the system and went on to create and market several of his own adventure games. These games and Adams' company, Adventure International have become industry standards.

A company in California, now known as Sierra On-Line Systems, created several unusual adventures for the Apple II. What made these adventures unusual was that they used the Apple high-resolution graphics display to show the player a picture of each location in the adventure as it was reached. Thus, textual descriptions and creative prose was replaced by graphics artistry. Several companies have now started writing and marketing adventure games in this style. Such adventures are referred to as *hi-res adventures* in honor of the original implementation.

Several adventure games that mimic the style and approach of the noncomputerized Dungeons and Dragons fantasy role-playing games are available. Dungeons and Dragons was admittedly the inspiration for the original adventure. However, the style of original adventure was unlike that of D and D. In the D and D style games characters are created or "rolled." (The terminology is derived from the fact that several different kinds of dice are used in the character creation process.) The characters have attributes such as strength, intelligence, wisdom, and charisma, with numerical values attached. These attributes play an integral part in the progress of the game.

In this book I will deal strictly with text-style adventures in the spirit of original adventure. The emphasis will be on the creation and solving of interesting problems. The nature of adventure game problems is discussed in detail. The methods of representing and handling problems using Pascal programming techniques are given extensive coverage in the text. It is my belief that the scope for creativity in text adventures is great. There are as many adventures out there waiting to be invented as there are adventure and fantasy novels waiting to be written. The range of possibilities is limited only by your imagination and your programming skills.

PASCAL

After BASIC, Pascal is the most popular programming language available for personal and microcomputers. It has been called by some the "language of the 80s." Since its creation in the late 1960s, it has spread throughout the world, growing in popularity and acceptance each year. When a committee was formed in late 1979 to investigate the standardization of the language, it attracted the attention of many of the leading companies in the computer and electronics fields. The interest in obtaining a language standard was almost unprecedented in the computer field.

In addition to being popular, Pascal is excellent for programming. Adventure game writing in Pascal is a satisfying experience as I hope to demonstrate. The features of the language greatly simplify the process of translating an adventure game into computer form. The existence of the set as a primitive data type in the Pascal language makes implementing the carry and drop commands almost a snap. That is just one example. Many more will appear during the course of our investigation.

Even though Pascal has been standardized by the International Standards Organization through the efforts of the British Standards Institute, the Joint ANSI/IEEE Pascal Committee in the United States, and computer standards committees in many other countries, there remain a large number of incompatible implementations of the language. In the microcomputer world, one implementation in particular has become immensely popular. That is the UCSD (University of California at San Diego) Pascal P-System implementation. It is not just a translator for the Pascal language, but an entire software development environment for use on micro and minicomputers. I shall use the UCSD implementation for all the examples in this book. If you use a different version of Pascal, you may have to make minor changes to implement the programs found here.

I am going to assume that you are familiar with Pascal. You should know how to write Pascal programs and should have written at least one or two of your own. You should have a textbook or reference that you can consult regarding matters of language syntax. I shall not attempt to teach the Pascal language from the ground up. There is a discussion of prerequisites in more detail in Chapter 4.

As you read this book, you will learn new programming techniques in Pascal. You should study the sample programs carefully—reading programs is almost as good a way to learn programming as writing programs is. Then you should reread the programs and try modifying them in simple ways. Finally, you should attempt to write your own adventure games using the techniques described.

ORGANIZATION OF THE BOOK

The book itself consists of five sections:

1. Adventure Game Concepts and Design—Chapters 1-5.
2. Adventure 1: Simple Pascal for Adventure Games—Chapters 6-11.
3. Adventure 2: A Complete Adventure Game in Pascal—Chapters 12-18.
4. MAKEDESC and BROWSE: A Simple Database for Adventure Games—Chapters 19-25.
5. Adventure 3: Advanced Adventure Game Techniques in Pascal—Chapters 26-30.

Section 1 deals with general adventure game ideas. You should read it regardless of your level of experience in Pascal. Chapter 4 tells you about Pascal and the UCSD system and should help you decide how much you need to know before starting serious study of the book.

If you are a beginner at Pascal, you should read all the sections carefully. If you are an intermediate Pascal programmer—you have taken a course in the language or have programmed in Pascal for at least a year—you may skim Section 2 and start reading in detail in Section 3. If you are an experienced Pascal programmer—two years or more of programming in the language—you may skim Sections 2 and 3 and start serious study with Section 4. If you have some UCSD experience, you may not need to read Chapter 17, which deals with the effective use of the UCSD system for developing Pascal programs.

The appendices of the book treat miscellaneous topics and include listings of the text of the descriptions databases used in Adventures 2 and 3.

1

The Elements of Adventure Games

In this chapter, I will discuss some of the ingredients necessary for creating adventure games. I will concentrate on games in the style of the original adventure; however, the techniques I describe apply to any adventure game.

A typical adventure game contains certain key stylistic ingredients that stamp it as an adventure. Among these are the following:

- Rooms or Locations

  Part of the raison d'etre of adventure is to explore a cave or similar adventure territory. Hence the rooms of the cave or the locations of the adventure territory and their interconnections form an important part in the design of the adventure.

- Objects and Treasures

  Most adventure games contain treasures. One of the objectives of these games is to locate the treasures and bring them to some "safe" place in the game map. Creating interesting treasures and hiding them in unusual ways adds to the excitement of inventing and playing new adventures.

  In addition to treasures, other objects may play a part in a typical adventure. For example, in the original adventure there are many objects that are not treasures but are necessary in order to make progress in the game. In this game, for example, both a little bird and a cage must be dealt with. It is the adventure writer's obligation to constantly invent new twists to the nature and use of objects.

- Beings and Monsters

  Adventure games usually contain other beings that the player may encounter. Usually these beings are adversaries, such as the fierce green snake, the troll, the dragon, and the pirate of the original adventure. However, there is absolutely no reason why a being in an adventure game could not be an ally as well as an adversary.

- Special conditions and Problems to solve.

  Part of the difficulty in winning adventure games lies in the problems that are incorporated. The player does not merely locate the treasure, carry it out, and win! On the contrary, various obstacles must be overcome. Many times dealing with these obstacles is a prerequisite even to locating a given treasure. Here is where the full scope of creativity and originality come into play in making a good adventure.

  There are various styles of "problems" in adventure games. Some players relish a fight in which there are odds of losing—for example, the dwarfs in original adventure, who, if you are careless, can kill you. On the other hand, some players prefer a strictly logical challenge—problems that can be solved totally with the intellect and involve no chance factors at all.

Now that I have enumerated the typical components of an adventure game, I will go into more detail in each category. The discussions below are intended to start your own creative processes going. They are not intended as a stock from which you merely choose a new combination to create your own adventure. To be truly successful at writing adventure games, in Pascal or whatever language, you must exercise your own individual creative powers. A definition of creativity that I especially like is the following:

To be creative—look around you at what everybody else is doing. Then don't do that!

ROOMS OR LOCATIONS

The classical environment for an adventure game is an underground warren of caves, tunnels, or mazes. There is something romantic about exploring an underground empire, looking for treasure. Many variations on the cave theme are possible. It is still possible to be creative by inventing new and unusual rooms. To take an analogy from music, Bach, Mozart, and Beethoven all used the same musical scales and keys to create their musical works. However, each composer produced art that was radically different from the other. There are many underground worlds still left to be invented that are as different from original adventure as Beethoven was from Bach!

What then are some general guidelines for creating the rooms of a new adventure? Let us consider a few:

Make Sure There is Variety. There should be a difference in character from one location to the next in a good adventure. There should be large rooms and small rooms. There should be rooms with lots of interest and others that are merely stops along the way. There should be objects spread around in a variety of rooms. It is probably a bad idea to put all the objects in one or two locations that are off in some distant and obscure corner of the map. The player of an adventure game likes to see progress being made.

By the same token, not all locations should be easy to find. Not all objects and treasures should be located right out in the open. Thus, even when the player reaches a given room, there may still be aspects of that room that are only revealed after the player solves a problem or two.

A good adventure map will have large territories that are easily accessible. It will also have one or two "chunks" of locations that are separated from the rest of the map by a narrow access path. There are various ways to achieve this goal:

- Make the only entrance to the "chunk" via a room that has a large number of exits. This means that the player has to try a large number of exits before finding the right one.

- Guard the only entrance to the "chunk". That is, require that the player solve some sort of problem in order to gain access to the entrance. An example of this sort of approach is the use of the fierce green snake in original adventure. It guards the only passageway to a large part of the cave. The only way to get through is to dispose of the snake.

- Make the first part of the "chunk" dull and boring so that the player is less likely to explore further in that direction.

Require Exploration. Don't create rooms in which everything is obvious from the very first description. There should always be rooms in which it takes some work to find out everything there is to know about them. There are many ways to accomplish this end. Some of them will be described later in this chapter. Here are just a few of them.

- Require that a special command be given in order to obtain the full description of the room. There might be hints that this is necessary, either in the ordinary description of the room or in some other aspect of the game.

- Require that certain conditions be met before giving the full description of the room or its contents. For example, the adventurer might be forced to possess a certain object or have accomplished a certain goal before being able to fully discern the nature of a given room.

- Require the discovery of information about a room from someplace else in the adventure. For example, a se et map giving necessary information might be found somewhere totally remote from the location in question.

OBJECTS AND TREASURES

A typical adventure game has a myriad of treasures that must be located. It also has a variety of objects, some useful and some merely window dressing. To be different, you might try an adventure that has just a single treasure. But, usually it will be wise to stick to tradition. In order to invent interesting treasures to find, you must simply be creative. As mentioned above, this involves inventing treasures that no one else has used before. Likewise, there are millions of objects that have never played a role in an adventure game. So being creative should be easy!

It should go without saying, but let's say it anyway:

Treasures should have some value.

This need not be an intrinsic value, but might be value derived in some way from the circumstances of the game. For example, the game might be set in some imaginary kingdom in which dandelions were of inestimable value. In such a situation, dandelions would be a legitimate treasure. Of course, it would be up to you, the adventure writer, to establish the value of dandelions. By inventing imaginary worlds, anything could potentially become a treasure. The ring of truth comes from the manner in which you set about convincing the adventurer that something ordinary could be of value in an imaginary setting. There is considerable scope here for inventiveness. As a challenge, try imagining something that you would ordinarily consider totally outrageous in the role of a treasure. Then try to invent an adventure setting and a description that makes that something utterly invaluable.

Objects are even easier to deal with than treasures. There are no requirements at all concerning objects. An object may be present simply because you will it to be so. No other explanation is necessary. In fact, it is your obligation to have at least some objects that have no use in the game whatsoever. Unless, of course, you are a classical purist who requires that every element of a game have a purpose no matter how small. Most of us are not purists and are quite willing to populate our adventures with stray incidental artifacts. It makes the game more challenging: the adventurer must discover, by reason or chance, which objects are useful and which are not.

Hints for Inventing Objects and Treasures

- Browse through the dictionary and the encyclopedia. You will come across an amazing amount of material in these works.

- Play other adventure games. You may get ideas by enlarging on what has been done before. Try a new variation on old themes.

- Read fantasy and science fiction novels for ideas. Don't plagiarize, but let your mind roam and wander. Start with what you read and extend by making new hypotheses and asking "What if?"

BEINGS AND MONSTERS

Good fiction contains good characters. Good adventure games will have interesting creatures inhabiting them. Here again, you may allow your imagination to run wild as you dream up monsters and other creatures to put into your games.

There are some practical considerations here, however.

- Beings, in general, may move around from location to location. The creation of moving beings is generally more difficult than the creation of creatures that stay in one location throughout the game.

- Animate beings exhibit behavior. Places or locations do not. It is a great challenge to incorporate behavior and reactions of creatures in your game. Most adventure games are limited in this regard.

In this treatment, I will have creatures whose behavior patterns are somewhat limited. Doing a really serious job of simulating behavior would require that I delve into advanced topics such as artificial intelligence, which I do not have the space to do.

PROBLEMS

To many players, it is the problems in a good adventure game that provide the true pleasure of playing them. I shall devote an entire chapter to this topic as I proceed. One aim will be to discuss not only the ingredients that go into creating good problems, but also the programming techniques needed to bring problem solving to life in Pascal adventures.

2

Notations for Describing Adventures

When you are creating an adventure game, it helps to draw maps. The adventure map summarizes the game in a concise notation that helps keep you organized. In this chapter, I describe my own notation—the one that I use in the maps reproduced herein. You may end up adopting a system totally different than mine. That is perfectly acceptable. The idea is to have some way of describing your own adventure games.

ROOMS OR LOCATIONS

Most of any adventure map consists of the rooms or locations in the adventure. They should be laid out on paper in a rough representation of their "actual" geographic relationships. You obviously have to use some conventions here, especially for dealing with up and down.

Pick a standard symbol for representing a location and always write the name of the location inside the symbol. I like the hexagon or elongated hexagon shape for most rooms, with circles or ovals for maze rooms or other crowded locations. You may also choose to use different symbols depending on the nature of the location. For example, a rectangle, as opposed to a hexagon, might represent a room containing a treasure.

TRAVEL INDICATORS

Adventure locations would be quite uninteresting if it were not possible to travel between them. Adventure maps show ways to travel between locations. Each possible path of travel may be indicated by a bold line joining the two locations. Arrowheads at the ends of the lines may be used to indicate whether or not the direction of travel is reversible. The absence of an arrowhead means that it is not possible or permissible to travel along this route in the direction indicated by the missing arrowhead.

Directions are part of the descriptions used in the play of the game itself. Each line of travel should be marked with a direction indicator. The usual directions are limited to n, s, e, w, u, and d. Occasionally, a minor compass point, such as NE or SW may be used.

Some travel paths may only be taken when

certain conditions are fulfilled. Some examples of this are

- The player is carrying a certain object.
- The player has solved some problems.
- The player has removed an obstacle to travel.

These conditions may be indicated on the map by a brief description of the condition in words. This description can be written near the affected travel line or can be placed in a footnote.

PROBLEMS

Much of the fun of adventure games lies in the problems they pose for the player to solve. I elaborate on this theme in a future chapter. For now, I only want to show you how to indicate that problems exist in various places on the adventure map.

Problems may be indicated by a special symbol. I use a balloon letter style question mark, enclosed in a circle as shown in Fig. 2-1.

Fig. 2-1. A problem indicator for adventure game maps.

This notation needs supplementation in order to distinguish one problem from another. One way is to assign a number to each of the problems in the adventure. Write the number of each problem near the appropriate question mark symbol. In a separate place, describe each problem in detail in words. Another possibility is to give each problem a name analogous to the placenames given to locations. The name of the problem could then be written near the ? symbol instead of a number. I use the numbering approach and write the number of the associated problem inside another full circle placed to the right of the circle containing the ? symbol.

OBJECTS

Objects usually start out at a fixed location at the beginning of the adventure. All such objects may be indicated on the map by writing the name of the object inside the box designating that location. Of course, this notation describes the adventure at the start of play. The player is free to pick up objects and move them around during play.

To indicate that there is a problem associated with an object, you can place a dash after the name of the object. Then a small ?, perhaps followed by the number of the problem, can be written after the dash. Occasionally, an object will have properties that are not part of the description of any problem. This situation can be handled by the use of footnotes that associate the textual description of the properties with the name of the object itself.

You may like drawing a cartoon style cloud around the name of each object. This serves to make a graphic distinction between the placename and the object name. While this is not strictly necessary, some may find it esthetically or psychologically pleasing.

BEINGS AND MONSTERS

These may be considered to be objects. They are animate objects, true. However, when you are drawing the adventure map, you can treat them just as you treat the inanimate objects.

EMBELLISHING THE MAP

The artistically minded may embellish their adventure maps much further than these simple instructions indicate. Pictures of locations, monsters, and objects all make interesting viewing. Perspective drawings of the locations and their relationships is also fun. All of this has nothing per se to do with programming adventure games, but their creation may well stimulate the imagination.

MAP LAYOUT AND ORGANIZATION

For complex and detailed adventure games, you will find that you have to draw a large map. You won't be able to fit this map on a single sheet of standard sized paper. If you don't want to go to the trouble of locating and purchasing oversized drawing paper, you will need to split your maps into multiple sheets. When you do this, try to group your locations into geographically and/or logically related "clumps." Then put one clump per page on your maps. Try to choose the clumps so that there is a minimum of possible travel paths between the different clumps. Then the connections between pages may be indicated with a symbol often used in drawing complex computer program flowcharts. The symbol in question is appropriately named the *off-page connector*. It looks like a pentagon with a number in it. The numbers in the pentagons are used to associate two connectors on different pages. They do not refer to any numbering of the map pages themselves. If a straight line leads into an off-page connector, look for a similar connector on another page. The matching connector should have a straight line leading out of it as shown in Fig. 2-2

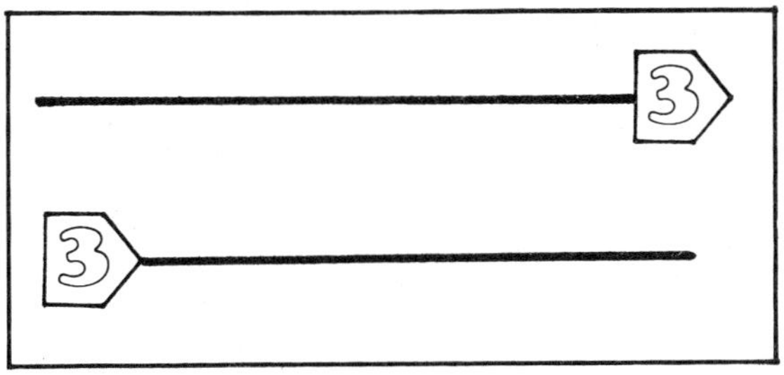

Fig. 2-2. An off-page connector for adventure game maps.

EXAMPLES

Each adventure game included in this book is mapped in detail using the techniques of this chapter. The resulting maps are included in the preview chapters that precede the complete listing of the Pascal source code for the game itself.

3

Adventures and Problem Solving

The essence of a good adventure lies in the problems it poses for the user to solve. They must be varied, original, interesting, challenging without being impossible, intricate without being arbitrary, and so on. This is truly an area where your creative impulses may be vented to their fullest. There is no cookbook approach to creating good problems. There are a number of guidelines, however. Let's do some exploring and see what we can discover.

CLUES TO PROBLEM SOLUTIONS

For each problem you contrive in an adventure, there should be at least one associated clue or hint. Such clues may take many forms:

- They may be hidden in the description of locations. Such clues should be subtle. In most cases the hint should be indirect. The player should be required to make some deduction based on the clue and other information. Only in rare cases and for extremely trivial and unimportant problems should you give away the answer directly.

  The player should have some way of telling that part of a description is in fact a hint. This can be done by making the hint somehow different in tone or style. Make it just slightly "jar" the player into recognizing it.

- Clues may be written on objects contained in the adventure. A clue may be written on a wall on a piece of parchment hidden in a closet or an old chest, on the bottom of a bottle, or just about anywhere. It may take an explicit command on the part of the adventurer to get at such clues. This gives you a chance to give hints about hints! You can take this more than one level deep in some cases. A few problems may even require an entire chain of clues in order to reveal their solution.

To get at a message hidden inside a container, the player should have to open the container, take out the object on which the message is written, and explicitly ask to read the message. How all this is represented in a computer program will be discussed later. Keep in mind that you will have to program your clues—so don't get too carried away.

- Clues may be implicit in the behavior of beings or entities within the adventure. The way a monster reacts to certain commands or situations may reveal weaknesses that the adventurer can exploit.

When you think of a good problem to include in your adventure, don't stop there. Work on ways of making the problem solution entertaining for the player. Really good clues will enhance this. Don't expect all this to magically come to you the instant you think of a problem. You should let the problem roll around in your subconscious for awhile. Write each problem on a separate sheet of paper and make notes as ideas come to you. Gradually crystallize these ideas into hints and clues. As you develop your adventure story line and structure, come back to these sheets again and again. Ask yourself if you can think of more or better clues. The effort you put into this will pay off in compliments from those who play your games.

PROBLEM DIFFICULTY: FROM THE OBVIOUS TO THE OBSCURE

Not all problems in an adventure should be equally difficult or easy. There should be a variety of levels of difficulty. There should be enough relatively easy problems in all parts of the game to keep the player coming back to the harder problems. The surest way to kill off interest in all but the most stubborn adventurers is to make all your problems next to impossible to solve.

How can the difficulty of a problem be estimated? One way is by the number of clues needed in order to solve the problem. The more information that must be gathered in order to figure out the solution, the harder the problem is likely to be to solve. Another factor is the individual clues themselves. A problem that has one very obscure clue is probably harder to solve than one that has several easy clues.

When you start writing real adventures, get others to play them. Then get feedback on the difficulty levels that you have put into them. If you have friends that are also writing adventures, so much the better. Trade adventures back and forth and then trade ideas about making problems both interesting and realistic in terms of their level of difficulty.

REPEATABILITY

There is a choice to be made in creating adventure problems. Do you want the solution to a problem to have an element of chance or not? For example, if you have to fight other beings, should there be an absolutely guaranteed method of winning or should there be some probability, however small, of failure even in the presence of perfect logic? This is a choice that you, the adventure writer, will have to make. It all depends on who will play your games and what their preferences are.

Absolutely repeatable problems will involve only logic in their solution. Problems that involve chance may still involve logic as well. The difference is that the player is not in complete control of the outcome. There is a middle ground here. You may create a problem in which the player may take certain actions in order to guarantee that the chance element is ruled out. For example, if the player attacks a certain monster first, that might guarantee that there is a completely logical way to avoid being a victim of the monster. Again, it may require other kinds of actions on the part of the adventurer to secure such results. The player may need to get killed off a few times in order to notice what these conditions are. Here you have another way of creating wheels within wheels effects. The player may through experience learn more and more about how to solve a problem. There may be progress through several levels where chance still plays a part, before the player reaches the absolute logical pinnacle consisting of the problem solution.

LOGIC

Good problems should allow a player's true problem-solving ability to be exercised. The solution to a problem should not be completely arbitrary, requiring the player to make wild or random guesses in order to arrive at a solution. In short, problems should be *logical*.

What is logic? For our purposes, it is a system of reasoning. The player may draw conclusions about the play of the game. Such conclusions may be based on information contained directly in the game. This may take the form of hints as discussed above. It may be hidden in descriptions of locations or objects. On the other hand, it may be necessary to draw conclusions based on common sense; that is, based on the normal properties of objects or behavior of objects in a natural setting. For example, water makes plants grow; dry wood may be set on fire with matches; doors must be opened in order to see what is behind them; and you may have to dig in order to uncover buried treasure.

In deducing information, it may be necessary for a player to make guesses. These guesses should always be reasonable, not arbitrary. And good guesses might be rewarded with the offer of further information.

A good way to require the use of logic is by including more than one hint or clue regarding a problem's solution. The player must discover two or more clues and connect them logically in order to solve the problem.

SURPRISE

I have just finished emphasizing that problems should have logical solutions. Having said that, I can now relax my position a bit and allow for the element of surprise.

There may be an inherent conflict between logic and surprise. What is totally logical is not surprising. What is surprising cannot be totally logical. What you wish to avoid is not illogical solutions, but arbitrary ones.

There is a fine line between a surprising solution to a problem and an arbitrary one. To illustrate this point, consider the original adventure game. In that game there are two problems that serve as perfect examples. First consider the one with the surprising solution.

There is a fierce green snake that bars you from entering a certain passageway. This tunnel turns out to be the only entrance to the rest of the cave. Therefore you must find a way to get rid of the snake. If you have played the game "correctly" up to that point, you reach the location of the snake carrying a cage containing a timid little bird. You try everything you can think of to get by the snake, but all efforts fail. What to do next? Now, using logic, you might engage in the following sort of dialogue:

Q. What means are at my disposal?
A. None.
Q. Really?
A. Well, I do have this bird in the cage.
Q. What might you do with it?
A. I could get it to sing—maybe that would frighten the snake away.
Q. Oh well, I suppose. Go ahead and try it.
A. OK.
Q. What happened?
A. Absolutely nothing.
Q. Well, what else can be tried?
A. I guess I could let the bird go. Maybe I could catch the snake in the cage.
Q. Good idea. Go ahead and do it.
A. OK.
Q. What happened?
A. Amazingly enough, the bird drove off the snake!

Surprise, surprise, surprise! You never thought the bird could have any positive effect on the snake. Nonetheless, you did discover the solution by a process of reasoning and common sense. (You thought the cage might be useful.)

Now for the problem with the arbitrary solution. When you get extremely good at the original adventure, you find that you have accumulated 349 points out of a possible 350. Unless you stumbled on the way to get the 350th point, you are now faced with the nasty problem: "How do I get the last point?" This problem is particularly nasty since its solution could lie almost anywhere. Some people spend hours and hours, for example, looking for a location that they have not visited that might net them the extra point.

There are some magazines that exist in the game. They seem to play no role. However, if you pick them up from their original location and carry them to Witt's End, you get the extra point! How utterly disappointing this turns out to be when you discover it—truly arbitrary, truly deflating, truly anticlimactic.

The moral of the story is—try to avoid totally arbitrary solutions. Don't make players of your game guess that your Uncle Harry's hair is brown in order to get a point! Don't require them to perform random acts in random locations in order to secure the last point!

4

UCSD Pascal Review

All of the programs presented in this book were written using the UCSD Pascal system. I used the version of this system as adapted by Apple Computer Co. for use on the Apple II and Apple *II*e. These programs should work with little if any modification on any computer using the UCSD P-System.

In this chapter I intend to accomplish the following:

- Tell you what you should know about Pascal before digging in further.
- Explain to those that are unfamiliar with it what the UCSD System is.
- Highlight some of the features of the UCSD System and some of the tricks of using it effectively.
- Give you some general suggestions that will be helpful when you start writing your own adventures.

WHAT YOU SHOULD KNOW ABOUT PASCAL

This is not an introduction to Pascal programming. I am going to assume that you know the basics. That means that you have written at least a few Pascal programs. It means that you are familiar with the syntax of Pascal and the mechanics of writing programs. You should at least have an idea of the meanings of the following terms:

- Procedures and functions.
- Block structure.
- Parameters: actual and formal.
- Types (user-defined, predefined), type checking.
- Structured statements, control structures.
- Declarations.
- Value parameters, var parameters.
- Files (sequential), get, put, readln, writeln
- Arrays.
- Records.

I will be using most of these concepts as well as some others in the programs. In many cases, I will give detailed explanations of how a particular usage works, and why it makes sense in Pascal. Thus, if you are not an expert, you should be able to learn more about how to use many Pascal features.

Just study the example programs diligently and try to follow the explanations.

I won't start out with the most basic topics, however. That is why I hope you are already conversant with these concepts.

If the preceding list makes you feel tired or intimidated, you should probably obtain a good beginning textbook on Pascal. Read it in parallel or slightly ahead of your study of this book. There are many books already out on Pascal and many more appearing all the time. The best places to seek them out are your local computer store or bookstore. When you buy a book make sure that it is not limited to a subset of Pascal or to an implementation that is peculiar to one or two computers.

WHAT IS THE UCSD SYSTEM?

The UCSD Pascal system was originally developed at the University of California at San Diego. It was intended to be used in the teaching of Pascal, and the goal was to implement the system on a variety of small computers, including microcomputers. The project was conceived and directed by Dr. Kenneth Bowles, a professor of computer science at UCSD.

The system is just that. It is a complete software development environment for Pascal, including not only a Pascal compiler but also a complete operating system and many utility programs. When you use the UCSD system, it is in complete control of your computer. Thus, if you have a system with CP/M, you must reboot the system in order to use UCSD Pascal, and you no longer have access to CP/M. The same is true for most micros that support a manufacturer's proprietary operating system. For example, when you run the UCSD system on the Apple II, you must forego access to the Apple DOS.

The UCSD system has been made into a commercial product by the SofTech Microsystems company in San Diego. It is now referred to as the P-System, and it runs on virtually every microcomputer currently manufactured. The system is based on an *interpreter* that executes a pseucode known as P-Code (whence the name P-System). The interpreter communicates with the hardware and the peripherals of the computer via a small set of programs known as the *BIOS* (Basic Input Output System).

The BIOS includes the machine code necessary for booting the system from a floppy disk. The booting process involves the reading in of the BIOS and the P-Code interpreter from the floppy disk. Then the operating system portion of the UCSD system is loaded. It is written in P-Code and is interpreted by the P-Code interpreter. Once it has been loaded, control is passed to the interpreter, and off you go.

The UCSD system is one of the early *menu-driven* systems. A menu is a list of choices coded by numbers or letters from which the user chooses. The UCSD system has a command line that lists the commands available in a given context and indicates their abbreviations. You have to know what each command will accomplish by reading the users' manuals, because there is no online help facility available.

In addition to the BIOS, the P-Code interpreter, and the operating system, the UCSD system provides

- A full-screen text editor.
- A filer for manipulating files on the floppy disk.
- A Pascal compiler for compiling Pascal programs into P-Code
- A linker for combining certain P-Code files into programs that are executable by the P-Code interpreter.
- A librarian program that enables you to create libraries of reusable pieces of P-Code. These pieces may then be incorporated into many different programs.

There are other features of the UCSD system, but these are the ones that I will be using the most.

In order to learn about the UCSD P-System, you will need the users' manuals for your particular implementation. I use the manuals for Apple Pascal as provided by Apple Computer. There are also textbooks available that discuss the use of the system, although they tend to be paraphrases of the UCSD documentation, organized differently and with different diagrams. Still they may in many cases be useful—you will have to decide for yourself.

This book is not intended to be a tutorial on the UCSD Pascal system. I assume that you know enough of the basics to use it. I will, however, give instructions on some techniques that you may not have picked up in your beginning use of the system. This will take the form of tips about general use of the system and some detailed instructions on preparing the programs in this book for actual use on your computer.

5

Preview of Adventure 1

In this book, I present substantial Pascal programs. Adventure games in Pascal tend to be large programs; there is no getting around that. My approach will be to introduce you to the goals and content of each program with a preview chapter. Following the preview you will find the complete listing of the Pascal program itself. After that will be several text chapters explaining the design of the program, the Pascal features used, and the way the Pascal programming techniques relate to the adventure game.

In order to get the most out of each program, here is how I suggest you read this book:

- Read the outline chapter, noting the mention of any Pascal features with which you are not already familiar. Pay particular attention to the outlines and diagrams. Try to grasp the overall design of the program.
- Skim through the program listing in back to front fashion—see the explanation of how to do this in the preview of Adventure 1 later in this chapter. Write down questions you may have about how the program works. Refer to these questions as you study the program in detail later on.
- Read and study the chapters devoted to explaining the program. As you read, refer frequently to the actual program listing. If possible enter the code for the program in your own computer as you proceed.
- After reading all the chapters pertaining to the specific program you are studying, go back and read the listing of the program once again. This time, read the program for details. Make notes of the particular coding techniques that you plan to use in your own adventures.
- Finally, design your own adventure game, using the techniques illustrated by the program you have finished studying. Implement it using your own computer and UCSD Pascal system. Compare your finished game to the illustrative program in the book. Review your lists of questions, and see how many you now can answer yourself.

PREVIEW CHAPTERS

Long programs can be intimidating, confusing,

and difficult to understand. So I would like to give you a perspective of a program before plunging into its details. By starting out with an idea of the overall structure of a program, you will be able to understand it more quickly. You will be able to fit details into the overall picture. Concentrating on program structure from the start will also encourage you to pay attention to the structure of the Pascal programs that you write yourself. This is an important point often overlooked by beginning or relatively inexperienced programmers.

I will include diagrams that show the static structure of the program. These diagrams will list the program elements (declarations, functions and procedures by name, main program, and so on) in the order in which they appear in the program listing. In addition to the static structure diagrams, I will include diagrams for each program revealing its *dynamic* structure. These diagrams will be modeled after the style of diagram used in the *structured design* technique of programming. Such diagrams reveal the relationships between the various procedures and functions in the program. They may also show how various pieces of data used by the program are passed around and modified by different parts of the program.

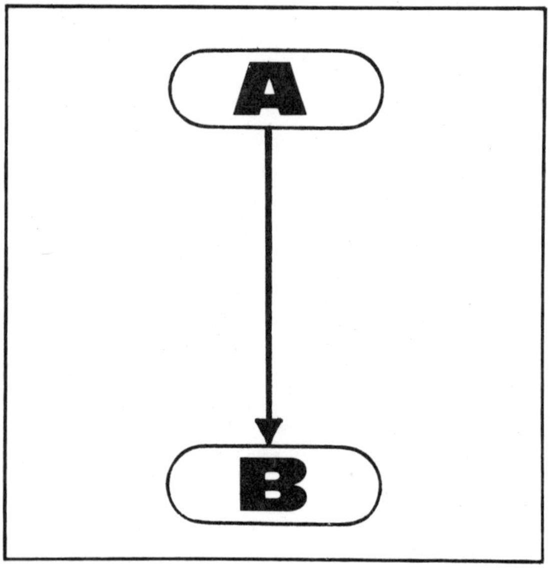

Fig. 5-1. A diagrammatic representation of a procedure call in structure diagrams.

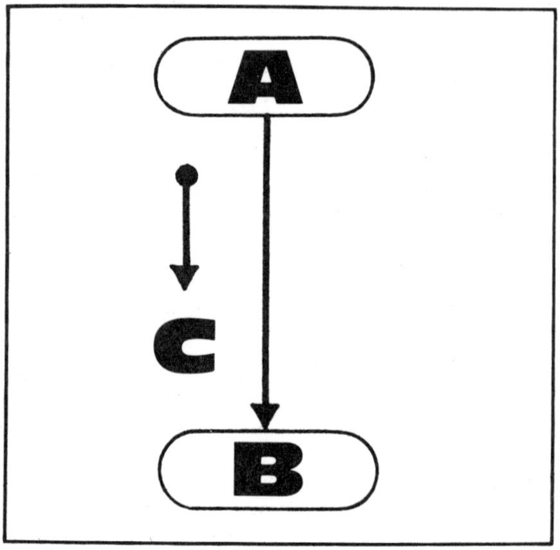

Fig. 5-2. Data connection in a structure diagram: A passes C to B.

Each procedure or function (as well as the main program itself) is represented in a structure diagram by an oval. The name of the procedure or function is written inside the oval. Lines with arrowheads connect various ovals in the diagram. A line that points from an oval named A to an oval named B, as shown in Fig. 5-1, indicates that procedure or function A *calls* procedure or function B. That is, the procedure or function A has in its program text (or code, if you prefer) an invocation of procedure or function B. If the tail of the line (the end without the arrowhead) has a diamond shape, ◆, it means that the call from A to B is *conditional*. The code in A will make some test. Depending on the outcome of the test, A may or may not call B. This information can be valuable in debugging a program; if there is a conditional call to B, but B is not called when it should be, there is no doubt a problem in the logic of A's code.

Some lines that connect ovals will be labeled with variable names. This means that the data represented by that variable passes between A and B. If A provides B with a variable named C, the diagram might look something like the one shown in Fig. 5-2.

Notice the smaller arrow beside C. The circle

PROGRAM miniadventure;

CONST, TYPE, and VAR declarations:

> This section of the program contains the declarations of the constants, types, and variables used by the rest of the program.
> See Figure 5-4

procedures and functions:

> This section consists of all the headers and code for all the procedures and functions accessible to the main program block and the outermost level of the program.
> See Figures 5-5 and 5-6

BEGIN

> This section of code is the first to be executed. It is referred to as the **main program block.** When reading a Pascal program, you should always start here.
> See Figure 5-7.

END.

Fig. 5-3. The code outline for Adventure 1: the program outline.

on the tail of this arrow points toward the provider of C, in this case A. This information is also of potential importance. Many bugs in programs are due to variables somehow obtaining incorrect values. A structure diagram can help reveal where a variable could be "going sour." Careful study of the diagram with your code at hand often reveals problems.

Structure diagrams give another viewpoint of a program, one that is more important in understanding how the code works. When you study structure diagrams, notice how groups of functions and procedures form logical chunks of a program. Notice also how each procedure and function accomplishes one logical task within a program. As you program in Pascal, this use of logical structure should be a conscious goal. It makes debugging and program modification considerably easier.

In addition to all the diagrams that attempt to reveal the structure of the program, I shall include a survey of the chapters that follow the program listing. Each chapter will be described briefly. You will be given an idea of what to expect from each chapter.

PREVIEW OF ADVENTURE 1

The full listing of Adventure 1 is presented in Chapter 6. After you finish reading this chapter, you should read the listing of Adventure 1 in back-to-front style. What does that mean? In standard Pascal programs, the so-called *main program block,* that is, the code that is executed first, is located at the end of the program text. So when you read a Pascal program, you should really start at the back.

CONST

user-defined constants

TYPE

user-defined types
rooms
represents the locations in Adventure 1
directions
represents the possible directions of travel

VAR

variables used by the program
command
holds command (direction to take) typed by the player
location
its value, of type rooms indicates where the player is located
visited
an array, indexed by rooms, which tracks the places in the game that the player has traveled to
turns
counts the number of turns taken by the player
done, quit, eaten, awake, readmsg, carrying, dropped, trapped, cooked
variables to keep track of events which have or have not occurred during the game.

Fig. 5-4. The code outline for Adventure 2: the data declarations.

PROCEDURE introduction;
Introduces the player to the game and the guide.

PROCEDURE initialize;
Assigns values to all program variables. The initial values reflect the state of the game at the beginning of play.

FUNCTION score: INTEGER;
Calculates the player's score at the end of the game.

FUNCTION whichway: directions;
Determines the direction the player wishes to take. It looks at the first letter of **command** for this purpose.
It makes sure **command** has letters!

PROCEDURE ogreaction;
Assists in handling the action at the ogre's den.

PROCEDURE pstart;
PROCEDURE pvestibule;
.
.
.
PROCEDURE piceroom;

} Procedures that handle the action at (including travel from) the locations start, vestibule, . . ., iceroom.

PROCEDURE pogreroom;
PROCEDURE pmaze;
Procedures that handle the action at the ogre's den and the maze. Each has one or more LOCAL functions and procedures. See Figure 5-6.

PROCEDURE pnarrow2;
PROCEDURE ppit;
.
.
.
PROCEDURE pdeadend;

} Procedures that handle the action at (including travel from) the locations narrow2, pit, . . ., deadend.

Fig. 5-5. The code outline for Adventure 1: the functions and procedures.

```
PROCEDURE pogreroom;
PROCEDURE general description;

        Local (or nested) procedure
        that is used to print
        the general description
        of the ogre's demesne.
```

```
PROCEDURE pmaze;
  Procedure that implements the maze. It is like a small
  adventure inside the larger adventure. It uses
  numerous local procedures and functions.

  FUNCTION bittest: BOOLEAN;
  PROCEDURE describe;
  PROCEDURE sameplace;
  PROCEDURE treasure;

      These procedures provide general
      support for the action in the maze.
  PROCEDURE pm1;
  PROCEDURE pm2;
  PROCEDURE pm3;
      •
      •
      •
  PROCEDURE pm 18;
  PROCEDURE pm19;
    Procedures pm1, pm2, . . ., pm19 are the location
    procedures for the nineteen maze rooms. They are
    analogous to the location procedures pstart, pvestibule,
    and so on. They handle travel and action inside
    the maze itself.
```

Fig. 5-6. The code outline for Adventure 1: the procedures with local procedures.

The last part of the listing will contain the main program block. The code there will invoke other parts of the program, in particular the procedures and functions whose text appears earlier in the listing. This means that as you see references to procedures and functions in the main program block, you will have to look for the listings of these procedures and functions closer to the front of the program. In turn, these procedures and functions may refer to other procedures and functions. Unless the author of the program has used FORWARD declarations (which I in general attempt to avoid in my adventure games), the procedures referred to will be listed even closer to the start of the listing. Now you can see what I mean by reading the program back-to-front.

Figures 5-3 through 5-7 present the code outline of Adventure 1. Figure 5-3 shows the entire program structure in brief, explaining the major parts of every Pascal program. It refers to the other figures that show various parts of the program in more detail. Figure 5-4 outlines the const, type, and var declarations of the entire program, giving brief descriptions of some of the more important declarations used by the program. Figure 5-5 outlines the procedures and functions used by Adventure 1. Again, there are brief comments regarding some of the more important of these. Figure 5-6

```
BEGIN

    introduction; \  Procedure invocations (once only) at the
    initialize;   }  start of the game play.

        REPEAT
          CASE location of
          start:   pstart;
          grandroom: pgrandroom;
               •
               •
               •
               flames: pflames;
          END;
        UNTIL quit OR done;

    Main control loop of the adventure game program.
    Various location procedures are repeately invoked
    until the game is complete. This is signaled by one of
    the two Boolean variables quit or done becoming TRUE.

    congratulations;
      Procedure called to wrap up the game and summarize
      the results including the score for the player.

END.
```

Fig. 5-7. The code outline for Adventure 1: the Main program block.

outlines one of the longer procedures of the program, pmaze. This procedure is notable for having many local procedures and functions. Finally, Fig. 5-7 outlines the main program block of Adventure 1.

Figure 5-8 is the dynamic structure diagram of Adventure 1. It shows the relationships between various groupings of procedures and functions used by the program.

CHAPTER PREVIEWS

Chapter 7 is entitled "Representing the Map." It discusses the use of enumerated types in Pascal programs generally an in adventure games specifically. You should pay special attention to this brief chapter. It lays groundwork for a technique that is used repeatedly in later adventures. At the end of Chapter 7, the map of Adventure 1 is presented in the graphic format explained in Chapter 2.

Chapter 8 is entitled "Controlling the Play" and deals with the use of enumerated types in conjunction with Pascal case statements. Chapters 7 and 8 go hand in hand. Go back and reread both chapters after you finish them the first time. The use of enumerated types in Pascal case statements is one of the most powerful Pascal coding techniques. Unfortunately, it is also one of the most underused. Master the technique, and you will have a valuable tool for all your Pascal coding, not just your adventure game writing.

Chapter 9 is entitled "Mazes in the Middle" and deals with the implementation of the maze in Adventure 1. It discusses the use of local procedures and functions as well as local declarations in general.

Chapter 10, entitled "Other Techniques Used in Adventure 1" discusses what I have termed the *ad hoc* code of Adventure 1. It explains how mis-

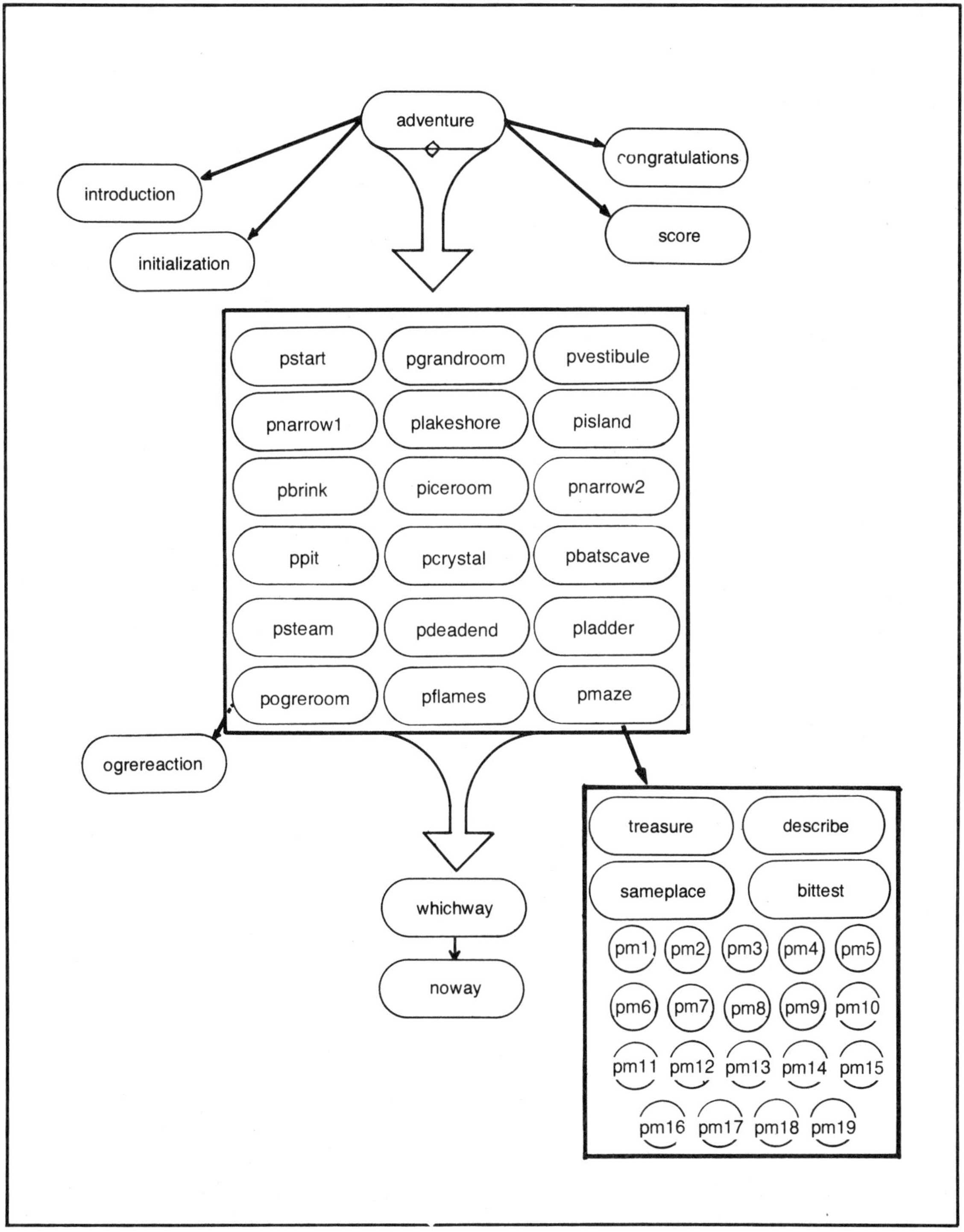

Fig. 5-8. The structure diagram for Adventure 1.

cellaneous features of the game were implemented by direct Pascal coding techniques. The techniques are ad hoc in the sense that they solve a specific problem in a very specific way and may not be as generally applicable as some of the techniques described in earlier chapters.

6

Pascal Adventure 1

This chapter presents the complete listing of the first Pascal adventure game. This example is meant more to illustrate features of Pascal than to be a serious game. To get the most out of this program, you should go through the following steps:

1. Skim read the program right now. Try to grasp the overall structure of the program and don't worry too much about the fine details. Refer back to the code outlines in Chapter 5 as you skim. Jot down any questions you may have about the overall organization of the program.
2. Read and study Chapters 7 through 10, which discuss the details of the Pascal coding of this adventure. As you read these chapters, study the listing of Adventure 1 and absorb the details. Imagine how you will apply the language features discussed to your own adventure game programs.
3. When you have finished Chapter 10, go back and reread the listing of Adventure 1 in detail. Check your list of questions from step 1, and see how many of them have now been answered.
4. Write an adventure of your own using the techniques illustrated by Adventure 1. Make up your own map and your own location descriptions. Notice what parts of the Pascal code you can use almost unchanged and what parts you have to alter radically.

LISTING 6-1. PASCAL MINIADVENTURE

```
(*************************************************)
(*                                               *)
(*   a   d   v   e   n   t   u   r   e     #  1  *)
(*                                               *)
(* This is an example of the Pascal language     *)
```

```
(* features that are useful in writing advent-   *)
(* games.  It is not really a serious game, but *)
(* more an instructional exercise.               *)
(*                                               *)
(************************************************)

(*$s+*)
PROGRAM miniadventure;
CONST

  ff     =      12;
  ew     =      12;
  nw     =       9;
  ne     =       5;
  sew    =      14;
  nonly  =       1;
  nsew   =      15;
  newud  =      61;
  sw     =      10;
  ns     =       3;
  donly  =      32;
  dn     =      33;
  ud     =      48;
  su     =      18;

TYPE

  rooms =  (start, grandroom, vestibule, narrow1,
            lakeshore, island, brink, iceroom,
            ogreroom, narrow2, pit, crystal,
            batscave, steam, deadend, ladder,
            maze, flames);

  directions = (n,s,e,w,u,d);

  byte        =  0..255;

VAR

  command:        STRING;
  (* holds user typed direction *)

  ch:             CHAR;

  dchars:         SET OF CHAR;
  (* characters which correspond TO the
```

```
    acceptable initial letters OF
    direction  commands.  initialized TO
    ['n','s','e','w','u','d']           *)

  location:       rooms;
  ogreloc:        rooms;
  visited:        ARRAY[start..flames] OF BOOLEAN;

  next:           directions;
  twopow:         ARRAY[n..d] OF INTEGER;

  turns:          INTEGER;
  done:           BOOLEAN;
  quit:           BOOLEAN;
  eaten:          BOOLEAN;
  awake:          BOOLEAN;
  readmsg:        BOOLEAN;
  carrying:       BOOLEAN;
  dropped:        BOOLEAN;
  trapped:        BOOLEAN;
  cooked:         BOOLEAN;

          (***********)
          (* w i p e *)
          (***********)
          PROCEDURE wipe;
          BEGIN
            write(chr(ff));
          END;

(*$imini1.text*)
(*$imini3.text*)
(*$imaze1.text*)
(*$imini2.text*)
(*(*
*)
(**************************************)
(* i  n  t  r  o  d  u  c  t  i  o  n *)
(**************************************)

PROCEDURE introduction;
BEGIN

  wipe;           (* clear screen *);

  writeln ('Welcome to miniadventure!');
```

```
  writeln ('Your goal will be to find a treasure');
  writeln ('and bring it to the starting point.');
  writeln ('You will also get points for finding');
  writeln ('each location in the adventure.');
  writeln ('Points will be deducted for various');
  writeln ('undesirable happenings: waking the');
  writeln ('ogre, getting eaten, getting toasted,');
  writeln ('etc.');
  writeln;
  writeln ('I will guide you and be your eyes and');
  writeln ('ears.  I will describe your location');
  writeln ('and give you special instructions');
  writeln ('from time to time.');
  writeln;
  writeln ('To command me, tell me a direction');
  writeln ('to take - north, south, east,');
  writeln ('west, up, or down.');
  writeln ('note: I only look at the first letter');
  writeln ('of the command, so abbreviations');
  writeln ('are acceptable.');
  writeln;
  writeln ('  When you are ready to begin your');
  writeln ('adventure, just press "return".');

  readln(command);

  wipe;

END (* PROCEDURE introduction *);

(***************************************)
(*   i  n  i  t  i  a  l  i  z  e     *)
(***************************************)

PROCEDURE initialize;
VAR
  loc:  rooms;
BEGIN

  location := start;
  dchars   := ['q','n','s','e','w','u','d'];
  done     := false;
  quit     := false;
  cooked   := false;
  eaten    := false;
  awake    := false;
```

```
  readmsg  := false;
  carrying := false;
  trapped  := false;
  dropped  := false;
  turns    := 0;
  twopow[n]:= 1;
  twopow[s]:= 2;
  twopow[e]:= 4;
  twopow[w]:= 8;
  twopow[u]:=16;
  twopow[d]:=32;
  FOR loc := start TO flames DO
    visited[loc] := false
  (* enddo *);

END (* PROCEDURE initialize *);

(*************************************)
(*     s     c     o     r     e     *)
(*************************************)

FUNCTION score: INTEGER;
VAR
  loc:  rooms;
  sc:   INTEGER;
BEGIN

  sc := 0;

  FOR loc := start TO flames DO
    IF visited[loc]
    THEN
      sc := sc + 10
    (* endif *)
  (* enddo *);

  IF NOT quit
  THEN
    sc := sc + 30;

  IF cooked
  THEN
    sc := sc - 50;

  IF eaten
  THEN
```

```
    sc := sc - 50;

  IF awake
  THEN
    sc := sc - 25;

  score := sc;

END (* FUNCTION score *);

(****************************************)
(*  c o n g r a t u l a t i o n s     *)
(****************************************)

PROCEDURE congratulations;
BEGIN

  IF NOT cooked
  THEN
  BEGIN
    IF NOT quit
    THEN
    BEGIN

      writeln (' ***** congratulations *****');
      writeln;
      writeln ('You got the treasure out in only');
      writeln (turns:4,' turns.');

    END;

    writeln ('You scored', score:4, ' points out');
    writeln (' of a maximum of 200 points.');
    writeln ('So long for now, come again soon!');

  END
  ELSE

    writeln ('Sorry about that - try again soon!')

  (* endif *);

  readln (command);
  wipe;

END (* PROCEDURE congratulations *);
```

```
(*************************************)
(*     w  h  i  c  h  w  a  y        *)
(*************************************)

FUNCTION whichway:directions;
BEGIN

  turns := turns + 1;

  REPEAT

    REPEAT

      writeln;
      write ('Which way?===>');
      readln (command);

    UNTIL length (command) > 0;

    ch := command[1];

    CASE ch OF

      'n':      whichway := n;
      's':      whichway := s;
      'e':      whichway := e;
      'w':      whichway := w;
      'u':      whichway := u;
      'd':      whichway := d;
      'q':          quit := true;

    END;

  UNTIL ch IN dchars;

  writeln;

end (* function whichway *);

(*************************************)
(*       n    o    w    a    y       *)
(*************************************)

PROCEDURE noway;
BEGIN
```

```
  writeln;
  writeln ('You cannot go in that direction.');

END;
(*(*
*)
(**************************************)
(*    o  g  r  e  a  c  t  i  o  n    *)
(**************************************)

PROCEDURE ogreaction;
BEGIN

  IF NOT awake
  THEN
  BEGIN

    writeln ('This is the ogre''s lair!');
    writeln ('If you are not careful, you''ll');
    writeln ('wake him.');

    IF (turns MOD 7)=0
    THEN
    BEGIN
      awake := true;
      writeln ('Now you''ve done it!');
      writeln ('You woke the ogre - better');
      writeln ('get out of here while you can');

    END (* IF *);

  END
  ELSE
  BEGIN

    writeln ('You wouldn''t listen to me would');
    writeln ('you?  You really better get out');
    writeln ('of here before you get eaten!');

    IF carrying
    THEN
      IF (turns MOD 2)=0
      THEN
      BEGIN
```

```
        writeln ('Too bad!!  The ogre caught you');
        writeln ('and roasted you for dinner.');
        writeln ('Better luck next time!!');

        eaten := true;
        quit  := true;

      END
      ELSE
      BEGIN

        writeln ('Get out fast if you don''t want');
        writeln ('to be a big-mac for the ogre!!');

      END
    ELSE
      IF (turns MOD 5)=0
      THEN
      BEGIN

        writeln ('Too bad - you''ve been eaten!');

        eaten := true;
        quit  := true;

      END

    (* endif *)

  END (* IF NOT awake *);

END (* PROCEDURE ogreaction *);

(****************************************)
(*     p    s    t    a    r    t      *)
(****************************************)

PROCEDURE pstart;
BEGIN

  IF carrying
  THEN
    done := true
  ELSE
  BEGIN
```

```
    writeln ('You are standing by a hole in');
    writeln ('the ground.  It looks big enough');
    writeln ('to climb down.');

    CASE whichway OF

      n,s,e,w:    noway;
      u: writeln ('You can''t jump to the clouds!');
      d: location := vestibule;

    END;

  END (* IF carrying *);

END (* PROCEDURE pstart *);

(**************************************)
(*   p  v  e  s  t  i  b  u  l  e   *)
(**************************************)

PROCEDURE pvestibule;
BEGIN

  writeln ('you are in the entrance to a cave');
  writeln ('of passageways.  there are halls');
  writeln ('leading off to the north, south,');
  writeln ('and east.  above you is a tunnel');
  writeln ('leading to the surface.');

  IF dropped
  THEN
  BEGIN

    writeln ('To the north, through a narrow crack,');
    writeln ('You can see the treasure.  If you');
    writeln ('stretch your arm through you might');
    writeln ('reach it.  Do you want to try?');

    readln (command);

    IF (command = 'yes') OR (command = 'y')
    THEN
    BEGIN
      carrying := true;
      dropped  := false;
    END (* IF *);
```

```
   END;
   CASE whichway OF

     n:    location := narrow1;
     s:    location := grandroom;
     e:    location := iceroom;

     w,d: noway;
     u:    location := start;

   END (* CASE whichway *);


END (* PROCEDURE pvestibule *);

(**************************************)
(*    p  g  r  a  n  d  r  o  o  m    *)
(**************************************)

PROCEDURE pgrandroom;
BEGIN

   writeln ('You are in a huge open room, with');
   writeln ('an immense expanse of ceiling.');
   writeln ('A dark passage leads west and a');
   writeln ('narrow crawl leads downward.');

   CASE whichway OF

     w:  location := brink;
     d:  location := iceroom;

     n,s,e,u:    noway;

   END;

END (* PROCEDURE pgrandroom *);

(**************************************)
(*     p  n  a  r  r  o  w  1         *)
(**************************************)

PROCEDURE pnarrow1;
BEGIN

   writeln ('You are in a narrow passage which');
```

```
  writeln ('continues to the north.  It is');
  writeln ('extremely narrow to the south.');
  writeln ('  A very tight crawl also leads east.');
  writeln ('A curious odor seeps through it.');
  writeln ('I would think twice before trying');
  writeln ('to go that way!');

  IF carrying
  THEN
  BEGIN

    writeln ('The treasure won''t fit through');
    writeln ('the crack going south.  Do you want');
    writeln ('to leave it here?');

    readln (command);

    IF (command = 'yes') OR
       (command = 'y')
    THEN
    BEGIN

      dropped  := true;
      carrying := false;

    END (* IF *);

  END (* IF carrying *);

  CASE whichway OF

    n:   location := lakeshore;
    e:   location := ogreroom;
    s:   writeln ('It''s too narrow to get through!');

    w,u,d:       noway;

  END (* CASE whichway *);

END (* PROCEDURE pnarrow1 *);

(*************************************)
(*   p   l   a   k   e   s   h   o   r   e    *)
(*************************************)

PROCEDURE plakeshore;
```

```
BEGIN

   writeln ('You are on the shore of a vast');
   writeln ('underground lake.  Narrow passages');
   writeln ('wind away to the east and south.');
   writeln ('A small island is visible in the');
   writeln ('center of the lake to the north.');

   CASE whichway OF

      n:  location := island;
      s:  location := narrow1;
      e:  location := narrow2;
      w,u,d:          noway;

   END;

END (* PROCEDURE plakeshore *);

(**************************************)
(*     p  i  s  l  a  n  d            *)
(**************************************)

PROCEDURE pisland;
BEGIN

   writeln ('You are on a small island in the');
   writeln ('center of a huge underground lake.');
   writeln ('Dark frigid waters surround you on');
   writeln ('all sides.  You can barely make out');
   writeln ('the shoreline to the south.');
   writeln ('A small message is scratched in the');
   writeln ('dirt here.  It says: ''The treasure');
   writeln ('may be found in the maze.''');
   CASE whichway OF

      n,e,w,u,d:  noway;
      s:          location := lakeshore;

   END;

   readmsg := true;

END (* PROCEDURE pisland *);
```

```
(****************************************)
(*    p    b    r    i    n    k        *)
(****************************************)

PROCEDURE pbrink;
BEGIN

  writeln ('You are on the brink of a steep');
  writeln ('incline.  The bottom of the pit');
  writeln ('is over fifty feet below you.');
  writeln ('You could probably slide down');
  writeln ('safely, but I won''t promise you');
  writeln ('that you could get back up.');
  writeln ('  To the west is a dark opening');
  writeln ('into a rubble-filled tunnel.  A');
  writeln ('vampire bat just flew out of it');
  writeln ('shrieking.');

  CASE whichway OF

    n,s,e,u:  noway;
    w:        location := ogreroom;
    d:        location := pit;

  END;

END (* PROCEDURE pbrink *);

(****************************************)
(*   p   i   c   e   r   o   o   m      *)
(****************************************)

PROCEDURE piceroom;
BEGIN

  writeln ('You are in a room whose walls are');
  writeln ('formed from a deep blue crystalline');
  writeln ('ice.  To the north a narrow tunnel');
  writeln ('opens.  From the other end of the tunnel');
  writeln ('an ominous growling sound may be');
  writeln ('heard.  To the east a sparkling ');
  writeln ('luminescence emanates from a broad');
  writeln ('opening.  To the west a passage');
  writeln ('leads back to the vestibule.');

  CASE whichway OF
```

```
    e:          location := crystal;
    n:          location := ogreroom;
    w:          location := vestibule;

    s,u,d:      noway;

  END;

END (* PROCEDURE piceroom *);

(*************************************)
(*   o   g   r   e   r   o   o   m   *)
(*************************************)

PROCEDURE pogreroom;
VAR
  i,j:  INTEGER;

  PROCEDURE generaldescription;
  BEGIN

    writeln ('You are in a low room whose walls');
    writeln ('are covered with ominous dark');
    writeln ('gouts of dried blood.  The center');
    writeln ('of the room is dominated by a');
    writeln ('firepit, which contains burned');
    writeln ('out coals and a long spit suspend-');
    writeln ('ed over its center.');
    writeln ('  From one dark corner emanates a');
    writeln ('horrible growling noise like that ');
    writeln ('of some unspeakable monster snoring');
    writeln ('during its dream of rending you limb');
    writeln ('from limb and making you its dinner!');

  END (* PROCEDURE generaldescription *);

BEGIN

  generaldescription;
  ogreaction;

  IF NOT eaten
  THEN
  BEGIN

    writeln ('There are exits to the east, west,');
```

```
   writeln ('north, and south.');

   CASE whichway OF

     w:            location := narrow1;
     e:            location := batscave;
     n:            location := narrow2;
     s:            location := iceroom;
     d: BEGIN

          quit  := true;
          eaten := true;
          writeln ('Oh no!! You dummy!!!');
          writeln ('You just fell in the firepit');
          writeln ('and made such a ruckus that');
          writeln ('you woke the ogre.  I hate to');
          writeln ('tell you this, but you are');
          writeln ('also trapped!');
          FOR i := 1 TO 5 DO
          BEGIN
            FOR j := 1 TO 1000 DO;
            write('.');
          END (* DO *);
          writeln ('You have been added to the');
          writeln ('ogre''s gourmet recipe library!');
          writeln ('Better luck next time.');

        END;

     u:     noway;

   END (* CASE whichway *);
   END (* IF NOT eaten *);

END (* PROCEDURE pogreroom *);
(*(*
*)
(*************************************)
(*        p    m    a    z    e       *)
(*************************************)

PROCEDURE pmaze;
TYPE

   mazerooms = (m1,m2,m3,m4,m5,m6,m7,m8,
```

```
                  m9,m10,m11,m12,m13,m14,
                  m15,m16,m17,m18,m19);
VAR

   mazeloc:       mazerooms;
   bitset:        ARRAY[directions] OF BOOLEAN;

   FUNCTION bittest
            (v: INTEGER; dir: directions): BOOLEAN;
   BEGIN

     IF ((v DIV twopow[dir]) MOD 2)=1
     THEN
       bittest := true
     ELSE
       bittest := false
     (* endif *);

   END (* FUNCTION bittest *);

   PROCEDURE describe(wh: INTEGER);
   VAR
     dir: directions;

   BEGIN

     writeln ('You are in a maze of featureless');
     writeln ('passages.  There are exits visible');
     writeln ('in the following directions:');

     IF bittest (wh,n) THEN write ('n ');
     IF bittest (wh,s) THEN write ('s ');
     IF bittest (wh,e) THEN write ('e ');
     IF bittest (wh,w) THEN write ('w ');
     IF bittest (wh,u) THEN write ('u ');
     IF bittest (wh,d) THEN write ('d ');

     writeln;

   end (* procedure describe *);

PROCEDURE sameplace;
BEGIN

  writeln ('You have crawled around some');
  writeln ('twisted tunnels and wound up');
```

```
  writeln ('where you began.');

END (* PROCEDURE sameplace *);

PROCEDURE treasure;
BEGIN

  IF NOT carrying
  THEN
  BEGIN

    IF readmsg
    THEN
    BEGIN

      writeln ('The treasure is here!!');
      writeln ('Do you want to take it now?');

      readln (command);

      IF (command = 'yes') OR
         (command = 'y')
      THEN
        carrying := true
      (* endif *);

    END
    ELSE
    BEGIN

      writeln ('The light is extremely dim here');
      writeln ('You better get out or risk');
      writeln ('falling into a pit.');

    END (* IF readmsg *);

  END (* IF NOT carrying *);

END (* PROCEDURE treasure *);

PROCEDURE pm1;
BEGIN

  writeln ('You are in a maze of featureless');
  writeln ('passages.');
  writeln ('from here you can go south, east,');
```

```
   writeln ('west, or up.');

   CASE whichway OF

     s:          location := ladder;
     e:          mazeloc  := m2;
     w:          mazeloc  := m4;
     u:          location := steam;
     n,d:        noway;

   END;

END (* pm1 *);

PROCEDURE pm2;
BEGIN

   describe(nw);

   CASE whichway OF

     n:          mazeloc := m1;
     w:          sameplace;
     e,s,u,d:    noway;

   END;

END (* PROCEDURE pm2 *);

PROCEDURE pm3;
BEGIN

   describe(ne);

   CASE whichway OF

     n:          mazeloc := m1;
     e:          sameplace;
     s,w,u,d:    noway;

   END;

END (* PROCEDURE pm3 *);

PROCEDURE pm4;
BEGIN
```

```
  describe(sew);

  CASE whichway OF

    s:          mazeloc := m7;
    e:          mazeloc := m3;
    w:          mazeloc := m5;
    n,u,d:      noway;

  END;

END (*  PROCEDURE pm4 *);

PROCEDURE pm5;
BEGIN

  describe(nonly);

  CASE whichway OF

    n:          mazeloc := m1;

    e,w,s,u,d:              noway;

  END;

END (* PROCEDURE pm5 *);

PROCEDURE pm6;
BEGIN

  describe(ne);

  CASE whichway OF

    n:          mazeloc := m4;
    e:          sameplace;

    s,w,u,d:  noway;

  END;

END (* PROCEDURE pm6 *);

PROCEDURE pm7;
BEGIN
```

```
   describe(nsew);

   CASE whichway OF

     n:          mazeloc := m5;
     s:          mazeloc := m9;
     e:          mazeloc := m6;
     w:          mazeloc := m8;

     u,d:        noway;

   END;

END (* PROCEDURE pm7 *);

PROCEDURE pm8;
BEGIN

   describe(nw);

   CASE whichway OF

     n:          mazeloc := m5;
     w:          sameplace;

     e,s,u,d:    noway;

   END;

END (* PROCEDURE pm8 *);

PROCEDURE pm9;
BEGIN

   describe(sw);

   CASE whichway OF

     s:          mazeloc := m11;
     w:          mazeloc := m10;

     n,e,u,d:    noway;

   END;

END (* PROCEDURE pm9 *);
```

```
PROCEDURE pm10;
BEGIN

  describe(ns);

  CASE whichway OF

    n:          mazeloc := m8;
    s:          sameplace;

    e,w,u,d:    noway;

  END;

END (* PROCEDURE pm10 *);

PROCEDURE pm11;
BEGIN

  describe(newud);

  CASE whichway OF

    n:          mazeloc := m9;
    e:          mazeloc := m6;
    w:          mazeloc := m10;
    u:          mazeloc := m1;
    d:          mazeloc := m12;

    s:          noway;

  END;

END (* PROCEDURE pm11 *);

PROCEDURE pm12;
BEGIN

  describe(dn);

  CASE whichway OF

    n:          mazeloc := m13;
    d:          mazeloc := m16;

    e,s,w,u:    noway;
```

```
  END;

END (* PROCEDURE pm12 *);

PROCEDURE pm13;
BEGIN

  describe(dn);

  CASE whichway OF

    n:          mazeloc := m14;
    d:          mazeloc := m17;

    e,s,w,u:    noway;

  END;

END (* PROCEDURE pm13 *);

PROCEDURE pm14;
BEGIN

  describe(dn);

  CASE whichway OF

    n:          mazeloc := m15;
    d:          mazeloc := m18;

    e,s,w,u:    noway;

  END;

END (* PROCEDURE pm14 *);

PROCEDURE pm15;
BEGIN

  describe(ud);

  CASE whichway OF

    u:          mazeloc := m1;
    d:          mazeloc := m19;

    n,s,e,w:    noway;
```

```
  END;

END (* PROCEDURE pm15 *);

PROCEDURE pm16;
BEGIN

  describe(ns);

  CASE whichway OF

    n:          mazeloc := m17;
    s:          sameplace;

    e,w,u,d:    noway;

  END;

END (* PROCEDURE pm16 *);

PROCEDURE pm17;
BEGIN

  describe(ns);

  CASE whichway OF

    n:          mazeloc := m18;
    s:          mazeloc := m16;
    e,w,u,d:    noway;

  END;

END (* PROCEDURE pm17 *);

PROCEDURE pm18;
BEGIN

  describe(ns);

  CASE whichway OF

    n:          mazeloc := m19;
    s:          mazeloc := m17;

    e,w,u,d:    noway;
```

```
    END;

  END (* PROCEDURE pm18 *);

  PROCEDURE pm19;
  BEGIN

    describe(su);
    treasure;

    CASE whichway OF

      s:          mazeloc := m18;
      u:          mazeloc := m15;

      n,e,w,d:    noway;

    END;

  END (* PROCEDURE pm19 *);

BEGIN  (* PROCEDURE pmaze *);

  mazeloc := m1;

  REPEAT

    CASE mazeloc OF

      m1:         pm1;
      m2:         pm2;
      m3:         pm3;
      m4:         pm4;
      m5:         pm5;
      m6:         pm6;
      m7:         pm7;
      m8:         pm8;
      m9:         pm9;
      m10:        pm10;
      m11:        pm11;
      m12:        pm12;
      m13:        pm13;
      m14:        pm14;
      m15:        pm15;
      m16:        pm16;
      m17:        pm17;
```

```
      m18:       pm18;
      m19:       pm19;

    END (* CASE mazeloc *);

  UNTIL location <> maze;

END (* PROCEDURE pmaze *);
(*(*
*)
(****************************************)
(*     p  n  a  r  r  o  w  2          *)
(****************************************)

PROCEDURE pnarrow2;
BEGIN

  writeln ('You are in a very narrow passage.');
  writeln ('To the west the passage opens out');
  writeln ('by a lake shore.  To the east it is');
  writeln ('even tighter.  You just might be');
  writeln ('able to squeeze through if you try');
  writeln ('real hard.');
  writeln ('  There is also a strange looking');
  writeln ('alcove in the south wall that seems');
  writeln ('to open into a very dark tunnel.');

  CASE whichway OF

    w:          location := lakeshore;
    e:          location := steam;
    s:          location := ogreroom;

    n,u,d:    noway;

  END;

END (* PROCEDURE pnarrow2 *);

(****************************************)
(*        p  p  i  t                   *)
(****************************************)

PROCEDURE ppit;
BEGIN
```

```
   writeln ('You are at the bottom of a fifty');
   writeln ('foot pit.  The walls are just a');
   writeln ('hair too steep to climb.  The pit');
   writeln ('is empty except for a few old');
   writeln ('dried bones - I can''t tell if they');
   writeln ('are human or not!!  In the center');
   writeln ('of the pit is a narrow shinny');
   writeln ('leading downward.');

   CASE whichway OF

     d: location := ladder;

     u: BEGIN
          writeln ('If you try to climb that,');
          writeln ('you''re sure to kill yourself!');
        END;

     n,s,e,w:    noway;

   END;

END (* PROCEDURE ppit *);

(*****************************************)
(*      p  c  r  y  s  t  a  l          *)
(*****************************************)

PROCEDURE pcrystal;
BEGIN

   writeln ('You are in a shining hall of crystal.');
   writeln ('It is intensely cold but also chill-');
   writeln ('ingly beautiful.  There are glass');
   writeln ('formations rising from the floor');
   writeln ('as if they had grown there, yet');
   writeln ('delicately sculptured with multi-');
   writeln ('faceted sides.  An intense white');
   writeln ('light shines brilliantly from the');
   writeln ('floor, which is also made of a');
   writeln ('mirror smooth lead crystal.  The light');
   writeln ('is almost blinding and the many');
   writeln ('reflections that it sets off among');
   writeln ('the crystal formations of the room');
   writeln ('make it almost impossible to tell');
```

```
  writeln ('where the room begins and where');
  writeln ('it ends. ');

  CASE whichway OF

    e:       location := maze;
    n,w:     location := ogreroom;

    s,u,d:  noway;

  END;

END (* PROCEDURE crystal *);

(*************************************)
(*     p  b  a  t  s  c  a  v  e     *)
(*************************************)

PROCEDURE pbatscave;
BEGIN

  writeln ('You are in a steep cavern filled');
  writeln ('with shrieking vampire bats.  They');
  writeln ('swoop and dive at you by the ');
  writeln ('thousands.  If I were you, I would');
  writeln ('get out as quick as I could.  There');
  writeln ('are openings to the west and north.');

  CASE whichway OF

    w:          location := ogreroom;
    n:          location := steam;

    e,s,u,d:    noway;

  END;

END (* PROCEDURE pbatscave *);

(*************************************)
(*     p   s   t   e   a   m         *)
(*************************************)

PROCEDURE psteam;
BEGIN
```

```
   writeln ('You have entered a hall filled with');
   writeln ('a stifling steamy vapor.  There are');
   writeln ('innumerable small geysers scattered');
   writeln ('about, each contributing its own steam');
   writeln ('to the general mist.');
   writeln ('To the west is a dark opening, as');
   writeln ('well as to the north.  Further out');
   writeln ('in the middle of the room is a dark');
   writeln ('opening in the floor into which some');
   writeln ('of the vapor seems to be seeping');

   CASE whichway OF

     w:          location := narrow2;
     n:          location := deadend;
     d:          location := maze;
     s:          location := batscave;

     e,u:        noway;

   END;

END (* PROCEDURE psteam *);

(****************************************)
(*     p l a d d e r                   *)
(****************************************)

PROCEDURE pladder;
BEGIN

   writeln ('You are at the base of a huge ladder');
   writeln ('reaching up out of sight.  It must');
   writeln ('extend up at least 500 feet, and it will');
   writeln ('take someone brave in heart to scale');
   writeln ('it.  There are also passages which');
   writeln ('lead north and down.');

   CASE whichway OF

     n: location := maze;
     d: location := flames;
     u: IF carrying
        THEN
        BEGIN
```

```
          writeln ('You can''t carry the treasure up the');
          writeln ('ladder - it''s much too heavy!');

        END
        ELSE
          location := vestibule
        (* endif *);

     e,s,w:    noway;

   END;

END (* PROCEDURE pladder *);

(****************************************)
(*    p    f    l    a    m    e    s    *)
(****************************************)

PROCEDURE pflames;
BEGIN

   writeln ('Unfortunately you have fallen into');
   writeln ('an underground fire pit.  It is the');
   writeln ('source of the heat that produces');
   writeln ('the geysers in the steam room.  You');
   writeln ('have been toasted to a crisp to put');
   writeln ('it politely.');

   cooked := true;
   done   := true;

END (* PROCEDURE pflames *);

(****************************************)
(*    p    d    e    a    d    e    n    d    *)
(****************************************)

PROCEDURE pdeadend;
BEGIN

   writeln ('Dead end.');

   CASE whichway OF

     s:  location := steam;
```

```
    n,e,w,u,d:  noway;

  END;

END (* PROCEDURE pdeadend *);

            (****************************)
BEGIN       (* =====> adventure <===== *)
            (****************************)

  introduction;
  initialize;

  REPEAT

    visited[location] := true;

    CASE location OF


      start:              pstart;
      grandroom:          pgrandroom;
      vestibule:          pvestibule;
      narrow1:            pnarrow1;
      lakeshore:          plakeshore;
      island:             pisland;
      brink:              pbrink;
      iceroom:            piceroom;
      ogreroom:           pogreroom;
      narrow2:            pnarrow2;
      pit:                ppit;
      crystal:            pcrystal;
      batscave:           pbatscave;
      steam:              psteam;
      deadend:            pdeadend;
      ladder:             pladder;
      maze:               pmaze;
      flames:             pflames;

    END (* CASE location *);

  UNTIL quit OR done;

  congratulations;

END.
```

7

Representing the Map

In this chapter, I begin to show you how to use the Pascal language to write adventure programs. The Apple version of UCSD Pascal has been used in all the examples in this book. These programs should run without major modifications on any system with UCSD Pascal.

Chapter 6 has presented the listing of Adventure 1 in Pascal. This adventure would not present much of a challenge to a seasoned adventurer. In fact, even beginners would probably find it boring. My purpose was not to write a serious game; I wanted to introduce you to some of the features of Pascal that are useful in writing adventures. By studying these techniques, you can learn to write your own adventures in Pascal. I hope that you also gain a deeper understanding of Pascal and become a better Pascal programmer as a result.

REPRESENTING THE ADVENTURE MAP

Figure 7-1 presents most of the initial map of Adventure 1. The notation for the map is explained in more detail in Chapter 2. Notice the use of the circled question marks and circled numbers to indicate the problems of the adventure. Figure 7-2 shows the map of the maze incorporated in Adventure 1. Finally, Fig. 7-3 lists the problems by number and gives explanations of each one.

There are 18 rooms shown on the map in Fig. 7-1, not counting all the individual maze locations. I will represent these rooms in Pascal by using an *enumerated type:*

```
TYPE
  rooms= (start, grandroom, vestibule, narrow1,
          lakeshore,island,brink,iceroom,
          ogreroom,narrow2,pit,crystal,
          batscave,steam,deadend,ladder,
          maze,flames) ;

VAR
  location:     rooms;
```

The concept of an enumerated type deserves a bit of discussion.

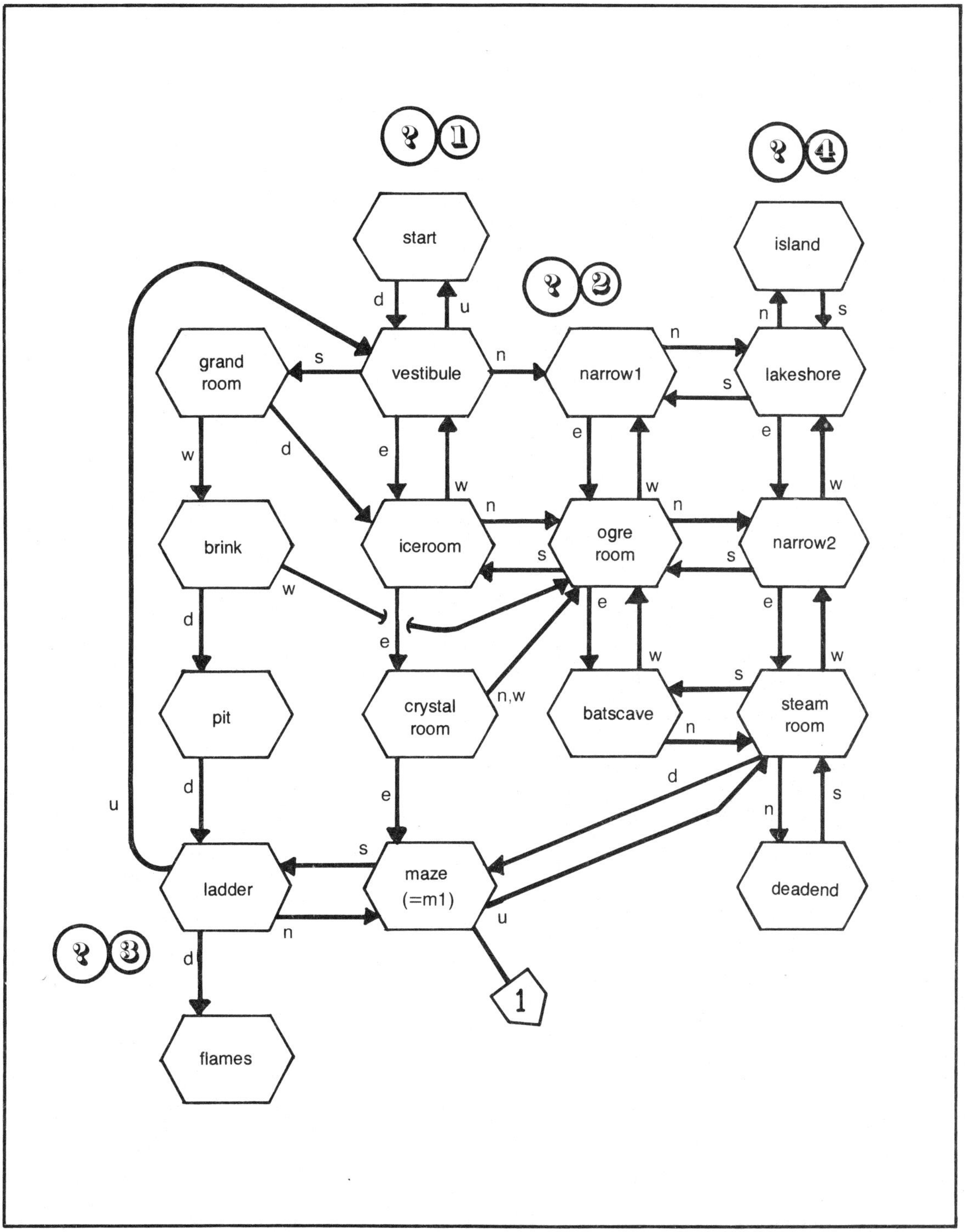

Fig. 7-1. The map of Adventure 1.

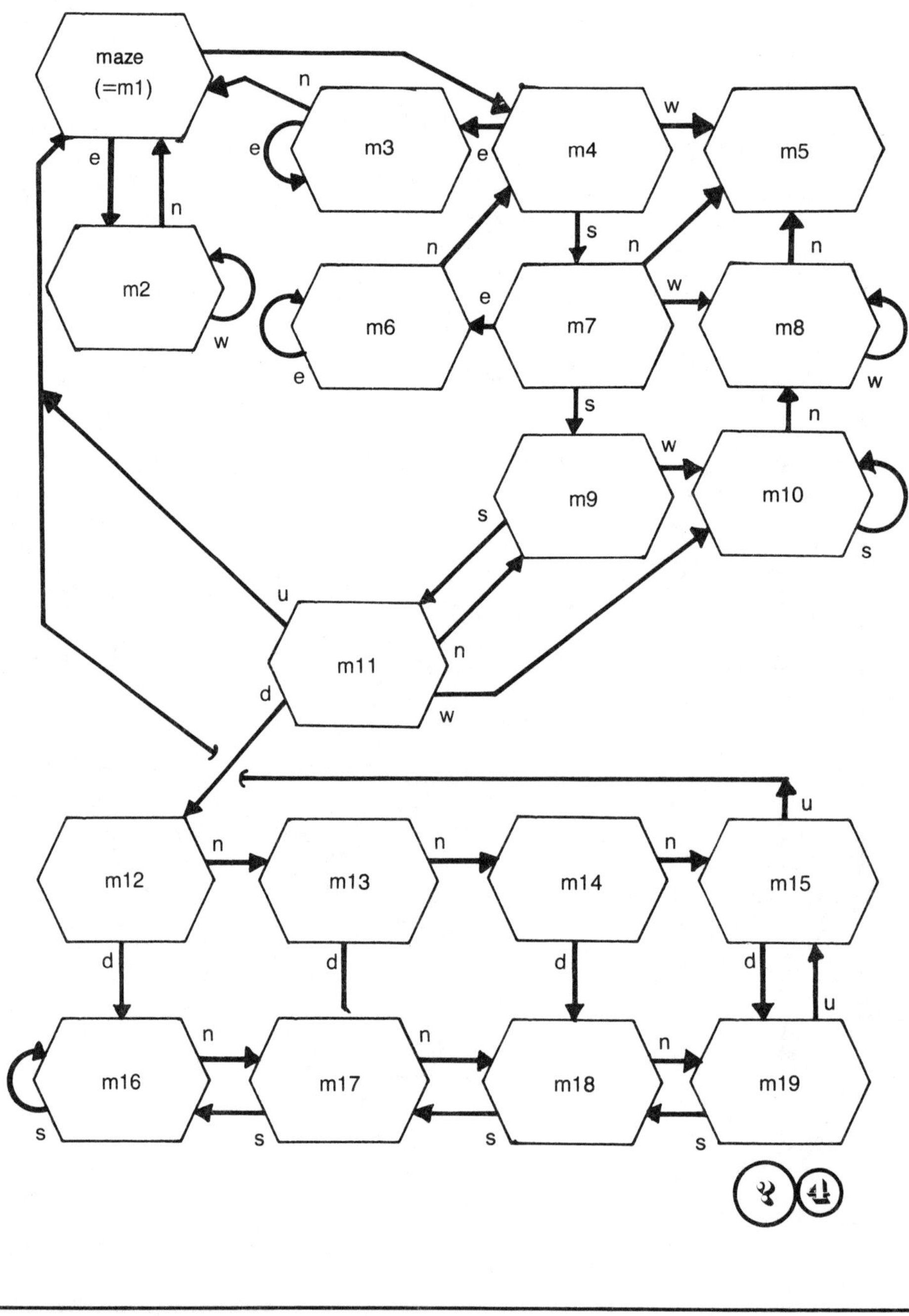

Fig. 7-2. The map of maze in Adventure 1.

You must bring the treasure to **start** in order to win.

To guarantee a win, you must carry the treasure to **narrow1** drop it, go around to the vestibule, and pull the treasure through the crack. You can get to the vestibule from the iceroom, but you must carry the treasure through the ogreroom, and you could be eaten in the process.

You cannot carry the treasure up the ladder—it's too heavy! You must find another way out while still carrying the treasure.

You must find the treasure deep in the **maze**. Before the treasure will be visible to you, you must discover the message on the island.

Fig. 7-3. The problems of Adventure 1.

ENUMERATED TYPES IN PASCAL

Programmers sometimes have difficulty coming to grips with the concept and use of enumerated types. The reason for this is a psychological one. A large part of traditional programming, whether it be in assembly language or in so-called "high-level" languages such as FORTRAN or BASIC, has dealt with the invention of *representations*. Programmers have become used to this necessity. In Pascal, the concept of enumerated type provides a facility which removes the need to invent representations in certain situations. Suddenly the very programming language itself solves part of the traditional representational problem. The programmer is not used to this. The programmer is fixated on solving all representational problems—indeed the programmer has come to love this aspect of programming. When faced with a ready-made solution, the circuits become overloaded.

To make this more concrete, suppose for the moment that you were writing a miniadventure in BASIC. You might use a variable to keep track of which room or location the player happens to be in at any given point in the game. Now BASIC can only manipulate two kinds of data—numbers and strings. Therefore, you must invent a correspondence between the set of rooms in your game and a set of numbers. The numbers will be used internally to represent the rooms. You might choose

start = 1
vestibule = 2
grandroom = 3

and so on.

On the other hand, it would be equally valid to use

start = 1001
vestibule = 1002
grandroom = 1003

and so on.

If the latter representation were chosen over the former, there is a likelihood that the choice would be based on some intended programming trickery. That is, part of the BASIC program might be written to "know" that numbers greater than 1000 represent rooms.

In general, unless you resort to coding tricks, the specific numbers chosen to represent the rooms are purely arbitrary. They only serve to distinguish one location from another and at some level, to identify which location is under scrutiny. The key points about these numbers are:

- They are explicity chosen by the programmer.
- They represent an external concept (rooms) in an internal form (numbers).
- They must be correlated mentally by the programmer; that is, the details of the representation are a factor in the coding of the program.

Pascal's enumerated type facility enables you to set aside the problem of representation in this case. The enumerated type given above effectively creates a new kind of data that Pascal can manipulate, a user-defined type called rooms. The variable location may be thought of as a variable that can take on any room as its value. The user may think of rooms in terms of their names as chosen in the type declaration. There is no need to choose a set of numbers to correlate to the names: the Pascal compiler takes care of this for you. Since you really don't care what the specific numbers are (unless you had planned on some clever trickery), it is better to let the details be swept under the rug of compilation. When you write your program, you can think in terms of room names, not numbers!

Since long years of training have made most programmers feel that we should be personally responsible for internal representations, it is difficult to make our minds let go of that feeling of responsibility. However, when we finally do let go, the freedom to think in terms of the problem instead of in terms of the computer is the result. Once you become accustomed to it, this can lead to an enormous feeling of power and relief.

If you read through Adventure 1, you will see that assignment statements such as:

```
location := vestibule;

location := flames;
```

are commonplace. How much more suggestive than:

```
location := 2;

location := 17;
```

Of course, the enumerated type rooms only represents the collection of locations in the adventure. It does not include information about the connections between locations. Figure 7-1 includes all the connections. This version of the adventure will only accept commands that indicate a direction in which to travel. In particular, it only recognizes six different directions represented by the single letters n, s, e, w, u, and d.

From any given location only certain directions lead to other locations. For example, from the Crystal room you may only proceed e, w, or n. There is no way to go u, d, or s. This information must be encoded in some fashion and interpreted by the adventure program in order for the game to be played. This has been accomplished by two techniques that I explain in the next chapter. In the process, I shall reveal how the general play of the game is controlled. Both the representation of the adventure map and the control of the game hinge on the use of the Pascal case statement.

8

Controlling the Play

In the last chapter, I discussed enumerated types in Pascal. The power of enumerated types is greatly enhanced by the use of the Pascal case statement. There are several examples of case statements in Adventure 1. They all are quite important in making the game work. I am devoting this chapter to a discussion of some of these statements.

CASE STATEMENTS IN PASCAL

The general form of a Pascal case statement may be indicated as follows:

```
case E of

l1:    a1;
l2:    a2;

   . . .

ln:    an;

  end;
```

In this general description, there are a number of elements that require further explanation.

case expression E

E must be an expression that evaluates to one of the elements of what in Pascal is referred to as a scalar type. In particular, enumerated types are examples of scalar types. In the context of adventure games, E could be a variable representing a value of type rooms. Or, it could be a call to a function that returns a value from the type directions= (n,e,s,w,u,d); More on this below.

The idea of the case statement is to allow a program to take different actions based on the particular values of an enumerated type. The elements 11,12, . . . ,ln of the general case statement represent the possible values of the enumerated type. Actually each li may be a list of elements from an enumerated type. The elements a1,a2, . . . ,an in the general description represent the Pascal code that is to be activated in response to the corresponding value or list of values li.

In Adventure 1 there are two major uses of the case statement. Both involve the flow of control through the game program.

CONTROLLING THE ADVENTURE GAME

If adventure were real, the player would either be in a location at a given time, or he would be traveling between two locations. In the act of traveling the player would leave one location for another by heading off in a specific direction, such as north, east, or down. Thus, in programming adventure these ideas must be represented in some way using Pascal code. Specifically, you must find ways to represent:

- The adventurer's location.
- The possible directions out of each location and the destinations they represent.
- The decision as to which direction to take.
- The changing of location from one room to another.

The Adventurer's Location

I have already discussed the use of an enumerated type (which I called rooms) to represent the possible locations. To store a specific value of the rooms type, I invented a variable called location.

```
var
location:     rooms;
```

At the beginning of the game, the location variable is assigned the value start. This represents the initial room or starting point of the adventurer. At various places in the adventure game code, assignments will be made to this variable. Such assignments will be dictated by the adventurer's choice of direction.

To organize the game, a separate Pascal procedure has been written for each value of the rooms type. These procedures have all been given names that consist of the letter p for procedure, followed by an identifier from the rooms type. For example, there are pstart, pflames, pgrandroom, pogreroom, and so on. Each of these procedures handles the activities that may take place in the corresponding location

The main program code consists largely of a case statement with case expression of type rooms:

```
case location of
  start:          pstart;
  grandroom:      pgrandroom;
  vestible:       pvestibule;
  narrow1:        pnarrow1;
  lakeshore:      plakeshore;
  island:         pisland;
  . . .
  end;
```

The meaning of this statement is extremely simple: When the player is in room x, activate the procedure px, which handles activities in that room. At any time during the game, one of these procedures will be in execution. The execution of that procedure corresponds to the adventurer actually being in that room in real life. The program's structure very closely reflects the way we imagine a real life adventure would happen.

Look back at the main program listing in Chapter 6 and notice that the case statement is enclosed within a while statement. This is necessary in order to ensure that the case statement is repeated over and over again. Otherwise, the game would cease after pstart was executed once.

The use of a case statement nested inside a while statement is common in Pascal programming. Remember it—you will probably use it often during your Pascal programming career.

Changing Locations

Part of the activity in each room is deciding which way to go next. The adventure map shows that in a given location it is impossible to proceed in all possible directions. Only a subset of the possible directions represent actual paths in the imaginary adventure world. The code must reflect this fact. In Adventure 1, each location procedure contains another case statement that handles the travel from location to location. The case statement also encodes the possible directions that may be taken. This is best explained by considering an example:

The following code is found in procedure plakeshore:

```
case whichway of
   n: location := island;
   s: location := narrow1;
   e: location := narrow2;
   w,u,d: noway;
end;
```

The identifier whichway is the name of a function that determines the direction the adventurer wishes to take. This is described in more detail below. The identifier noway is the name of a procedure that simply prints the message:

"There is no way to go in that direction."

on the game player's display screen.

The operation of the case statement is once again quite simple.

- A direction is chosen by the adventurer. This is accomplished by a call to whichway.
- If the direction chosen represents a possible avenue of travel, the new room is assigned to the variable location in the appropriate section of the case statement. This will cause a new location procedure to be invoked on the next cycle of the main case statement.
- If the direction chosen does not represent a possible route in the adventure map, the noway procedure is called. The value of the variable location does not change. This means that the same location procedure will be invoked on the next cycle. The adventurer gets another chance to find a way out.

Deciding on a Direction

In this adventure, only very simple commands are used; only one of the six directions n, s, e, w, u, or d may be specified. The function whichway is responsible for this interaction with the player. It prompts by "asking"

```
Which way?===>
```

The player responds by keying in a "command." This may be any string of characters. The Pascal code examines only the first character of the string:

```
command[1]
```

If this character is one of the letters n, s, e, w, u, or d, whichway sets its return value to the corresponding value from the enumerated type direction. For example, if the adventurer types in never, whichway will return n as the direction to try.

Protecting Against Empty Responses

There is one problem that the Pascal code in whichway must solve. If the adventurer simply pushes the RETURN key the variable command, which is used to store the response, will contain an empty string. The length of the empty string is, of course, 0. The character to be assigned to ch using command[1] is then nonexistent. If a statement in the program attempts to access this character, the Pascal run time system will complain with a cryptic message. The adventurer will be yanked from pleasant fantasy back to mundane computer reality. You must avoid this if at all possible, and it turns out to be quite simple to do so. The program simply checks the length of command and refuses to touch it until the length is greater than 0.

Changing Location

The act of changing location is represented by a simple assignment statement giving a new value to the variable location. If you now go back to the listing again, you will find that such assignments are scattered all over the case statements that begin with

```
case whichway of
```

These assignments collectively determine the map of the adventure. That is, the connections between different locations is implicit in these assignments.

This last point is worth a minute's reflection. If you were writing adventure games in a language like BASIC, you would probably encode the map as an array of numbers. The array would probably have two dimensions, with any pair of subscripts representing a pair of locations. The contents of the array for each such pair would be yet another number. This number would be a code representing one of two things:

1. The direction to take to get to the room represented by the second subscript from the room represented by the first subscript.

or

2. A number that means there is no connection between the pair of locations in question.

In terms of Adventure 1, you could imagine an array MAP[18,18]. The rooms start, grandroom, vestibule, narrow1, and so on would be represented by the numbers 1 to 18. Then the pair of subscripts 1,3 would represent start, vestibule; the pair of subscripts 4,17 would represent narrow1, flames; the pair of subscripts 5,9 would represent lakeshore; ogreroom; and the pair of subscripts 5,6 would represent lakeshore, island.

The directions n,s,e,w,u,d, and noway might be represented by the numbers 1,2,3,4,5,6, and–1. Then MAP[1,3] would equal 6; MAP[4,17] would equal–1; MAP[5,9] would equal–1; and MAP[5,6] would equal 1.

I could have taken an approach like this in Adventure 1. However, it was unnecessary to do so, because the Pascal implementation I have chosen was available and was so much easier to understand and work with.

9

Mazes in the Middle

Adventure 1 has a maze in it. The original adventure game had not one but two mazes in it. Many subsequent adventures, especially those of the underground or cave variety, also contain mazes.

The maze offers a good opportunity for introducing more of the structural features of Pascal. The maze is conceptually like a single location. Yet in practice it contains many individual locations. While you are in the maze you are "trapped" in a miniature adventure within an adventure.

The entire adventure in Pascal is implemented by a program. The maze is implemented by a single procedure, pmaze. By analogy, because the maze is like a miniature adventure, pmaze must be like a miniature program. Indeed as you shall see, procedures can have almost all of the features that a Pascal program can have.

Although pmaze is a single procedure that controls play in the maze, it has its own *local* or *nested* procedures and a *nested* function. Local procedures and functions are just like the procedures and functions that contain them, as far as Pascal syntax rules are concerned. However, they may only be invoked from the procedure or function that contains them or from other functions and procedures that are also local in the same sense.

The pmaze procedure also contains a local TYPE and VAR section. The types and variables thus declared may only be used inside pmaze. They are not "visible" outside pmaze; pmaze is referred to as the *scope* of these declarations. The scope includes any nested procedures or functions that do not redeclare the types or variables in question.

The concept of scope is fundamental to Pascal and other languages like it, which are referred to as *block structured* languages. It is beyond the scope (pun intended) of this chapter to go into a full discussion. For full detail on this subject, consult your authoritative Pascal language textbook. However, by imitating these program layouts you should not run afoul of the scope rules.

Local or nested declarations, including procedures and functions, are provided in the language to allow for better program structure. If a variable logically belongs only to a certain procedure, it is best to declare it there and there only. Then it cannot interfere with other variables that have been declared in the outermost part of the program. A good example of this (in general) is a loop control variable for a counting loop. Such a variable should be a VAR declared locally within the procedure or function that uses it. In some implementations UCSD Pascal allows you to violate this guideline. The International Standards Organization (ISO) standard for Pascal does not.

Local procedures and functions are useful for breaking down the code of a large procedure or function. Good program design requires that each procedure perform a single logical purpose. The name of the procedure should suggest that purpose in a simple way. pmaze is a good example, although the name is somewhat cryptic. It would have been more understandable if I could have called it something like handle_the_play_while_the_adventurer_is_in_the_maze, but UCSD Pascal limits the significance of an identifier to its first eight characters. So if I ever named another procedure with a long name beginning with handle_the_play_while_the_player_is_in_. . . , I would have a name conflict. In any case, the procedure pmaze handles a single purpose that is easy to state and to comprehend. Nevertheless, it is useful to be able to write procedures and functions that are *subordinate* to pmaze and that help pmaze carry out parts of its task. I shall discuss these subordinate functions and procedures later.

LOCAL DECLARATIONS

The procedure pmaze declares an enumerated type called mazerooms. The identifiers in this type represent the individual maze locations. It is used in a fashion analogous to the rooms enumerated type in the main program. The maze rooms are not given individual names, nor are they given individual descriptions. Thus, I just call them m1, m2, m3, and so on.

There is a single local variable declared in pmaze—mazeloc. It is of the type mazerooms. Its value represents the current location of the player in the maze. The value is always one of the elements of the local enumerated type mazerooms. The variable mazeloc is entirely analogous to the global variable location.

I could have implemented the maze by simply extending the global type rooms to include the maze locations and using the variable location to keep track of them as well as of the other locations. In fact, this is what I do in the next adventure later on. For now, I have chosen the local approach to illustrate a point about Pascal. I shall let you decide which implementation of the maze you like better when you have seen both.

LOCAL PROCEDURES AND FUNCTIONS

The pmaze procedure has a large number of local procedures and a local function. The procedures fall into two classes—"location" procedures and "support" procedures. The support procedures carry out general tasks. They may be invoked from several places within the overall pmaze code, or as in the case of treasure, they may simply serve to make the program more understandable.

The support procedures are describe, sameplace, and treasure. They perform functions that are suggested by their names. The describe procedure is used to print the general description displayed when the player visits any of the maze locations. The sameplace procedure is used when a move by the player results in landing in the same maze location as before the move was made. The treasure procedure handles the discovery of the treasure that is located in one of the maze rooms. In addition, describe tells the player in which directions it is possible to continue from any given maze location. This makes it easier to map the maze.

The location procedures of pmaze are pm1 pm2, . . .,pm19. Each of these procedures corresponds to one maze location. They are analogous to the location procedures of the entire adventure (pmaze itself is one of these). However, pm1 through pm19 handle only the maze locations, which are sublocations within the maze. All of these procedures perform the following duties:

- Print a description by calling describe.
- Determine the direction of travel desired by the player, by calling whichway.

- Determine the resulting maze location or adventure location after the player's move is carried out. This is accomplished in each procedure by using a case statement as discussed in the previous chapter.

The location procedure pm1 does a little extra. In response to a player's directions, it allows not only mazeloc but also location to change. This is the way the player gets out of the maze—by returning to pm1 and then giving a direction that goes out of the maze.

The only local function in pmaze is bittest. It is an example of poor Pascal coding practice. It is included because I wrote it that way originally, and because it illustrates the kind of thinking habits that FORTRAN and assembly-language programmers fall into. It uses so-called "bit-fiddling" techniques that are better represented in Pascal using set variables.

10

Other Techniques Used in Adventure 1

In this book, I make every attempt to implement the adventures using "general" code. That is I want procedures and functions to serve as many parts of the adventure as possible. I also want to write procedures and functions that may be used as patterns. Some, like whichway, can be used directly in other adventures. Others like the location procedures provide a *skeleton* or *template*. The same general approach may be used in other adventures to accomplish the same goals.

There are many times, however, when you just have to give up on generality. There are cases in which you need fairly elaborate code in order to implement some feature of the game, and that code cannot be used for anything but that single feature. There are examples of this kind of code in Adventure 1.

The location procedure pstart, pvestibule, pnarrow1, pisland, pogreroom, ppit, pladder, and pflames each contain one or more sections of special code. Let's just go through them to get a flavor of the kind of things that are possible.

The pisland Procedure

This procedure provides the simplest possible example. The procedure pisland contains the statement

```
readmsg: = TRUE;
```

What this represents in the game is the fact that the adventurer has read the message to be found on the island. This is important later on—in the maze—because the treasure cannot be found until the message has been read. This is an extremely simple example of solving a problem. In this case, the adventurer solves the problem just by visiting the island. Later, when you add commands to your adventures, you might require the adventurer to explicitly command the guide to READ MESSAGE or something like that.

There is a general principle in this example, as well. The variable readmsg is of the Boolean type. This means that its value may either be true or false. Such variables are useful for representing events in adventure games. More precisely, a Boolean variable may be used to record the occurrence of an event. In this example, the event was the reading of the message. As long as readmsg has the value false, the event has not occured. When and if the value becomes true, the event has occurred.

The pflames Procedure

This procedure is similar to the pisland procedure. It sets two Boolean variables, namely, cooked and done to true. This effectively says that the adventurer has been cooked and that the adventure is over. Not much more to say, is there?

The pstart and ppit Procedures

Both of these procedures have slightly different case statements than the other location procedures in Adventure 1. In each, there is one direction that causes a special message to be printed. This happens rather than either the location being changed or the noway message being printed. In each case, the difference is not important to the way the game is played or to the result. The only purpose for the extra messages is to add interest.

In ppit, if the player tries to go u, the message:

Try to climb that, and you'll kill yourself.

appears. This message is consistent with the earlier description in location brink. There, the player is warned that sliding down into the pit is possible, but climbing back out doesn't seem possible. The ppit special message confirms this message.

The pvestibule, pnarrow1, pladder, and pstart Procedures

In each of these procedures, one or more Boolean variables is examined in order to detect conditions that require special action. In each case, further setting of Boolean variables may take place depending on what happens.

In pladder, the variable carrying is examined. If carrying is true, it indicates that the adventurer has located the treasure and is carrying it. In this case, it is impossible for him to climb the ladder, because the treasure is too heavy. Otherwise, going up the ladder is allowed.

In pnarrow1, the variable carrying is examined again. If it is true here, the guide tells the adventurer that going south with the treasure is not feasible, because the crack in that direction is too narrow. The adventurer is then given a chance to drop the treasure. If the answer is yes, carrying is set to false and the variable dropped is set to true. The latter variable is used in pvestibule later on.

In pvestibule, if dropped is true, the treasure is sitting abandoned in location narrow1. The guide tells the adventurer this and allows the treasure to be reached for through the crack. If the adventurer agrees to try to reach for it (can you imagine anyone who would not agree to do that?), carrying is set back to true and dropped is set back to false. This allows the adventurer to win the game by then returning to location start.

In pstart, the variable carrying is looked at. If it is true, the variable done is set to true, which means that the game is over. The fact that carrying is true when the game ends means that the adventurer has succeeded in finding the treasure and getting it back to the starting location. In short, the adventurer has won.

The pogreroom Procedure

This location contains the most elaborate special case code of any location. In fact, there is a subsidiary procedure, ogreaction, which is invoked to handle a lot of the action.

The procedures pogreroom and ogreaction deal with the adventurer's interactions with the ogre. There are only bad experiences to be had in the ogreroom! The Boolean variables awake, and eaten control these. If awake is true, you risk being eaten by the ogre. Your chances are 1 to 5 if you are not carrying the treasure, but 1 in 2 if you are carrying it! If the ogre is not yet awake, each time you visit his lair, you stand a 1 in 7 chance of waking him.

If you should be silly enough to ask to go in direction d while you are in the ogreroom, you will also be eaten. This corresponds to walking directly into the ogre's fire-pit.

11

Preview of Adventure 2

The second example of a Pascal adventure game is based on the first. The map has been extended considerably, and many additional capabilities have been added. This is the first "real" adventure game, because it allows the player to issue commands and control the play much more directly than the first game did. In many ways, Adventure 2 is the heart of the book. I shall continue to discuss it in one way or another up until Chapter 25.

MAPS, DIAGRAMS, AND CODE OUTLINES

Figures 11-1 through 11-9 present the code outlines, structure diagram, and maps of Adventure 2. Because Adventure 2 is an extension and modification of Adventure 1, you should compare Figs. 11-1 through 11-9 to Figs. 5-1 through 5-8. The map of Adventure 2 is similar to that of Adventure 1, with some extensions. Figure 11-7 shows the differences between the map of Adventure 1, which was presented in Figs. 7-1 and 7-2, and the map of Adventure 2. Figure 11-8 presents the map of the additions to Adventure 1.

CHAPTER PREVIEWS

Chapter 13 is called "Command Processing in Adventure 2" and discusses the use of enumerated types in representing commands. It shows how the cmdlookup function uses a linear search with a sentinel to determine which command the player has entered. In the process, it deals with arrays indexed by an enumerated type, the input of values of an enumerated type, the Pascal succ function, and other related topics.

Chapter 14 is called "Carry and Drop: Pascal Sets." It deals with the use of the Pascal set types to represent collections of objects in the adventure game. In particular, it shows how the player's "stash," that is, the objects being carried at a given time, is represented by a Pascal set. It also shows how the collection of items at each location is represented in a similar fashion. A comparison of the use of Pascal sets with the implementation of sets in ad hoc BASIC code presented. Finally, the use of the set operators in Pascal is discussed in the course of presenting the implementation of the

PROGRAM miniadventure;

CONST, TYPE, and VAR declarations:

This section of the program contains the declarations of the constants, types, and variables used by the rest of the program.
See Figure 11-2

procedures and functions

This section contains the headers and code for the procedures and functions accessible to the main program block and the outermost level of the program.
See Figures 11-3 and 11-4

BEGIN

The main program block of Adventure 2.
See Figure 11-5

END.

Fig. 11-1. The code outline for Adventure 2: the program outline.

carry and drop commands in the adventure game.

Chapter 16 is entitled "Problems in Adventure 2." Problems, as I have emphasized, are the soul of adventure games. The techniques for representing problems and their solutions in Pascal code are therefore paramount. This chapter deals with the use of Boolean variables and Boolean expressions in the problem-solving process. It discusses the particular problems posed by Adventure 2 and both their *external* face, the way the player views them, and their *internal* representation, the way they are implemented.

The Pascal set membership operator, IN, and its role in Boolean expressions is discussed. Other elements of Boolean expressions are explained including numeric relationships, and the AND, OR, and NOT operators.

Chapter 16 deals with the ad hoc techniques of Adventure 2. It is called "Other Techniques Used in Adventure 2." The Pascal coding solutions for

CONST

TYPE

rooms
directions } As in Adventure 1

cmds
represents the commands the user may issue in Adventure 2 apart from directions

objects
represents the objects found in Adventure 2

collection
represents any subset of objects

placerec
a record type describing entries in the index part of the descriptions database

VAR

xfile
narrate
file variables corresponding to the descriptions database index and text data files, respectively

places: ARRAY [rooms] of placerec;
an array to hold a copy of the descriptions database index in memory

whatshere: ARRAY [rooms] of collection;
an array corresponding to the set of objects present at each location—modified by the carry and drop commands.

stash
represents the objects carried by the player

cmdnames, objnames
arrays of strings used to match command names and object names typed by the player

hasdug
counts the number of times the player has dug

done, quit, carrying, dropped, chgloc, etc.
variables to track the occurrence of various events during game play

Fig. 11-2. The code outline for Adventure 2: important data declarations.

counting the number of turns the player has taken, displaying the contents of a set, scoring the game, dealing with the lamp, and implementing the eat and dig commands are explained. The handling of the ogre character in the game is discussed. The simplification of the process of changing locations is explained, in particular, the function of the new procedure **travel**.

Adventure 2 uses files for some of its information. This is hinted at in Chapter 16. However, the information in files is a complete data base of descriptions of all the locations in the adventure game. How this database is created and all the techniques associated with it are dealt with in great detail in the next section of the book starting with Chapter 18.

Chapter 17 is a collection of helpful hints regarding the use of the UCSD Pascal system. It is

PROCEDURE introduction; **PROCEDURE initialize;**	} As in Adventure 1

PROCEDURE showobjects;
Tells the player what objects are present, if any, at the location currently being visited.
PROCEDURE show;
Prints the full description of the location just entered.

FUNCTION score: INTEGER; } As in Adventure 1
FUNCTION objlookup: objects;
Determines which object name, if any, a user-typed string matches; returns the internal value of said object.

FUNCTION ckobject (it: objects) : BOOLEAN;
Determines if a given object is present in the current location; returns true if it is; false, otherwise.

PROCEDURE pcarry; **PROCEDURE pdrop;** **PROCEDURE phelp;** **PROCEDURE plight;** **PROCEDURE pinventory** **PROCEDURE ppush;** **PROCEDURE pdig;** **PROCEDURE popen;** **PROCEDURE plook;** **PROCEDURE peat;**	} Procedures used to support the execution of specific commands in Adventure 2

FUNCTION cmdlookup:cmds;
Similar to **objlookup**, but determines commands rather than objects.

PROCEDURE listen;
FUNCTION docommand:CHAR;
FUNCTION whichway: directions;
PROCEDURE noway;
PROCEDURE travel (nloc,sloc,eloc,wloc,uloc,dloc:rooms);

Procedures and functions for general command handling and changing player's location from one "room" to another.
PROCEDURE cklamp;
Monitors the lamp; warns player about staying in the dark, and so on.

Fig. 11-3. Code outline for Adventure 2: the procedures and functions: Part I.

```
PROCEDURE oreaction;
PROCEDURE pstart;
PROCEDURE pvestibule;
PROCEDURE pnarrow1;
PROCEDURE pisland;
PROCEDURE pogreroom;
PROCEDURE ppit;
PROCEDURE pladder;
PROCEDURE pflames;
```

Location procedures as in Adventure 1. Because **travel** is itself a procedure in Adventure 2, many locations no longer need a location procedure. (See Figure 11-5)

```
PROCEDURE pmaze;
```

Location procedure for the maze.

```
PROCEDURE describe;
PROCEDURE sameplace;
```

Local procedures as in Adventure 1.

```
PROCEDURE travel (nloc,sloc,eloc,wloc,uloc,dloc:rooms);
```

Local proceure—handles travel within the maze.

```
PROCEDURE pm1;
```

Local procedure—handles travel within the maze.

```
BEGIN
  REPEAT
    CASE location OF
      maze,m1: pm1;
      m2: travel (m1,same,m0,m0,m0,m0);
      .
      .
      .
      m19: travel (m0,m18,m0,m0,m15,m0);
    END;
  UNTIL (location<maze) or (location-flames);
END(* PROCEDURE pmaze *);
```

Function block for **pmaze** handles travel inside the maze. A REPEAT statement invokes the local travel procedure until the player gets out of the maze.

Fig. 11-4. The code outline for Adventure 2: the procedures and functions: Part II.

entitled "UCSD Pascal Development Techniques." There are discussions of how to manage your files effectively and UCSD tricks and pitfalls. Organizing your files, entering them into the system using the UCSD Editor, splitting a large program into multiple files, and using the include option in the com-

```
BEGIN

   introduction; }
   initialize;   } As in Adventure 1

   REPEAT
      visited [location] := TRUE;
      show (location);
      cklamp;

      Perform general processing associated with changing locations.

      CASE location OF
        start: pstart;
        grandroom: travel (nowhere, nowhere, nowhere,
                           brink, nowhere, stairs);
        vestibule: pvestibule;
        narrow1: pnarrow1;
        lakeshore: travel (island, narrow1, narrow2,
                           nowhere, nowhere, nowhere);
        •
        •
        •
        flames:pflames;
      END;
    UNTIL quit OR done;

   Main control loop of Adventure 2. If a visit is made to a
   location for which no special handling is required,
   the travel procedure is invoked to process commands
   and move to a new location. Other locations, for
   example maze and narrow1 still require location procedures.
   These location procedures handle special conditions
   as well as invoke travel.

   congratulations; } As in Adventure 1

END.
```

Fig. 11-5. The code outline for Adventure 2: the main program block.

piler are all touched on in the discussion. A couple of filer tricks involving the prefix command and the K(runch command are introduced—these tricks can save you time and trouble in your day to day use of the UCSD system. Finally, a general discussion of pitfalls in software development under the UCSD system is presented.

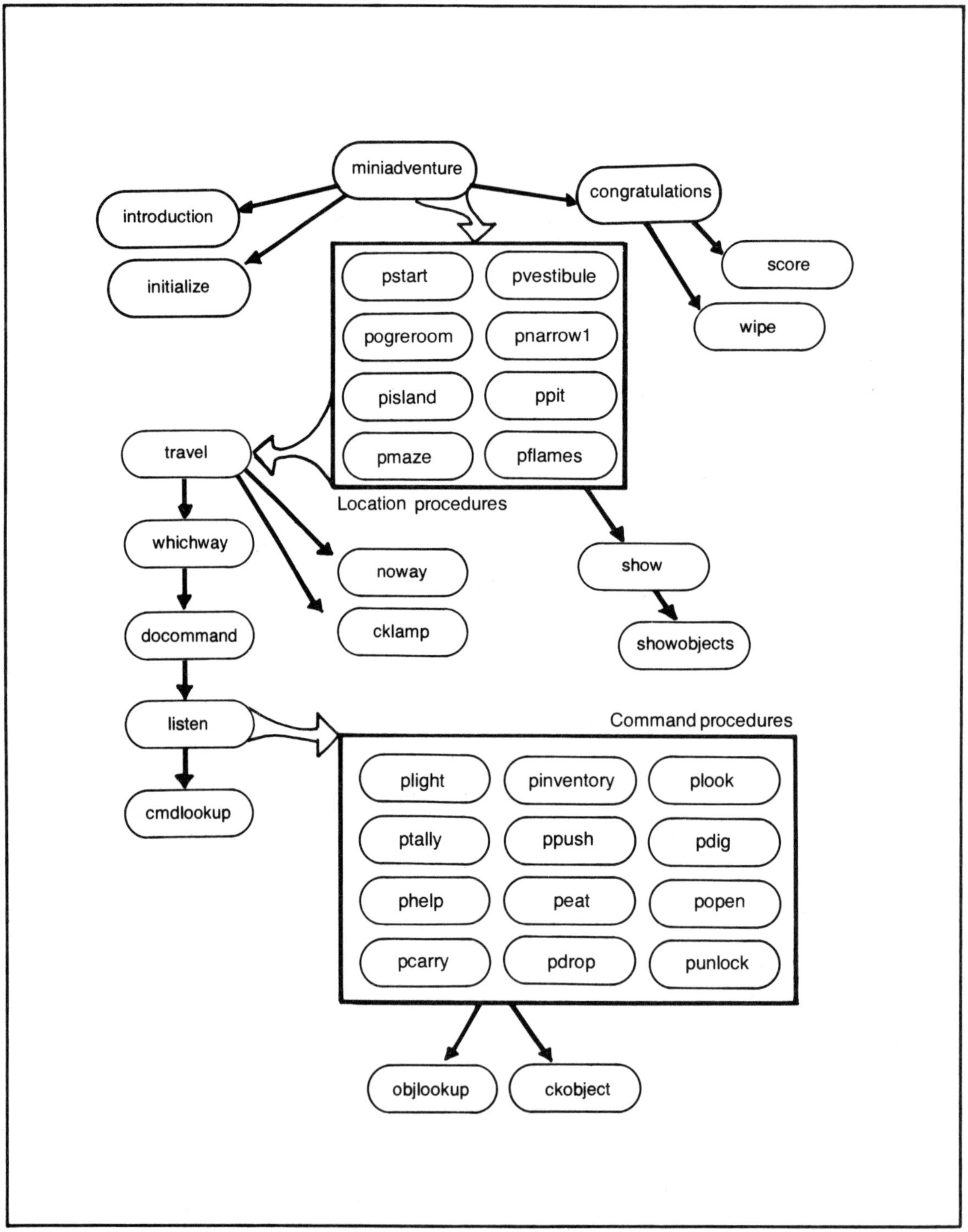

Fig. 11-6. Structure diagram for Adventure 2.

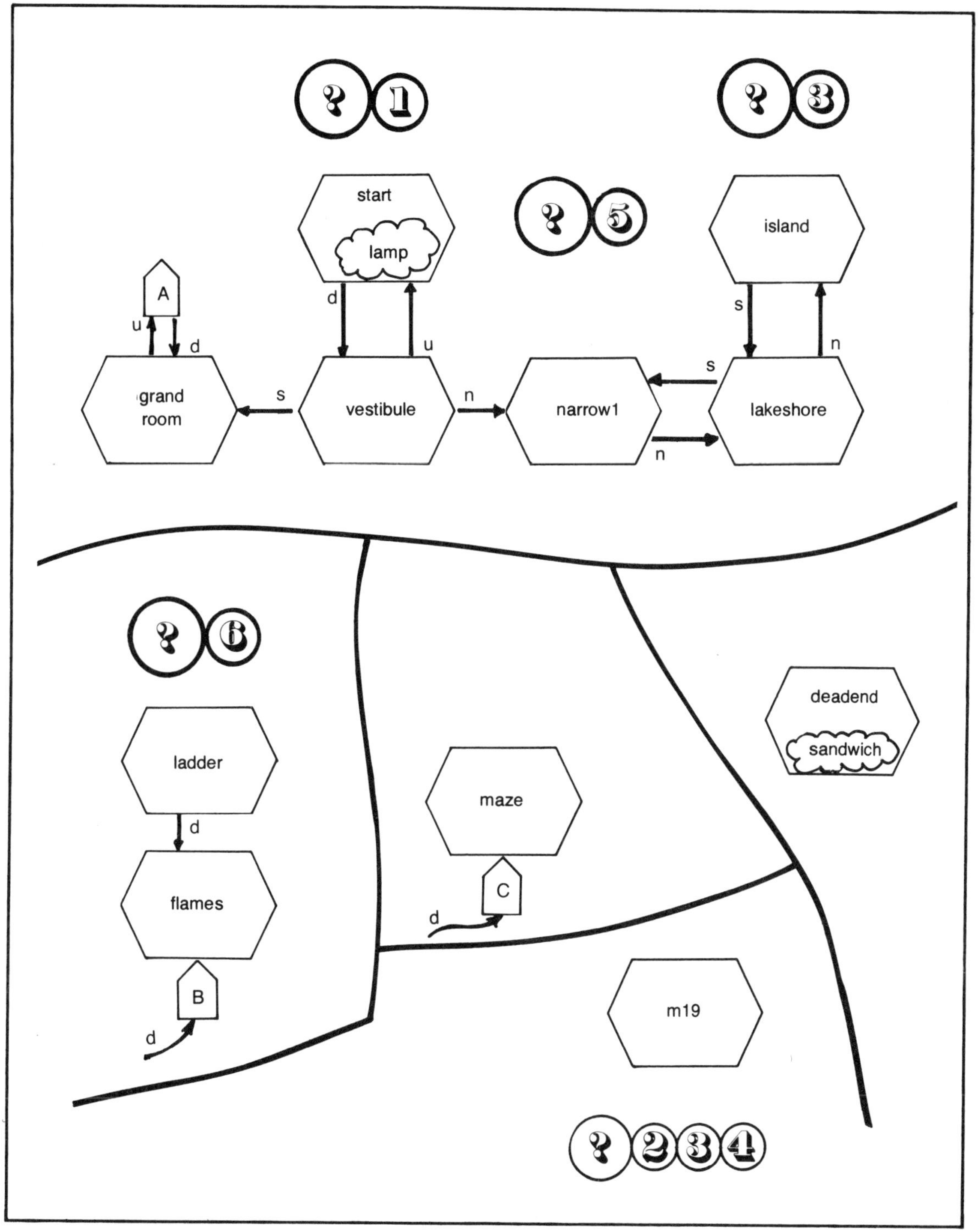

Fig. 11-7. Map of Adventure 2: Page 1.

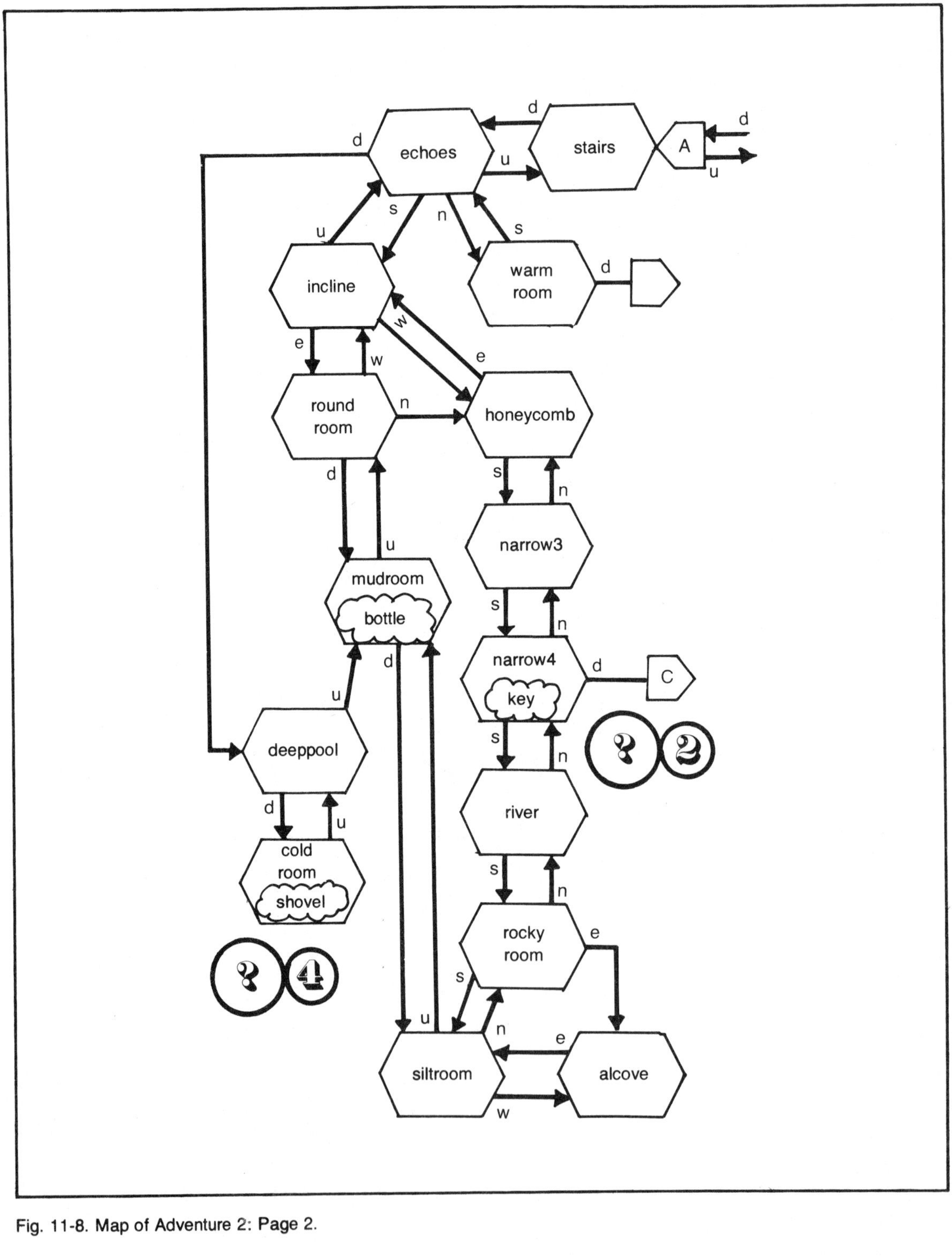

Fig. 11-8. Map of Adventure 2: Page 2.

1. You must carry the lamp and light it in order not to fall into a pit. You must bring the treasure to **start** in order to win the game.

2. The treasure in Adventure 2 is locked in a chest. You must find and carrv the key—otherwise, you cannot open the chest when you dig it up.

3. You must visit the island and read the message before you can dig up the treasure.

4. The treasure in Adventure 2 is buried. In order to be able to dig for it, you must locate and carry the shovel. When you dig for the treasure, you must dig three times to fully reveal the chest.

5. You must drop the treasure at narrow1 and **push** it through the crack leading to the vestible. There is no other way to get it out.

6. You cannot carry the treasure up the ladder—it is too heavy. You must discover the trick of Problem 5.

Fig. 11-9. Problems of Adventure 2.

12

Pascal Adventure 2

```
{$s+}

PROGRAM miniadventure;
CONST

  ff     =        12;

TYPE

  rooms =  (start, grandroom, vestibule, narrow1,
            lakeshore, island, brink, iceroom,
            ogreroom, narrow2, pit, crystal,
            batscave, steam, deadend, ladder,
            maze, stairs, echoes, warmroom,
            incline, honeycomb, roundroom,
            mudroom, deeppool, coldroom, narrow3,
            narrow4, river, rockyroom, siltroom,
            alcove, flames, m0, m1, m2, m3, m4,
            m5, m6, m7, m8, m9, m10, m11, m12,
            m13, m14, m15, m16, m17, m18, m19,
            same, nowhere);

  directions    =  (n, s, e, w, u, d);
```

```
  cmds              =  (carry, drop, help, light,
                        invent, take, tally, push,
                        dig, look, open, unlock,
                        eat, nocmd);

  objects           =  (lamp, treasure, key,
                        sandwich, bottle, shovel,
                        noobj);

  collection        =  SET OF objects;

  pname             =  STRING[40];
  storyline         =  STRING[80];
  byte              =  0..255;

  whichsect         =  (indexsection, descsection);

  placerec          =

    RECORD

      CASE section:whichsection OF

        indexsection:    ( tableentry:    INTEGER);

        descsection:     ( name:        pname;
                           id:          INTEGER;
                           dbegin:      INTEGER;
                           dend:        INTEGER;
                           link:        byte    );

    END;


VAR

  xfile:          FILE OF placerec;
  narrate:        FILE OF storyline;

  places:         ARRAY[rooms] OF placerec;
  whatshere:      ARRAY[rooms] OF collection;
  visited:        ARRAY[rooms] OF BOOLEAN;

  stash:          collection;

  command:        STRING;
```

```
{ holds user typed direction }

head,
tail:            STRING;
{ hold SEPARATE words OF command }

cmdnames:        ARRAY[cmds] OF STRING;
objnames:        ARRAY[objects] OF STRING;
ch:              CHAR;

dchars:          SET OF CHAR;
{ characters which correspond TO the
  acceptable initial letters OF
  direction  commands.  initialized TO
  ['n', 's', 'e', 'w', 'u', 'd']       }

location:        rooms;
ogreloc:         rooms;

special1:        SET OF rooms;

next:            directions;

turns:           INTEGER;
i:               INTEGER;
indark:          INTEGER;
hasdug:          INTEGER;

done:            BOOLEAN;
quit:            BOOLEAN;
lit:             BOOLEAN;
eaten:           BOOLEAN;
awake:           BOOLEAN;
readmsg:         BOOLEAN;
carrying:        BOOLEAN;
dropped:         BOOLEAN;
trapped:         BOOLEAN;
cooked:          BOOLEAN;
candig:          BOOLEAN;
chgloc:          BOOLEAN;

        {*********}
        { w i p e }
        {*********}
        PROCEDURE wipe;
        BEGIN
```

```
            write(chr(ff));
          END;

{$ia2.u1.text}
{$ia2.u2.text}
{$ia2.m2.text}
{$ia2.maze.text}
{$ia2.main.text}
 { source FILE: a2.u1.text }
{*********************************}
{ i  n  t  r  o  d  u  c  t  i  o  n }
{*********************************}

PROCEDURE introduction;
BEGIN

   wipe;          { clear screen };

   writeln;
   writeln ('Welcome tó miniadventure!');
   writeln ('Your goal will be to find a treasure');
   writeln ('and bring it back to your starting');
   writeln ('point.  You will also get points');
   writeln ('for finding each location in the');
   writeln ('adventure.  Points will be deducted');
   writeln ('for various undesirable happenings:');
   writeln ('waking the ogre, getting eaten,');
   writeln ('getting toasted, etc.');
   writeln;
   writeln ('I will guide you and be your eyes');
   writlen ('and ears.  Command me with one or');
   writeln ('two word phrases, such as');
   writeln ('"CARRY KEY" or "NORTH".');
   writeln ('I only look at the first letter');
   writeln ('of commands that tell me which');
   writeln ('direction to take.  Thus, i take');
   writeln ('"NORTH" and "N" to be the same.');
   writeln;
   writeln ('  When you are ready to begin your');
   writeln ('adventure, just press RETURN');

   readln (command);

   wipe;

END { PROCEDURE introduction };
```

```
{***********************************}
{   i  n  i  t  i  a  l  i  z  e    }
{***********************************}

PROCEDURE initialize;
VAR
  loc:  rooms;
BEGIN

  location := start;
  dchars   := ['q','n','s','e','w','u','d'];
  done     := false;
  quit     := false;
  cooked   := false;
  eaten    := false;
  lit      := false;
  awake    := false;
  readmsg  := false;
  carrying := false;
  trapped  := false;
  dropped  := false;
  candig   := false;
  chgloc   := true;
  turns    := 0;
  indark   := 0;
  hasdug   := 0;

  FOR loc := start TO nowhere DO
  BEGIN

    visited[loc] := false;
    whatshere[loc] := [];

  END { DO };

  stash := [];
  whatshere[start]      := [lamp];
  whatshere[coldroom]   := [shovel];
  whatshere[narrow4]    := [key];
  whatshere[deadend]    := [sandwich];
  whatshere[mudroom]    := [bottle];

  cmdnames[carry]   := 'carry';
  cmdnames[drop]    := 'drop';
  cmdnames[help]    := 'help';
  cmdnames[light]   := 'light';
```

```
  cmdnames[invent]   := 'inventory';
  cmdnames[take]     := 'take';
  cmdnames[tally]    := 'score';
  cmdnames[push]     := 'push';
  cmdnames[dig]      := 'dig';
  cmdnames[look]     := 'look';
  cmdnames[open]     := 'open';
  cmdnames[unlock]   := 'unlock';
  cmdnames[eat]      := 'eat';
  cmdnames[nocmd]    := 'sentinel';

  objnames[lamp]     := 'lamp';
  objnames[treasure]:= 'treasure';
  objnames[shovel]   := 'shovel';
  objnames[key]      := 'key';
  objnames[sandwich]:= 'sandwich';
  objnames[bottle]   := 'bottle';
  objnames[noobj]    := 'sentinel';

  reset (xfile, 'a2.db80.x');
  reset (narrate, 'a2.db80');

  loc := start;
  seek (xfile,31);
  get (xfile);
  places[loc] := xfile^;

  REPEAT

    loc := succ (loc);
    get (xfile);
    places[loc] := xfile^;

  UNTIL loc = flames;

  close (xfile);

END { PROCEDURE initialize };

{***********************************}
{    s  h  o  w  o  b  j  e  c  t  s }
{***********************************}

PROCEDURE showobjects;
VAR
  lobj: objects;
```

```
BEGIN

  FOR lobj := lamp TO noobj DO
    IF lobj IN whatshere[location]
    THEN
    BEGIN

      write ('There is a ');
      write (objnames[lobj]);
      writeln (' here.');

    END { IF lobj IN .. }
  { enddo };

END { PROCEDURE showobjects };

{************************************}
{        s     h     o     w         }
{************************************}

PROCEDURE show(where: rooms);
VAR
  i:     INTEGER;
BEGIN

  IF (chgloc AND lit)
      OR
     (location = start)
  THEN
  BEGIN

    WITH places[where] DO
    BEGIN

      FOR i := dbegin TO dend DO
      BEGIN

        seek (narrate,i);
        get (narrate);
        write (narrate^);

      END { DO };

    END { WITH places };

  END { IF chgloc };
```

```
  showobjects;

END { PROCEDURE show };

{***********************************}
{      s     c     o     r     e          }
{***********************************}

FUNCTION score: INTEGER;
VAR
  loc:  rooms;
  sc:   INTEGER;
BEGIN

  sc := 0;

  FOR loc := start TO flames DO
    IF visited[loc]
    THEN
      sc := sc + 5
    { endif }
  { enddo };

  IF NOT quit
  THEN
    sc := sc + 140;

  IF cooked
  THEN
    sc := sc - 50;

  IF eaten
  THEN
    sc := sc - 50;

  IF awake
  THEN
    sc := sc - 25;

  score := sc;

END { FUNCTION score };

{***********************************}
{  c o n g r a t u l a t i o n s    }
{***********************************}
```

```
PROCEDURE congratulations;
BEGIN

  IF NOT cooked
  THEN
  BEGIN

    IF NOT quit
    THEN
    BEGIN

      writeln (' ***** Congratulations *****');
      writeln;
      write ('You got the treasure out in only ');
      writeln (turns:4,' turns.');

    END;

    writeln ('You scored ', score:4);
    writeln (' points out of a maximum of 300 pts.');
    writeln ('So long for now, come again soon!');


  END
  ELSE

    writeln ('Sorry about that - try again soon!')

  { endif };

  readln (command);
  wipe;

END { PROCEDURE congratulations };

{**********************************}
{    o b j l o o k u p           }
{**********************************}

FUNCTION objlookup: objects;
VAR
  lobj: objects;
BEGIN

  objnames[noobj] := tail;
  lobj := lamp;
```

```
   WHILE tail <> objnames[lobj] DO
   BEGIN

     { old debug statements - leave in
       for historical edification.
     write (tail);
     write ('<>');
     writeln (objnames[lobj]);
     }
     lobj := succ(lobj);

   END { DO };

   objlookup := lobj;

 END;

 {***********************************}
 {     c  k  o  b  j  e  c  t        }
 {***********************************}

 FUNCTION ckobject(it:objects): BOOLEAN;
 BEGIN

   ckobject := false;

   IF it IN whatshere[location]
   THEN

     ckobject := true
   { endif };

END { FUNCTION ckobject };
 { source FILE: a2.u2.text }
{************************************}
{      p    c    a    r    r    y     }
{************************************}

PROCEDURE pcarry;
VAR
  it:   objects;
BEGIN

  it := objlookup;

  IF NOT ckobject (it)
```

```
  THEN
  BEGIN

    write ('I don''t see any ');
    write (tail);
    writeln (' here.');

  END
  ELSE
  BEGIN

    writeln ('Ok');
    stash := stash + [it];
    whatshere[location] :=
        whatshere[location] - [it]

  END { IF NOT it IN ... };

END { PROCEDURE pcarry };

{***********************************}
{        p   d   r   o   p          }
{***********************************}

PROCEDURE pdrop;
VAR
  it:   objects;
BEGIN

  it := objlookup;

  IF NOT (it IN stash)
  THEN
  BEGIN

    write ('You are not carrying any ');
    writeln (tail);

  END
  ELSE
  BEGIN

    writeln ('Ok');
    stash := stash - [it];
    whatshere[location] :=
        whatshere[location] + [it];
```

```
  END { IF NOT it IN stash };

END { PROCEDURE drop };

{***********************************}
{          p  h  e  l  p            }
{***********************************}

PROCEDURE phelp;
BEGIN

  IF readmsg
  THEN
  BEGIN

    writeln ('The treasure is deep in the maze');

  END
  ELSE
  BEGIN

    writeln ('There are hints to be found');
    writeln ('near the lake and in the alcove.');

  END { IF readmsg };

END { PROCEDURE phelp };

{***********************************}
{        p   l   i   g   h   t      }
{***********************************}

PROCEDURE plight;
VAR
  cmd:  STRING;
BEGIN

  IF NOT (lamp IN stash)
  THEN
    writeln ('You are not carrying the lamp.')
  ELSE
  BEGIN

     IF (tail = 'on')
        OR
        (tail = 'lamp')
```

```
        OR
         (tail = '')
     THEN
       lit := true
     ELSE
       lit := false
     { endif };
   END { IF NOT lamp IN stash };

   IF lit
   THEN
     writeln ('Your lamp is now on.')
   ELSE
     writeln ('Your lamp is off.');
   { endif };

END { PROCEDURE plight };

{************************************}
{    p  i  n  v  e  n  t  o  r  y    }
{************************************}

PROCEDURE pinventory;
VAR
  lobj: objects;
BEGIN

   IF stash <> []
   THEN
   BEGIN
     writeln ('You are currently holding: ');
     FOR lobj := lamp TO noobj DO
     BEGIN

       IF lobj IN stash
       THEN
         writeln (objnames[lobj])
       { endif }

     END { FOR lobj := ... };
   END { IF stash <> [] };

END { PROCEDURE pinventory };

{************************************}
{        p  p  u  s  h               }
{************************************}
```

```
PROCEDURE ppush;
VAR

  newtail: STRING;
  p:       INTEGER;
BEGIN

  p := pos (' ', tail);
  IF p = 0
  THEN
    newtail := ''
  ELSE
  BEGIN

    newtail := copy(tail,p+1,length(tail)-p);
    tail := copy(tail,1,p-1);

  END { IF p=0 };

  IF (tail = 'treasure')
  THEN
  BEGIN

    IF (treasure IN whatshere[narrow1])
       AND
       (location = narrow1)
    THEN
    BEGIN

      writeln ('Ok');
      whatshere[vestibule] :=
          whatshere[vestibule] + [treasure];
      whatshere[narrow1]   :=
          whatshere[narrow1]   - [treasure];

    END { IF treasure ... };

  END
  ELSE
  BEGIN

    writeln ('Sorry, but I don''t think');
    writeln ('I can do that.');
  END { IF tail = 'treasure' };

END { PROCEDURE ppush };
```

```
{************************************}
{           p   d   i   g            }
{************************************}

PROCEDURE pdig;
BEGIN

  candig := (shovel IN stash)


           AND
           (readmsg);

IF (location = m19)
   AND
   candig
THEN
  hasdug := hasdug + 1
{ endif };

IF (location <> m19)
THEN
  writeln ('You can''t dig here at all.')
ELSE
  IF hasdug = 0
  THEN
  BEGIN

    writeln ('You can''t dig here yet.');

  END
  ELSE
    IF hasdug = 1
    THEN
    BEGIN

      writeln ('That''s a nice pile of dirt you');
      writeln ('have shovelled.  Be careful');
      writeln ('not to block your way out!');

    END
    ELSE
      IF hasdug = 2
    THEN
    BEGIN
```

```
  writeln ('I see the top of a weather-');
  writeln ('beaten chest.');

END
ELSE
  IF hasdug = 3
  THEN
  BEGIN

    writeln ('You have unearthed an old');
    writeln ('treasure chest.  It is');
    writeln ('secured with a massive');
    writeln ('brass lock.');

  END
  ELSE
      IF hasdug = 4
      THEN
      BEGIN

        writeln ('There''s nothing else here.');
        writeln ('but if you try hard, you');
        writeln ('might dig down to the');
        writeln ('lava pits!');

      END
      ELSE

        IF hasdug > 4
        THEN
        BEGIN

          cooked := true;
          done   := true;
          show (flames);
          location := flames;
          chgloc   := true;

        END { IF hasdug > 4 }
      { END IF hasdug > 3 }
    { END IF hasdug = 3 }
  { END IF hasdug = 2 }
{ END IF hasdug = 1 }
```

```
    { END IF hasdug = 0 }
   { END IF (location <> m19 };

END { PROCEDURE pdig };

{**********************************}
{         p  o  p  e  n            }
{**********************************}

PROCEDURE popen;
BEGIN

  IF (location = m19)
     AND
     (hasdug >= 3)
     AND
     (key IN stash)
  THEN
  BEGIN

    writeln ('Ok');
    whatshere[m19] := whatshere[m19] + [treasure];
    writeln ('The chest is full of treasure');

  END { IF };

  IF (location = m19)
     AND
     (hasdug >= 3)
     AND
     ( NOT (key IN stash))
  THEN
  BEGIN

    writeln ('I''m afraid you''ll need a key');
    writeln ('to open that brass lock!');

  END { IF };

  IF location <> m19
  THEN

    writeln ('There''s nothing here to open!')

  { endif };
END { PROCEDURE popen };
```

```
{**********************************}
{          p  l  o  o  k           }
{**********************************}

PROCEDURE plook;
VAR
  savchg:        BOOLEAN;
BEGIN

  savchg := chgloc;
  chgloc := true;

  IF location <= flames
  THEN
    show (location)
  ELSE
    show (maze)
  { endif };

  chgloc := savchg;

END { PROCEDURE plook };

{**********************************}
{          p   e   a   t           }
{**********************************}

PROCEDURE peat;
BEGIN

  IF sandwich IN stash
  THEN
  BEGIN

    writeln ('Oh, yummy!!');
    stash := stash - [sandwich];

  END
  ELSE
    IF tail = 'sandwich'
    THEN
      writeln ('You don''t have a sandwich')
    ELSE
      writeln ('Don''t be ridiculous!!')
    { endif }
```

```
  { endif };

END { PROCEDURE peat };

{*********************************************************}
{       c  m  d  l  o  o  k  u  p       }
{*********************************************************}

FUNCTION cmdlookup: cmds;
VAR
  p: INTEGER;
  lcmd : cmds;
BEGIN

  writeln;
  write ('===>');
  readln (command);
  p := pos (' ', command);

  IF p=0
  THEN
  BEGIN
    head := command;
    tail := '';
  END
  ELSE
  BEGIN
    head := copy (command, 1, p-1);
    tail :=
        copy (command, p+1, length (command)-p);
  END { IF p=0 };

  cmdnames[nocmd] := head;
  lcmd := carry;

  WHILE head <> cmdnames[lcmd] DO
    lcmd := succ (lcmd)
  { END DO };
  cmdlookup := lcmd;

END { FUNCTION cmdlookup };

{*********************************************************}
{         l  i  s  t  e  n          }
{*********************************************************}
```

```
PROCEDURE listen;
VAR
  lcmd: cmds;

BEGIN

  REPEAT

    lcmd := cmdlookup;
    CASE lcmd OF

      carry:    pcarry;
      drop:     pdrop;
      help:     phelp;
      light:    plight;
      invent:   pinventory;
      take:     pcarry;
      tally:    BEGIN

                  write ('Should you quit now,');
                  writeln ('your score would be ');
                  writeln ((score-140):3);
                  writeln (' points of a possible 300.');

                END;
      push:     ppush;
      dig:      pdig;
      look:     plook;
      open:     popen;
      unlock:   popen;
      eat:      peat;
      nocmd:    ;

    END;

  UNTIL lcmd = nocmd;

END { PROCEDURE listen };

{***********************************}
{     d  o  c  o  m  m  a  n  d      }
{***********************************}


FUNCTION docommand: CHAR;
BEGIN
```

```
  head := '';
  tail := '';
  REPEAT

    listen

  UNTIL length (head) > 0;
  docommand := head[1];

END { PROCEDURE docommand };

{***********************************}
{     w   h   i   c   h   w   a   y        }
{***********************************}

FUNCTION whichway:directions;
BEGIN

  turns := turns + 1;

  REPEAT

    ch := docommand;

    CASE ch OF

      'n':       whichway := n;
      's':       whichway := s;
      'e':       whichway := e;
      'w':       whichway := w;
      'u':       whichway := u;
      'd':       whichway := d;
      'q':           quit := true;

    END;

  UNTIL ch IN dchars;

  writeln;

end { function whichway };

{***********************************}
{       n   o   w   a   y              }
{***********************************}
```

```
procedure noway;
begin

  writeln;
  write ('There is no way to go');
  writeln ('in that direction.');
  chgloc := false;

END;

{*********************************}
{    c    k    l    a    m    p         }
{*********************************}

PROCEDURE cklamp;
BEGIN

  IF (location <> start)
     AND
     NOT lit
  THEN
    indark := indark + 1
  { endif };

  IF indark > 4
  THEN
  BEGIN

    quit := true;
    cooked := true;
    done   := true;

    writeln ('You fell into a pit and were');
    writeln ('killed. Too bad!! Maybe next');
    writeln ('time you''ll listen to me');
    writeln ('and keep your lamp on!');

  END
  ELSE

    IF (indark > 0)
       AND
       (NOT lit)
       AND
       (location <> start)
```

```
    THEN
    BEGIN

      writeln ('It is now pitch dark.');
      writeln (' I wouldn''t go too far.');
      writeln ('You might fall into a pit AND be');
      writeln ('killed.');

    END { IF indark > 0 };

  { END IF indark > 4 };

  IF (turns >= 75)
     AND
     (turns < 80)
  THEN
  BEGIN

    writeln ('I would think about wrapping this');
    writeln ('up, since your lamp is getting dim.');

  END
  ELSE
    IF turns > 150
    THEN
    BEGIN

      writeln ('You''re in trouble now!');
      writeln ('Your lamp just went out!');
      lit := false;

    END { IF turns > 150 }
  { END IF turns >= 75 ... };

END { PROCEDURE cklamp };

{***********************************}
{     t   r   a   v   e   l         }
{***********************************}

PROCEDURE travel(

            nloc,
            sloc,
            eloc,
            wloc,
```

```
            uloc,
            dloc: rooms);

  PROCEDURE newloc(loc:rooms);
  BEGIN

    IF loc=nowhere
    THEN
      noway
    ELSE
    BEGIN
      location := loc;
      chgloc   := true;
    END { IF };

  END { PROCEDURE newloc };

BEGIN  {** travel **}

  CASE whichway OF
    n:  newloc (nloc);
    s:  newloc (sloc);
    e:  newloc (eloc);
    w:  newloc (wloc);
    u:  newloc (uloc);
    d:  newloc (dloc);

  END { CASE whichway };

END { PROCEDURE travel };
 { source FILE: a2.m2.text }
{***********************************}
{    o  g  r  e  a  c  t  i  o  n   }
{***********************************}

PROCEDURE ogreaction;
BEGIN

  IF NOT awake
  THEN
  BEGIN
    writeln ('This is the ogre''s lair!');
    writeln ('If you are not careful, you''ll');
    writeln ('wake him.');

    IF (turns MOD 3)=0
```

```
  THEN
  BEGIN

    awake := true;
    writeln ('Now you''ve done it!');
    writeln ('You woke the ogre - better');
    writeln ('get out of here while you can');

  END { IF };

END
ELSE
BEGIN

  writeln ('You wouldn''t listen to me would');
  writeln ('you?  You really better get out');
  writeln ('of here before you get eaten!');

  IF treasure IN stash
  THEN
    IF (turns MOD 2)=0
    THEN
    BEGIN

      writeln ('Too bad!!  The ogre caught you');
      writeln ('and roasted you for dinner.');
      writeln ('Better luck next time!!');

      eaten := true;
      quit  := true;

    END
    ELSE
    BEGIN

      writeln ('Get out fast if you don''t want');
      writeln ('to be a big-mac for the ogre!!');

    END
  ELSE
    IF (turns MOD 2)=0
    THEN
    BEGIN

      writeln ('Too bad - you''ve been eaten!');
```

```
        eaten := true;
        quit  := true;

      END

    { endif }

  END { IF NOT awake };

END { PROCEDURE ogreaction };

{***********************************}
{     p   s   t   a   r   t         }
{***********************************}

PROCEDURE pstart;
BEGIN

  IF treasure IN stash
  THEN
    done := true
  ELSE
  BEGIN

    CASE whichway OF

      n,s,e,w:    noway;

      u: writeln ('You can''t jump to the clouds!');
      d: location := vestibule;

    END;

  END { IF carrying };

  chgloc := (location <> start);

END { PROCEDURE pstart };

{***********************************}
{   p   v   e   s   t   i   b   u   l   e   }
{***********************************}

PROCEDURE pvestibule;
BEGIN
```

```
   IF treasure IN whatshere[narrow1]
   THEN
   BEGIN

     write ('To the north, through a narrow');
     writeln ('crack,');
     writeln ('you can see the treasure. ');

   END { IF treasure ... };

   travel (narrow1,grandroom,iceroom,
           nowhere,start,nowhere);

END { PROCEDURE pvestibule };

{***********************************}
{     p  n  a  r  r  o  w  1        }
{***********************************}

PROCEDURE pnarrow1;
BEGIN

   CASE whichway OF

     n:  location := lakeshore;
     e:  location := ogreroom;
     s:  writeln ('It''s too narrow to get through!');

     w,u,d:      noway;

   END { CASE whichway };

   chgloc := (location <> narrow1);

END { PROCEDURE pnarrow1 };

{***********************************}
{       p  i  s  l  a  n  d         }
{***********************************}
PROCEDURE pisland;
BEGIN

   travel (nowhere,lakeshore,nowhere,
           nowhere,nowhere,nowhere);

   readmsg := true;
```

```
END { PROCEDURE pisland };

{**********************************}
{     o   g   r   e   r   o   o   m   }
{**********************************}

PROCEDURE pogreroom;
VAR
  i,j:  INTEGER;
BEGIN

  ogreaction;

  IF NOT eaten
  THEN
  BEGIN

    writeln ('There are exits to the east,');
    writeln ('north, and west');

    CASE whichway OF

      w:            location := narrow1;
      e:            location := batscave;
      n:            location := narrow2;
      d:

      BEGIN

        quit  := true;
        eaten := true;

        writeln ('Oh no!! You dummy!!!');
        writeln ('You just fell into the firepit');
        writeln ('and made such a ruckus that');
        writeln ('you woke the ogre.  I hate to');
        writeln ('tell you this, but you are');
        writeln ('also trapped!');

        FOR i := 1 TO 5 DO
        BEGIN
          FOR j := 1 TO 1000 DO;
          write ('.');
        END { DO };
        writeln;
        writeln ('You''ve just been added to the');
```

```
        writeln ('ogre''s gourmet recipe library!');
        writeln ('Better luck next time.');

      END;

      s,u:  noway;

    END { CASE whichway };

  END { IF NOT eaten };

  chgloc := (location <> ogreroom);

END { PROCEDURE pogreroom };

{ source FILE: a2.maze.text }
{***********************************}
{       p   m   a   z   e           }
{***********************************}

PROCEDURE pmaze;
TYPE
  mazerooms = m0..same;
VAR
  mazeloc:      mazerooms;

  PROCEDURE describe;
  BEGIN

    writeln ('You are in a maze of
    writeln ('featureless passages.');
    writeln;

  end { procedure describe };
  procedure sameplace;
  begin

    writeln ('You have crawled around');
    writeln ('some twisted tunnels and');
    writeln ('wound up where you began.');

  END { PROCEDURE sameplace };

  PROCEDURE travel (

            nloc,
            sloc,
```

```
            eloc,
            wloc,
            uloc,
            dloc: rooms);

   PROCEDURE newloc (loc:rooms);
   BEGIN

      IF loc=m0
      THEN
        noway
      ELSE
        IF loc=same
        THEN
          sameplace
        ELSE
          location := loc
        { endif }
      { endif };

   END { PROCEDURE newloc };

BEGIN  {** travel **}

   CASE whichway OF

     n:  newloc (nloc);
     s:  newloc (sloc);
     e:  newloc (eloc);
     w:  newloc (wloc);
     u:  newloc (uloc);
     d:  newloc (dloc);
   END { CASE whichway };

END { PROCEDURE travel };

PROCEDURE pm1;
BEGIN

   writeln ('From here you can go south, east,');
   writeln ('west, or up.');

   CASE whichway OF

     s:         location := ladder;
     e:         location := m2;
```

```
    w:          location := m4;
    u:          location := steam;
    n,d:        noway;

  END;

END { pm1 };
BEGIN  { PROCEDURE pmaze };

  REPEAT

    IF (location <> m1)
       AND
       (location <> maze)
    THEN
      describe
    { endif };
    showobjects;
    cklamp;

    CASE location OF

      maze,
      m1:         pm1;
      m2:         travel (m1,same,m0,m0,m0,m0);
      m3:         travel (m1,m0,same,m0,m0,m0);
      m4:         travel (m0,m7,m3,m5,m0,m0);
      m5:         travel (m1,m0,m0,m0,m0,m0);
      m6:         travel (m4,m0,same,m0,m0,m0);
      m7:         travel (m5,m9,m6,m8,m0,m0);
      m8:         travel (m5,m0,m0,same,m0,m0);
      m9:         travel (m0,m11,m0,m10,m0,m0);
      m10:        travel (m8,same,m0,m0,m0,m0);
      m11:        travel (m9,m0,m6,m10,m1,m12);
      m12:        travel (m13,m0,m0,m0,m0,m16);
      m13:        travel (m14,m0,m0,m0,m0,m17);
      m14:        travel (m15,m0,m0,m0,m0,m18);
      m15:

      BEGIN

        writeln ('I seem to remember buried');
        writeln ('treasure near this location.');
        travel (m0,m0,m0,m0,m1,m19);

      END ;
```

```
    m16:       travel  (m17,same,m0,m0,m0,m0);
    m17:       travel  (m18,m16,m0,m0,m0,m0);
    m18:

    BEGIN

      writeln ('I seem to remember a treasure');
      writeln ('near here.');
      travel  (m19,m17,m0,m0,m0,m0);

    END;
    m19:       travel  (m0,m18,m0,m0,m15,m0);

   END { CASE location };

  UNTIL (location < maze) OR (location = flames);
  chgloc := true;

END { PROCEDURE pmaze };
 { source FILE: a2.main.text }

{************************************}
{          p   p   i   t            }
{************************************}

PROCEDURE ppit;
BEGIN

  CASE whichway OF
    d:          location := ladder;
    u:   writeln ('Try to climb that');
         writeln ('and you''ll kill yourself!');

    n,s,e,w:    noway;

  END;
  chgloc := (location <> pit);

END { PROCEDURE ppit };

{************************************}
{     p   l   a   d   d   e   r     }
{************************************}

PROCEDURE pladder;
BEGIN
```

```
  CASE whichway OF

    n:          location := maze;
    d:          location := flames;
    u:

      IF treasure IN stash
      THEN
      BEGIN

        writeln ('You can''t carry the treasure');
        writeln ('up the ladder -');
        writeln ('it''s much too heavy!');

      END
      ELSE

        location := vestibule
      { endif };

    e,s,w:    noway;

  END;

  chgloc := (location <> ladder );

END { PROCEDURE pladder };
{***********************************}
{     p   f   l   a   m   e   s     }
{***********************************}

PROCEDURE pflames;
BEGIN

  cooked := true;
  done   := true;

END { PROCEDURE pflames };


          {*************************}
BEGIN     { =====> adventure <===== }
          {*************************}

  introduction;
  initialize;
```

```
REPEAT

  visited[location] := true;
  show(location);
  cklamp;

  CASE location OF

    start:        pstart;
    grandroom:    travel (nowhere, nowhere,
                          nowhere, brink,
                          nowhere, stairs);
    vestibule:    pvestibule;
    narrow1:      pnarrow1;
    lakeshore:    travel (island, narrow1,
                          narrow2, nowhere,
                          nowhere, nowhere);
    island:       pisland;
    brink:        travel (nowhere, nowhere,
                          nowhere, ogreroom,
                          nowhere, pit);
    iceroom:      travel (ogreroom, nowhere,
                          crystal, vestibule,
                          nowhere, nowhere);
    ogreroom:     pogreroom;
    narrow2:      travel (nowhere, ogreroom,
                          steam, lakeshore,
                          nowhere, nowhere);
    pit:          ppit;
    crystal:      travel (ogreroom, nowhere,
                          maze, ogreroom,
                          nowhere, nowhere);
    batscave:     travel (steam, nowhere,
                          nowhere, ogreroom,
                          nowhere, nowhere);
    steam:        travel (deadend, batscave,
                          nowhere, narrow2,
                          nowhere, maze);
    deadend:      travel (nowhere, steam,
                          nowhere, nowhere,
                          nowhere, nowhere);
    ladder:       pladder;
    maze:         pmaze;
    stairs:       travel (nowhere, nowhere,
                          nowhere, nowhere,
```

```
                         grandroom, echoes);
    echoes:     travel (warmroom, incline,
                        nowhere, nowhere,
                        stairs, deeppool);
    incline:    travel (nowhere, nowhere,
                        roundroom, honeycomb,
                        echoes, nowhere);
    warmroom:   travel (nowhere, echoes,
                        nowhere, nowhere,
                        nowhere, flames);
    roundroom:  travel (honeycomb, nowhere,
                        nowhere, incline,
                        nowhere, mudroom);
    honeycomb:  travel (nowhere, narrow3,
                        incline, nowhere,
                        nowhere, nowhere);
    mudroom:    travel (nowhere, nowhere,
                        nowhere, nowhere,
                        roundroom, siltroom);
    deeppool:   travel (nowhere, nowhere,
                        nowhere, nowhere,
                        mudroom, coldroom);
    coldroom:   travel (nowhere, nowhere,
                        nowhere, nowhere,
                        deeppool, nowhere);
    narrow3:    travel (honeycomb, narrow4,
                        nowhere, nowhere,
                        nowhere, nowhere);
    narrow4:    travel (narrow3, river,
                        nowhere, nowhere,
                        nowhere, maze);
    river:      travel (narrow4, rockyroom,
                        nowhere, nowhere,
                        nowhere, nowhere);
    rockyroom:  travel (river, siltroom,
                        alcove, nowhere,
                        nowhere, nowhere);
    siltroom:   travel (rockyroom, nowhere,
                        nowhere, alcove,
                        mudroom, nowhere);
    alcove:     travel (nowhere, nowhere,
                        siltroom, nowhere,
                        nowhere, nowhere);
    flames:     pflames;

  END { CASE location };
```

```
  UNTIL quit OR done;

  congratulations;

END.
```

13

Command Processing in Adventure 2

This chapter is one of the most important of the book. It deals with topics that, taken one at a time, are pretty simple, but when put all together form a major part of all our subsequent adventure game implementations. You will probably want to read it more than once. It is also a good idea to refer to the actual Pascal code frequently while reading.

The first example of an adventure game would be considered a mere "toy" by devotees. Why? Mainly because it did not allow the player to use traditional adventure game commands. It limited the player to travel commands or directions. The consequence of this was the fact that "solving" all the problems was totally unchallenging. It was simply a matter of answering yes or no questions (with most of the successful answers obviously being yes). Of course, you want your own adventure games to allow "real" command processing.

Commands are important because they add a sense of control to the game. The player is participating. Not everything is yes or no. Even the commands that the guide will recognize and carry out must be guessed by the player. Beyond that, commands provide the vehicle by which players solve the problems posed by the adventure game. This is the essence of true adventure, and without it adventures are not really worth playing.

In Adventure 2 I have included commands that take the form of one or two word sentences. These are simple verbs or verbs with a single noun as object. Such commands provide adequate complexity. More advanced adventure games allow a variety of multiple word commands. Such games often claim that the player can use English commands. This is an overstatement. Most English sentences will completely befuddle such adventure games. In any case, implementing a parser for such commands is a much greater challenge than I am prepared to attempt in this book. So I will stick to our one or two word commands. Even these will allow you to implement interesting problems in your adventures.

The commands that have been added to the game are carry, drop, help, light, inventory, take (synonym for carry), tally, push, dig, look, open, unlock (synonym for open), and eat.

There is one support procedure for each possible command. These procedures are named by prefixing the letter p to the command name itself. So for example, there are the procedures pcarry, pdrop, plight, and so on. The command suppon procedures are to commands, what the location procedures are to locations. They provide all the Pascal code needed to carry out the corresponding command. The commands that are synonyms for other commands use the same support procedures as the commands for which they are synonyms.

AN OVERVIEW OF THE COMMAND HANDLING CODE

Figure 13-1 shows the procedures and functions used by Adventure 2 for command processing. The top levels of this diagram duplicate Adventure 1. What is new are the functions and procedures below travel and whichway—docommand, listen, and cmdlookup, which are various procedures designed to do special processing for individual commands. Much of the code that I describe in this chapter can be reused in all of your adventure games.

The travel Procedure

The travel procedure causes either a new location to be determined or the message "There is no way to go in that direction" to be printed. The travel procedure invokes the whichway function to determine which direction the player desires to take. I discuss travel in more detail in Chapter 16.

The whichway Function

The whichway function is also similar to the one used in Adventure 1. It differs in that it does not contain the code for prompting the user. Rather it invokes a new function called docommand; docommand returns a single character that indicates the direction the player wants to go. There is the possibility that this character does not correspond to one of the legal travel indicators. In such a case, the command is simply ignored and the player is reprompted for a command.

There are two weaknesses with the command processing in Adventure 2 that will be remedied in Adventure 3:

- Any word beginning with a travel letter (n, s, e, w, u, or d) is taken to be equivalent to the travel command. Thus, if the player types NEVERMORE, the command processor will assume that the command was n, or north.
- If a command that is neither a legitimate command nor a direction indicator is typed, the player is simply reprompted. There is no indication given that the guide failed to understand. This can be misleading at times—the player may assume that the command was understood. For example, TURN ON LIGHT will be ignored, and the lamp, if not yet lit, will stay unlit.

The docommand Procedure

The docommand procedure is really a "front" for listen, which does the real work. the docommand procedure sits in a while loop calling the listen procedure. The listen procedure eventually returns, having set the variables head and tail. The docommand procedure returns the first character of the head string. It makes sure this is valid by first determining that there is something in the string to return. This is accomplished by using the intrinisic function length:

```
length (head) > 0
```

The listen Procedure

The listen procedure is the *command dispatcher* for Adventure 2. It supervises the process of determining which command the player wants to have executed. It invokes the appropriate command procedure for each command entered.

The cmdlookup Function

The parts of a compiler that read, interpret, and verifiy the syntax of a program are called *scanners* and *parsers*. The cmdlookup function provides a very rudimentary scanner and parser combination for Adventure 2. It prompts for the players command and breaks that command into two pieces—head and tail. The head string always determines which command will be executed. The tail string will contain the object of the command verb if there

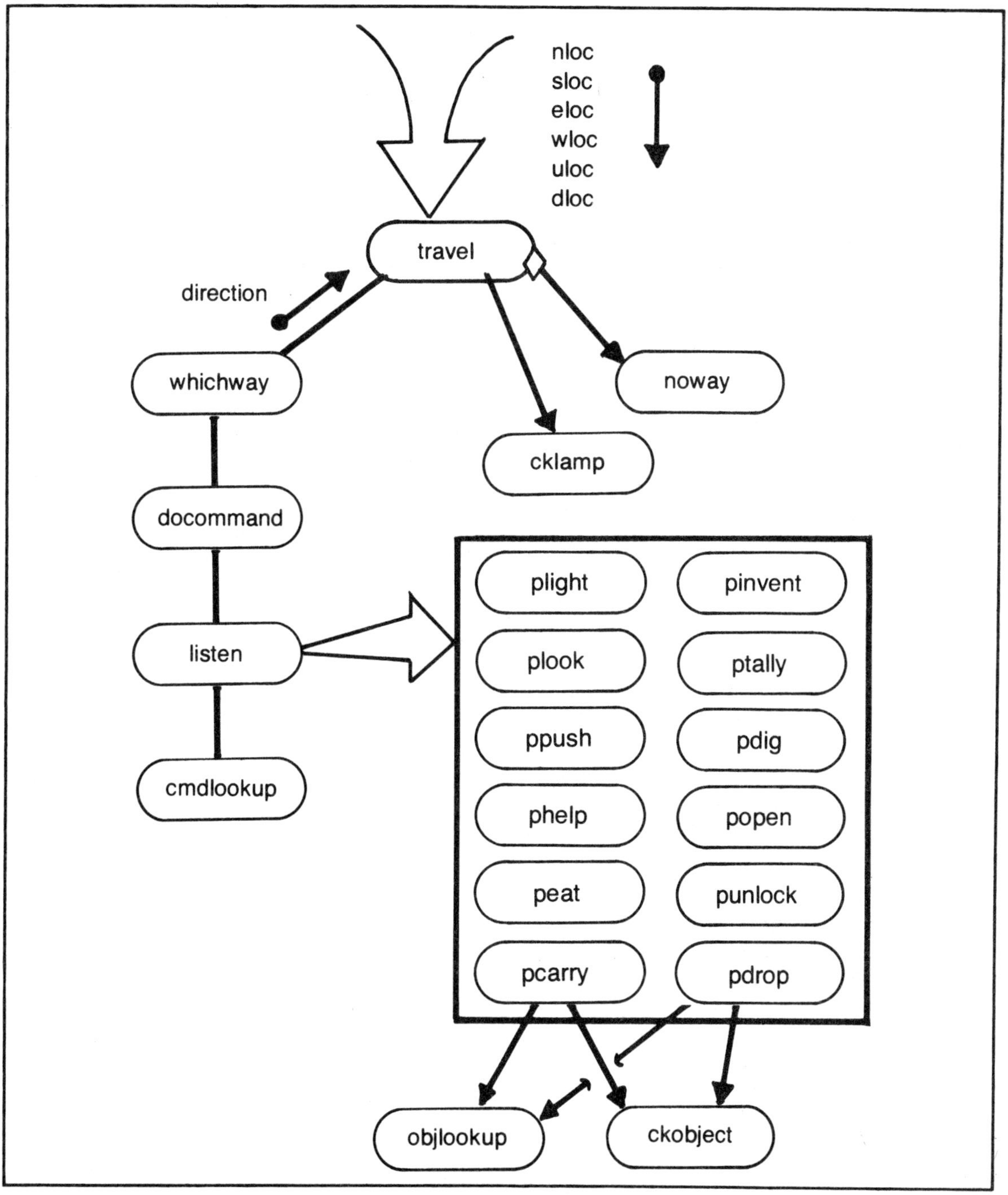

Fig. 13-1. The structure diagram of the command processing in Adventure 2.

is any. It is always possible for tail to be the empty string: length (tail) = 0.

As I hinted earlier, cmdlookup is not at all sophisticated. It doesn't even bother to make sure that the character strings in head and tail are sensible for command and object names. It will blithely allow you to type:

*&∧%$#@!(/?>< ---++==

as a command. When it fails to match the string & %# !(/?>< to the name of any legal command or direction, it will reprompt you for another command. It is monumentally stupid! However, it is just smart enough to do the required job.

COMMAND PROCESSING IN DETAIL

Parts of the command processing code involve some rather complex but very useful programming techniques. These programming strategies are detailed in the following pages.

docommand: Calling listen in a Loop

There really isn't much more to say about docommand. It conveniently separates an enclosing loop around listen. That loop could have been incorporated into listen itself. The only difference would be a miniscule gain in efficiency. Because docommand is involved in direct response to interactive commands, you probably wouldn't even notice the difference. If you are the curious type, making that modification would be a good exercise to try.

listen: Another Case Statement for Control

The listen procedure uses a local variable lcmd of type cmds to control its case statement. The cmds type is an enumerated type that names all the commands available to the player:

```
cmds = (carry, drop, help, light, inventory,
        take, tally, push, dig, look, open,
        unlock, eat, nocmd);
```

I shall discuss the use of this type and the setting of the variable lcmd in detail below.

The REPEAT . . . UNTIL loop in listen ensures that the player's commands are carried out until a command that is either a direction or an unrecognizable sequence is entered. All of the fun takes place inside the cmdlookup function, and I devote the remainder of this chapter to its workings.

The cmdlookup Function

The cmdlookup function is not very long—a little over half a page of well-spaced Pascal source code. Yet it packs a lot of wallop. In the course of unraveling its inner mysteries, I shall delve into the following subjects:

- The input of enumerated types.
- Arrays indexed by enumerated types.
- The conversion of values—external to internal.
- The method of searching an array using a linear search.
- Arrays of strings and string comparison.
- Sentinels in a linear search.
- The succ function and its use in searching.

There is a lot to cover. The only way to reach the end is to plunge ahead. So, here we go!!

The Input of Enumerated Types. I have done more than a little to give Pascal's enumerated types "rave reviews." Now I come to one of the annoying weaknesses of enumerated types in many Pascal implementations: it is usually impossible to READ or WRITE a value of an enumerated type directly, that is, using the identifiers contained in the declaration of the enumerated type.

In Adventure 2, this is exemplified by the array of strings that I have called cmdnames. cmdnames is indexed by the enumerated type cmds:

```
cmdnames: ARRAY[cmds] of STRING;
```

In order to really understand what is going on here, I need to elaborate on this declaration and its implications for the Pascal language. Bear with me while I digress from the consideration of the actual code of cmdlookup.

Arrays Indexed by an Enumerated Type. I am assuming that you know what an array is. I also assume that you have used arrays before in your Pascal programs and are familiar with the syntax for declaring arrays. However, the idea of using an enumerated type as the index for an aray may be new to you.

Ordinarily, the index of an array is simply a range of integers

```
x: ARRAY[1 . . 100] OF STRING;
```

and individual elements of an array are referenced using single values from the range as subscripts—x[1], x[5], x[29], and so on. An array corresponds to a list of items. The index is like the number indicating the position of the item in the list. Because the identifiers of an enumerated type are assigned numeric values by the Pascal compiler, you may think of the enumerated type itself as being just like a range of integers. Therefore, using an enumerated type as the index of an array in a declaration is a normal thing to do.

When an array is indexed by an enumerated type, you can think of the array as a whole as a "named list" of items. To illustrate, consider the following list of men's nicknames. The list is enumerated by the names for which nicknames are being listed:

Name	Nickname
Richard	Dick
Thomas	Tom
Lawrence	Larry
William	Bill
John	Jack
Arnold	Arnie
James	Jim

This list may be represented in Pascal as an array of strings indexed by the enumerated type:

```
name = (Richard, Thomas, Lawrence, Wil-
        liam, John, Arnold, James);
```

The array declaration would look like this:

```
nicknames:   ARRAY[name] OF STRING;
```

Then assignment statements such as

```
nickname[Richard] := 'Dick';
nickname[Lawrence] := 'Larry';
nickname[James] := 'Jim';
```

are perfectly legitimate. Each one constructs one of the entries in the original list of nicknames given above.

The Conversion of Values: External to Internal. The identifiers in a Pascal enumerated type represent *external* values. The numbers assigned to the identifiers in an enumerated type represent *internal* values. They are the values that the Pascal compiler prefers to use when manipulating the enumerated type inside the computer.

In the best of all possible Pascal implementations, you should be able to write the following sort of code:

```
writeln ("Your wish is my command > ");
read (lcmd);
CASE lcmd OF

   carry: pcarry;
   drop: pdrop;
   help: phelp;
   light: plight;
   invent: pinventory;
```

and so on. That is, given a variable of type cmds, such as lcmd, you should be able to read a value of lcmd. The user of the program containing the above code should be able to type one of the identifiers in the enumerated type in response to the prompt, for instance

```
Your wish is my command > carry keys
```

This should have the effect of the identifier carry being read and the corresponding internal value of the enumerated type being stored in the variable lcmd. (The second part of the input line would be ignored until another read command was issued by the program—presumably this would take place in the pcarry procedure.)

This is an example of the concept of *conversion of representations.* It is worth talking about this a little further to give you an idea of why our "best of all implementations" scenario is usually not the reality.

What kind of values are stored in a variable like lcmd? In the guts of the actual Pascal program, they are whole numbers: 1, 2, 3, and so on. The actual numbers are not guaranteed to be any particular values. The definition of Pascal only requires that the numbers assigned be consecutive. It is true that 90% of all Pascal compilers will assign values beginning with 0. I would venture to say 100%, but then I am not personally acquainted with every Pascal compiler ever written! The correspondence between the identifiers in the declaration and the numbers chosen to represent these identifiers is maintained by the Pascal compiler. So whenever your program refers to one of the identifiers in the enumerated type, the right numeric value is substituted for it in the translated program.

Once a Pascal program has been compiled, the identifiers of an enumerated type are forgotten. They have all been assigned their internal numeric values. This is fine as long as you never wish the program to input or output a value of any enumerated type. Should you wish to do so, you are faced with the following fact: the identifiers (as they appear in the declaration of the enumerated type) are character strings, but the internal values corresponding to those identifiers are numbers. For example, the cmds enumerated type might be assigned internal values as follows:

External (identifier)	Internal (number)
carry	0
drop	1
help	2
light	3
inventory	4
take	5
tally	6
push	7
dig	8
look	9
open	10
unlock	11
eat	12
nocmd	13

The question becomes how do you "compute" a variable whose type is a user-defined enumerated type? In particular, how do you input such a value in response to a user's command that is typed as a character string. The answer is basically pretty boring. You input the external representation of such a value and convert that value to its internal form yourself. This requires writing explicit Pascal code to do the job. In Adventure 2 the procedure cmdlookup performs this task.

The first piece in solving the puzzle of enumerated type input is an array of strings. The array must be indexed by the enumerated type. The strings in the array are the identifiers used in the declaration of the enumerated type. Thus for cmds, you have the array cmdnames, mentioned above. For example, cmdnames[inventory] := inventory ; The array cmdnames is set up in the procedure initialize. This is similar to the example of nicknames that I gave earlier.

How do you use the string array? You use it to match a string typed by the user to one of the identifiers in the cmds type. This is the lookup aspect of cmdlookup.

Actually, the strings read by cmdlookup may consist of more than just the command name itself. This is true because many command verbs take objects: carry keys, drop treasure, light lamp, eat crow, and so on. Also, the player may perversely type anything at all that forms a legal string: "Take me to your leader," or "Come with me to the Casbah." cmdlookup must first dissect the input string into two parts, which I have called head and tail. So cmdlookup first reads the player's response to the prompt into the string variable command. It dissects command into two pieces by locating the first blank in the command string (if any). The part of the command preceding the first blank is stored in the variable head. The part of the command after the first blank (but not including it) is stored in the variable tail.

The variable head will be used in the command lookup process. The variable tail is used by the various command support procedures to determine the details of specific commands. For example, if head is the command carry, tail will be used to determine what, if anything, will be carried.

Figure 13-2 illustrates the picking apart of command. There is a "bug" in this code. Can you spot it? Can you fix it?

Searching an Array Using the Linear Search. Searching is a technique used in many different computer programs. More often than not, it is a list that is searched. This is the case in Adventure 2. There are many kinds of search techniques, but I shall concentrate on one of the simplest, the ***linear search.***

The general technique of linear search assumes the existence of a linearly ordered collection of items. In this case the collection is the list of strings represented by the array cmdnames.

Any collection of "things" organized in a lineup of some kind may be subjected to linear search. Here are some examples from real life:

- A pile of magazines on a coffee table.
- A bin of watercolor paintings on sale at the art gallery.
- A pile of essays waiting to be graded by an English teacher.
- A collection of recipes on 3×5 cards.

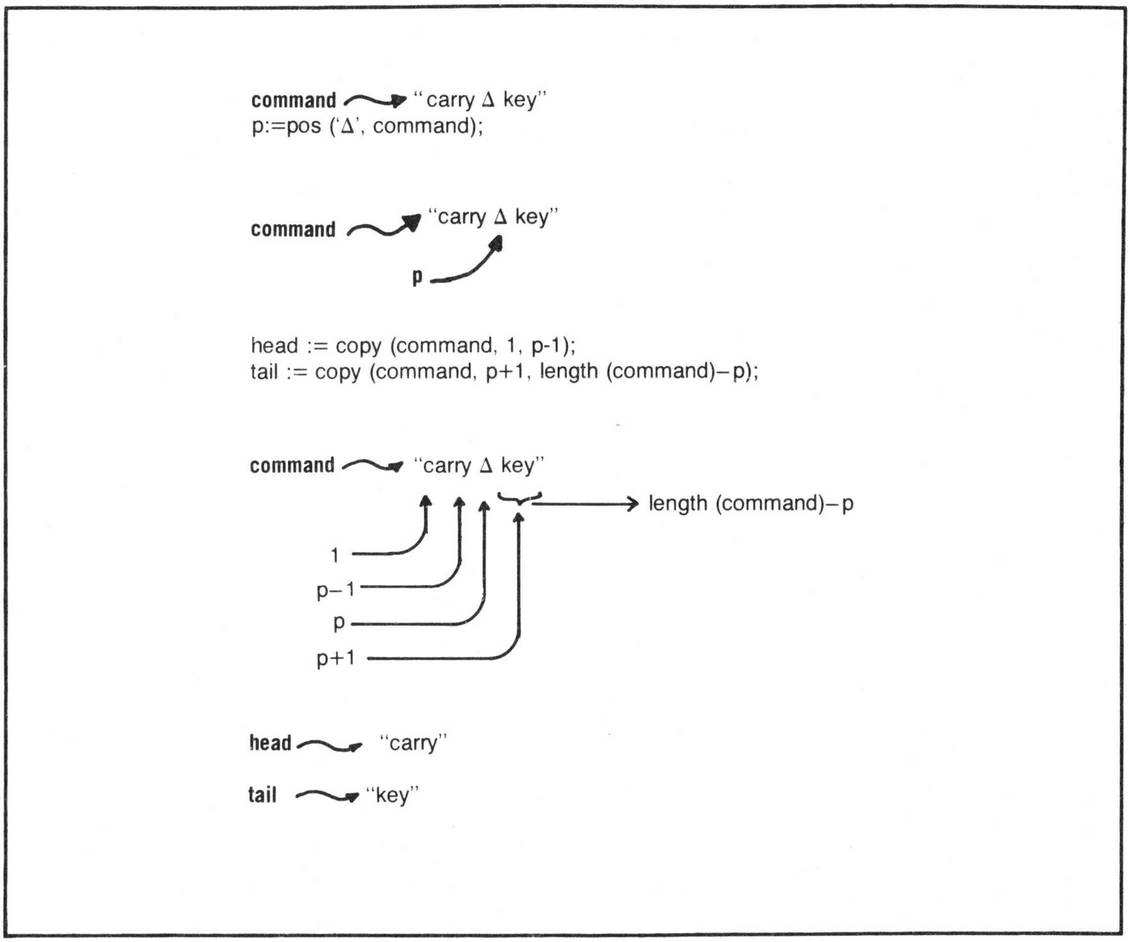

Fig. 13-2. The dissection of a command into head and tail.

■ The want ads in your local newspaper.

In all these examples, if you were searching for a specific item such as last month's issue of your favorite computer magazine, a painting by a specific artist, an essay by your favorite pupil, a recipe for shrimp jambalaya, or an ad for a used printer for your computer, you would be apt to start at the beginning and search through the collection one item at a time. You would look at each item to see if it was the one you wanted, and continue until you either found that item or came to the end of the collection.

In some cases, you might take advantage of extraneous information to speed up your speech. For example, you might remember the color of the cover of the magazine and limit your search to magazines whose covers were of that color. You might look for a painting that had the recognizable style of the specific artist you were interested in. You might look for certain key words in the newspaper ad, such as *printer* or *computer*.

Because you are human, you have sophisticated pattern matching abilities with which a computer cannot yet compete. A computer, searching a list of items, is not able to use such cues in most cases. It has to take each item in turn to see whether or not it is the one being sought. This is always true when the list being searched has no other structure than that of a list. Our arrays are simply big unsorted piles—like a collection of twenty years' worth of *LIFE* magazines, well shuffled from use.

Here's how to search:

1. First ask whether or not there are any more items left in the pile you are searching. If the answer is yes, continue the search by doing step 2. If the answer is no, stop the search.
2. Is the next item in the pile the item for which you are looking? If it is, you have succeeded, so quit. If it is not, do step 3.
3. Put aside the item you just examined and rejected. Continue the search from step 1.

The following easy-to-remember names can be given to the three steps in the above procedure: 1. TEST, 2. COMPARE, and 3. LOOP. I shall refer to these steps in the following discussion.

Arrays of Strings and String Comparison. To be able to perform searches of string arrays, you must be able to compare one string to another. For cmdlookup, you must be able to compare strings in cmdnames with the string in head. UCSD Pascal allows you to make comparisons of string variables for equality and inequality:

S1 = S2 is true <=> S1 and S2 contain the same character string.

S1 <> S2 is true <=> S1 and S2 differ in at least one character position.

It is also possible to compare two character strings *lexicographically*. This is a fancy word for "in dictionary order." The mathematical comparison symbols < and > are used to mean the following:

S1 < S2 is true <=> The string in S1 would come before the string in S2, if both strings were in the dictionary.

S1 > S2 is true <=> The string in S1 would come after the string in S1, if both strings were in the dictionary.

The search in cmdlookup only uses the comparison for inequality.

The test for the completion of a linear search, "Are we out of items to consider?" is not conceptually part of the search itself. It seems like unwanted extra baggage. You will soon see that it really is.

Suppose you knew ahead of time that what you were searching for definitely was one of the items in the collection being searched; or to put it another way, suppose you knew at the start that a successful search was guaranteed. Then the TEST part of the procedure would be superfluous. You might think the whole search would be superfluous! Leaving that issue aside for a moment, let's see if we can

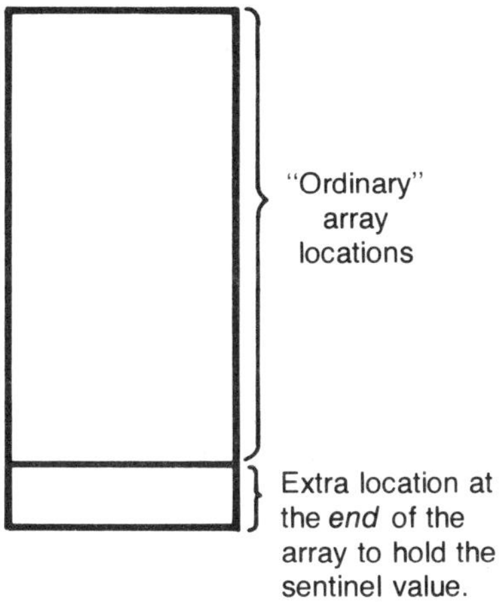

Fig. 13-3. A picture of an array set up for the sentinel search technique.

think of a way to guarantee that all your linear searches have happy endings.

Figure 13-3 gives the basic idea—an extra location in the search collection. Now why would you want to increase the number of items to be searched through? To guarantee success, of course. You will always use the extra location to store a "copy" of the item you are looking for. Then if that item turns out not to be in the collection proper, you will still find it in the extra location at the end. You won't have to worry about testing to determine whether or not any items are left. At the very worst, you will find what you are looking for just before you run out of items to consider.

The extra item added to the collection is known as a *sentinel.* It "stands guard" against the possibility of failure.

You now have a slightly different problem to solve with your search. There are now two possible ways to "succeed."

1. Find the sentinel.
2. Find the item you are searching for before reaching the sentinel.

In the first case, even though you succeed in one sense, you fail in the larger sense. Case 2 could be dubbed "real success." How do you know if you "really" succeed? Simple! After you succeed (which you know you will, because you have a sentinel), you check to see if you are at the sentinel location. If you are not, then you really did succeed. If you are at the sentinel you were only helped over the finish line. Real success awaits in some future search.

You may have been wondering why nocmd was one of the identifiers in the enumerated type cmds. After all, you probably couldn't imagine typing nocmd as a command. It is there as a place holder for the sentinel that will be used in the linear search in cmdlookup. The cmdlookup function guarantees the success of the linear search by storing the string contained in head in cmdnames [nocmd]:

```
cmdnames[nocmd] := head;
```

The search is a very simple while loop:

```
WHILE head <> cmdnames[lcmd] DO
```

```
    lcmd := succ (lcmd)
  (* END DO *);
```

When this loop terminates, the value stored in lcmd will either be the value of cmds corresponding to the command the player typed or the value nocmd.

The succ Function. In order to cause lcmd (a variable of type cmds) to take on the "next" value of its enumerated type, the intrinsic function succ is provided. Its action corresponds to picking the next identifier from the list of identifiers given in the declaration of the enumerated type. It is analogous to saying x := x + 1 for a variable x of the integer type. For example,

```
succ (carry) = drop
succ (tally) = push
succ (eat) = nocmd
succ (open) = unlock
```

The succ function is undefined for the last element in an enumerated type. For cmds, succ (ncmd) is undefined. An attempt to use succ (nocmd) in an expression will cause an error when that expression is evaluated at run time.

14

Carry and Drop: Pascal Sets

In the last chapter I discussed the overall implementation of command processing in Adventure 2. In this chapter I will look more closely at two of the commands themselves: carry and drop. Both of these commands make use of the Pascal concept of a *set*.

The Pascal language allows for variables of type set. Very few languages allow the programmer to create and manipulate sets. This is somewhat surprising, because the idea of a set is a common one in the real world and is often used in programs. I shall discuss the concept briefly below and show how it is simulated in languages that do not support it directly.

WHAT ARE SETS AND HOW CAN THEY BE USED?

The concept of the set may be given a very precise mathematical definition. I will not subject you to such a treatment, however. Let us define set by giving some synonyms: collection, group, and aggregate, etc. Try to understand *set* by considering some examples:

- A stamp collection.
- A set of tools.
- A set of silverware.
- A collection of books.

Any group of similar items may be considered to be a set.

Sets occur in many natural situations. In our adventures, the collection of objects that the player is carrying at any given time is a set. It turns out to be very easy to represent this in Pascal. In other languages, it is not so easy. Let us briefly consider how a set can be represented in BASIC.

Sets in BASIC

In adventure games, the player can pick up and carry various objects. Consider the problem of keeping track of which objects are being carried. First of all, you need to represent the objects themselves. In Pascal, this is best done by an enumerated type:

```
object = (lamp, treasure, key, sandwich, bottle, shovel, noobj);
```

In BASIC, there is no best or natural way to represent the objects. One straightforward way is to choose numeric variables whose values are similar to those that might be assigned to the identifiers in the Pascal enumerated type:

```
LA = 1
TR = 2
KE = 3
SA = 4
BO = 5
SH = 6
NO = 7
```

Most BASIC interpreters will allow you to spell out longer variable names, even though only the first two characters are significant:

```
LAMP = 1
TREASURE = 2
KEY = 3
SANDWICH = 4
BOTTLE = 5
SHOVEL = 6
NOOBJ = 7
```

Now, how do you represent the set of objects that the player is carrying? A simple way is to use an array:

```
DIM CARRY(7)
```

Each entry in the array corresponds to one object. The value of the array entry represents whether or not that object is being carried. The value of 1 means that the object is being carried, the value of 0 means that the object is not being carried. The collection of values stored in the array represents the set of items being carried by the player.

For example, if CARRY(6) = 0, the player is not carrying the shovel. If CARRY(1) = 1, the player is carrying the lamp.

Storing several values, each of which is either 0 or 1, in an array is wasteful of memory. Another technique for representing a set using 0s and 1s is to use a *bit string* instead of an array. A bit string is nothing more than an ordinary whole number thought of in its *binary* form. The 0s and 1s in the binary numeral for the number may be used in the same way the 0s and 1s in the array are used.

In this simple example, you can get by with a number between 0 and 63 to represent any possible collection of the 6 objects. The "object" noobj is not something the player can carry. It is used in a fashion similar to that of nocmd in the last chapter. Thus, it can be ignored when you consider the set representation problem.

Each object is assigned to a particular power of two between 1 and 32:

```
LAMP     <===> 1 = 2 to the 0th power
TREASURE <===> 2 = 2 to the 1st power
KEY      <===> 4 = 2 to the 2nd power
SANDWICH <===> 8 = 2 to the 3rd power
BOTTLE   <===>16 = 2 to the 4th power
SHOVEL   <===> 32 = 2 to the 5th power
```

Then, each number between 0 and 63 can be represented by adding together some collection of these powers of two. The number obtained by adding the values assigned to a given collection then represents the situation in which the player is carrying the objects that correspond to the powers of two chosen. For example, if the player is carrying the key, sandwich, and shovel, the corresponding number would be 4 + 8 + 32 or 44. If, the player is carrying the lamp and the bottle, the corresponding number would be 1 + 16 or 17. If the player is carrying nothing, this is represented by the number 0. If the player is carrying all six objects, this is represented by the number 1+2+4+8+16+32 or 63.

Using bit strings in BASIC would require special code to calculate and interpret the various numbers. All this is very cumbersome and I will not carry our treatment any further. In fact, UCSD Pascal (and many other Pascal systems as well) uses bit strings to represent its set variables, but it handles all the interpretation of them automatically.

The programmer can think in terms of the set itself and in terms of concepts naturally allied to sets.

In Adventure 2, you find the following type declarations:

```
objects = (lamp, treasure, key, sandwich,
           bottle, shovel, noobj);

collection = SET OF objects;
```

This is so "natural," so close to the way we think about the real situation that it takes some time for us to realize that this is programming language code. A collection is exactly that—a set of objects. The enumerated type **objects** represents the objects in terms of their names, not as numbers or powers of two. Set variables may be thought of directly in terms of the set concept. The programmer may ignore all problems of representation.

Set Variables Used In Adventure 2

There are two **collection** variables declared in Adventure 2. One is a scalar variable called **stash**. **stash** is the set of objects that the player is carrying at any given time during the game. The other variable is an array of sets called **whatshere**. This array is indexed by the enumerated type **rooms**. An entry in this array corresponds to the set of objects that happens to exist in a given adventure location at any time. Thus, **whatshere[start]** represents the objects that are at the **start** location. **whatshere[m19]** represents the objects that are at location **m19** (the nineteenth room in the maze).

The Use of Set Variables: pcarry and pdrop

As the adventurer moves around, he will issue commands to carry and drop objects. The adventure guide notes which objects are at which locations as those locations are visited. This cues the adventurer that carrying some object is possible. For example, at the **start** location the guide says:

```
There is a lamp here.
```

The adventurer may in turn say:

```
carry lamp
```

If the player wishes to leave an object somewhere, he or she can use the command **drop**. Of course, you cannot drop something you are not carrying.

The **pcarry** and **pdrop** procedures contain the Pascal code that manage the carry and drop commands. They make use of Pascal capabilities regarding set variables. In addition, the **initialize** procedure determines the original values for all the set variables in the program. In particular, the variable **stash** must initially be the empty set, that is, the collection of no objects at all. This initialization is accomplished by the Pascal assignment:

```
stash := [ ];
```

In general, set constants are represented by lists of items inside square brackets:

```
setvar := [item1, item2, item3];
```

In addition to simple items, you may also use the Pascal subrange notation in order to include several items in a set constant. For example: suppose **mazerooms** was a variable of type **SET OF rooms**. Then the assignment:

```
mazerooms := [m1 . . m19];
```

would assign to **mazerooms** the set of rooms consisting of **m1**, **m2**, **m3**, **m4**, **m5**, **m6**, **m7**, **m8**, **m9**, **m10**, **m11**, **m12**, **m13**, **m14**, **m15**, **m16**, **m17**, **m18**, and **m19**. The subrange notation **m1 .. m19** is more compact for this purpose than listing all the individual rooms themselves.

In addition to setting **stash** to **[ ]**, **initialize** also determines where each object is by assigning objects to various **whatshere** entries:

```
whatshere[start]     :=  [lamp];
whatshere[coldroom]  :=  [shovel];
whatshere[narrow4]   :=  [key];
whatshere[deadend]   :=  [sandwich];
whatshere[mudroom]   :=  [bottle];
```

Notice that there is no assignment:

```
whatshere[m19] := [treasure];
```

This is because the player cannot see the treasure until certain problems have been solved. I will discuss this further in the next chapter.

The pcarry Procedure. The pcarry procedure makes use of two subsidiary functions, objlookup and ckobject. When the player types a carry command, there is an object named after the verb carry: carry key, carry treasure, carry sandwich, and so on. The Pascal code must analyze the command string. It must determine whether or not the string stored in tail (see the preceding chapter for details of how tail is determined) corresponds to one of the objects in the game. This is accomplished by another linear search with the sentinel algorithm, just like the one used by cmdlookup. See the last chapter for a detailed discussion of this algorithm.

The objlookup function uses an array objnames[objects], which is to objects what the array cmdnames was to commands. That is, objnames contains strings of all the names of objects in the game. These strings are used in comparisons with the variable tail. The code in objlookup is strictly analogous to that in cmdlookup. The value returned by objlookup is a value of the enumerated type objects. This includes the possible value noobj. If objlookup returns noobj, it means that the string in tail is not the name of one of the objects in the game. This can happen, for example, if the player types the command carry beans or carry knife.

The function ckobject simply checks to see whether or not the object requested by the player is in the current location. This is accomplished using the Pascal set operator IN.

In general, if S is a set variable and O is a variable whose value is one of the possible "items" in the set, the Pascal expression

```
O IN S
```

is either true or false depending on whether or not the particular item represented by the value of O happens to one of the items stored in S. So for example,

```
key IN [shovel, lamp] is FALSE
treasure IN [sandwich, shovel, treasure] is
TRUE
noobj IN [lamp . . shovel] is FALSE
```

ckobject uses the expression

```
it IN whatshere[location]
```

where, it is the particular value of type objects determined by objlookup. Because the value noobj can never be one of the values in any of the whatshere entries, the ckobject expression will always be false if the player requests a nonexistent object.

If ckobject (it) turns out to be false, pcarry informs the player

```
I don't see any "it" here
```

where, of course, it is filled in with the specific object the player requested. This can either mean that the object is not at that particular location (even though it does exist) or that the object simply does not exist. The player can't tell which is the case merely by reading the message. That is, if the player says

```
carry baloney
```

and the guide replies:

```
I don't see any baloney here.
```

the player cannot tell whether or not any baloney exists in the game. All that is revealed is that there is no baloney at this particular location.

If, on the other hand, ckobject (it) is true, the object not only exists, but is present at the player's current location. This means that the carry command should be "carried out." This involves changing the value of two different set variables; stash and whatshere[location]. For this purpose, there are two Pascal operators available for adding an object to a set or for removing an object from a set: + and −. The specific Pascal statements used are stash := stash + [it];, which adds the object it to the collection represented by stash, and whatshere[location] := whatshere[location] − [it];, which removes the object it from the collection represented by whatshere[location]. These assignments reflect the real situation being modeled: the player is adding the object to the collection being carried, and the same object is being removed from the location being visited.

The pdrop Procedure. The pdrop procedure is quite similar in spirit to pcarry. It calls objlookup to determine the object requested. It checks to see whether or not the player is carrying that object:

```
IF NOT (it IN stash)
```

If the player is not carrying the object, the guide replies:

You are not carrying any 'it.'

Otherwise, the object is removed from the player's collection:

```
stash := stash - [it];
```

and added to the collection of objects at the current location:

```
whatshere[location]: = whatshere[location]
  + [it];
```

15

Problems in Adventure 2

Adventure 2 contains the first examples of real problems. In this chapter, I will present techniques for representing problems and handling their solutions within the play of the game.

In Chapter 3 I began our discussion of adventure game problems. There I covered general characteristics of problems from the players' point of view. I talked about clues and hints. I delved into the topics of problem difficulty and repeatability. I discussed the use of logic in problem solution and the element of surprise.

Now is the time to think about problems more from the perspective of implementation. What are the key features of problems and how do you "map" them into Pascal code?

EVENTS

Many problems revolve around the simple concept of an *event*. An event is just that—something that may or may not occur. An event may happen once or it may represent a situation that may flip-flop. For example, the act of carrying something is an event. The act of dropping the same thing is the opposite of the same event, that is, the act of carrying has not occurred if the act of dropping has occurred. This is an example of an event that reflects the current situation.

Some other examples of events are

- The player has not found the treasure.
- The player is or is not in a specific location.
- The player has or has not dug a hole.
- The ogre has or has not been awakened.
- The ogre has or has not eaten the player.

and so on. The occurrence of an event may be recorded by setting a Boolean variable to the value true. The same variable may have the value false if the event has not occurred. This approach can be used for the events that are really situations as well. One side of the situation (the player is carrying the treasure) may be represented by the value true, while the other side (the player is not carrying the treasure) may be represented by the value false. This is basically the technique used in Adventure 1.

BOOLEAN EXPRESSIONS AND EVENTS

If you can use Boolean variables to represent simple events, what kind of code can you use to compute values for those variables? The answer is that you can use *Boolean expressions*. Boolean expressions are Pascal expressions whose values can be reduced to either true or false. Boolean expressions may also be used to represent more complicated events that depend on more than one situation.

Numeric Relationships

Two numbers may be compared using any of several *relational operators:*

```
=       turns = 0
<>      turns <> 0
<       turns < 25
>       turns > 75
<=      turns <= 100
>=      turns >= 50
```

In all these examples, the variable turn is compared to some number. Other examples might compare the values of two variables. In all such examples, the result of the comparison is true or false: either the two values being compared stand in the relationship used or they do not.

Numeric relationships may also be used to represent events or to "compute the value of an event." For example, the relationship

```
turns >= 75
```

could represent the situation in which the player's lamp runs out of energy or the player runs out of time.

Set Relationships: Set Membership

The Pascal operator IN yields a result which is either true or false. IN is a binary operator (not symmetric). The first operand of IN is a possible set member, one of the elements that could be in the set represented by a given set variable. The second operand of IN is a specific set variable. The result of the set membership relationship: O IN S is true if the element represented by the value of O is an element of the set that is the present value of S.

I have already discussed sets extensively in the previous chapter. You have seen how the set membership relationship may be used to represent the event of carrying or not carrying an object, for example, key IN stash or treasure IN whatshere[start].

Equality for Enumerated Types

A special case of the = (equals) relationship occurs for variables whose type is an enumerated type. An identifier of the enumerated type may be used as one of the operands of an = operator. The other operand will be a variable of the enumerated type. This is used frequently in adventure games in Pascal; for examples location = start, it = treasure, and so on. Again, these relationships represent events in the ways that have just been discussed.

Building Boolean Expressions: Boolean Operators

The relationships just explained, plus simple Boolean variables, are the building materials of Boolean expressions. The nails and fasteners that stick these materials together are called *Boolean operators*. The Boolean operators are AND, OR, and NOT.

The Boolean operators are used in a way that is similar to the way the same words, (*and, or,* and *not*) are used in making declarative statements in ordinary English. In such a context, the words *and, or,* and *not* are usually referred to as *logical connectives*. This is the grammatical equivalent of the Pascal term Boolean operators.

Think about the declarative statements

It is raining.
It is cold.
I am a millionaire.
The stock market went up today.
Apples are red.

A Buick is an automobile.

and so on. Such statements are either true or false. In ordinary speech, people compose more complex declarative statements by combining such simple statements using *and, or,* and *not:*

It is raining and it is cold.
It is snowing or it is hot.
It is not raining.
It is sunny and either the stock market went up today or the New York Yankees lost a baseball game today.

The truth or falsity of such statements depends on the truth or falsity of the simple statements involved and the particular connectives used. For example, the statement

I weigh 175 pounds and I weigh 200 pounds

is always false. But, the statement:

I weigh 175 pounds or I weigh 200 pounds

may sometimes be true and other times be false. The use of *or* instead of *and* changes the way in which the truth or falsity of a statement is determined.

In Pascal, the relationships and Boolean variables are the analogues of simple declarative statements. They may be combined to form expressions, which are the analogues of more complex statements:

```
(turns > 0) AND (location = start)
(treasure IN stash) AND (NOT eaten)
NOT (treasure IN whatshere[location])
```

Notice the difference in syntax. Pascal does not read exactly like English. The two major things to watch for are

- The use of parentheses.
- The prefixing of NOT.

In general, it is a good idea to put parentheses around each operand of an AND, OR, or NOT operator. There are times when they may be omitted, but their proper use never hurts. For example, the expression

```
turns > 0 AND location = start
```

will cause Pascal to issue a syntax error message, while

```
(turns > 0) AND (location = start)
```

is correct.

The technical details regarding this matter involve the concept of *operator procedure*. That is a topic for a textbook dealing strictly with Pascal language rules and regulations. Consult your favorite manual of this type for those details. Meanwhile, if you imitate the code in the sample adventures and use parentheses liberally, you should avoid most problems with syntax errors.

PROBLEMS IN ADVENTURE 2

To conclude this chapter, I discuss the specific problems of Adventure 2 and their Pascal encoding. In each case, I shall describe the general problem in English. The description is from the point of view of the adventurer. Then I give a set of *preconditions* and *postconditions*. The preconditions describe what must take place in order for the player to be able to solve the problem. This includes events that must take place and commands that must then be issued. These are generally described in Pascal, with English comments when deemed necessary.

Problem 1

You must go to the island in order to read the message.

Precondition

```
location = island
```

The preconditions in this problem are fulfilled merely by the player arriving at the island. The pisland procedure is not invoked unless the precondition is met.

Postcondition

readmsg = TRUE

The code in pisland causes this to occur.

Problem 2

You must find and carry the shovel in order to later be able to dig for the treasure.

Precondition

location = coldroom
command issued is "carry shovel"

Postcondition

(shovel IN stash) = TRUE

The support procedure pcarry, of course, guarantees that this is the case.

Problem 3

You must dig three times in order to find the treasure chest.

Precondition

(location = m19) AND (shovel IN stash) AND readmsg
command is "dig"

Postcondition

The integer variable hasdug is one larger than before.

Each time the preconditions of this problem are met (including the issuance of the dig command, the value of hasdug is increased by 1.

Problem 4

If you dig four times, you fall into the flames.

Precondition

hasdug = 4

Postcondition

cooked = TRUE

If you keep on digging, you eventually dig a hole into the flames room. You get a warning after the third time you dig. By that time, you have been told that a chest has been uncovered. If you are greedy and keep digging, you get "toasted."

Problem 5

You must find the key and carry it in order to open the treasure chest.

Precondition

location = narrow4
command is "carry key"

If you arrive at the treasure location without the key, you will be unable to open the chest when it is uncovered. Of course, you can always go back and find the key after you have dug up the treasure, but this may take more turns.

Problem 6

You must push the treasure through the crack between narrow1 and the vestibule.

Precondition

location = narrow1
treasure IN whatshere[narrow1]
command is "push treasure"

Postcondition

treasure IN whatshere[vestibule]

The treasure is too heavy to carry up the ladder. The only other way to get it back to the start is to get it into the vestibule by means of this command. This is the most difficult problem in Adventure 2.

There is a hint about what to do. If you visit the location deadend, you will be able to read the message "Good things go through small places."

Problem 7

You must carry the treasure to the start location and drop it there in order to win.

Precondition

treasure IN whatshere[vestibule]
location = vestibule
command sequence is "carry treasure" and then "up"

Postcondition

treasure IN stash

16

Other Techniques Used in Adventure 2

In this chapter I discuss miscellaneous techniques used in Adventure 2. The approach is similar to that of Chapter 10. You should read the explanations here and then study the relevant sections of code in the listing of Adventure 2. This is a chapter to be dipped into at random and over and over again.

COUNTING TURNS

The counter turns keeps track of the number of turns a player has taken. If you look through the code, you will see that it is only changed in one place, namely in the whichway function. What this means is that the player takes one turn for each direction or travel command given. Other commands, such as, carry, drop, eat, or dig do not count as turns. This is a somewhat arbitrary decision. It gives the player slightly more time to play. On the other hand, it is not the most liberal policy of counting I could have adopted. I could have counted only those travel commands that succeed. A good exercise is to change the code to use this more liberal rule. See if you can figure out how to do it. If you like that rule better, then put it in!

DISPLAYING THE CONTENTS OF A SET

The procedures pinvent and showobjects both cause the contents of a set variable to be printed out. This involves the use of the string array objnames, which was discussed in Chapter 13.

The technique is simple: the IN operator is used to check for the presence or absence of each possible item. This can be done in a FOR loop:

```
FOR lobj := lamp TO noobj DO
```

If an object is present in the set, its identifier is printed out using the objnames array:

```
write (objnames[lobj]);
```

The pinvent procedure goes through the set variable stash in this fashion. The showobjects procedure goes through the variable whatshere[location]. The latter clearly depends on where the player happens to be at a given time.

SIMPLIFICATION OF TRAVEL

Adventure 2 contains a new procedure called travel, which simplifies the changing of location during the play of the game. It replaces most of the case statements that were used in Adventure 1 for that purpose.

The travel procedure takes six parameters of type rooms:

```
PROCEDURE travel  (
                        nloc,
                        sloc,
                        eloc,
                        wloc,
                        uloc,
                        dloc: rooms);
```

A typical call of travel might look like

```
travel (deadend, batscave, nowhere, nar-
  row2, nowhere, maze);
```

which means that from the current location (which happens to be the location steam), the possible destinations are deadend going north, batscave going south, nowhere going east, narrow2 going west, nowhere going up, and maze going down. The travel procedure uses a nested procedure called newloc. The newloc procedure checks the requested destination. If it is nowhere, it prints the message "There is no way to go in that direction." If it is not nowhere, it changes the value of the variable location and sets the Boolean variable chgloc to true—I'll say more about chgloc shortly.

The travel procedure uses a case statement that resembles those used in Adventure 1. This case statement uses a call to newloc for each case label:

```
CASE whichway OF

    n: newloc (nloc);
    s: newloc (sloc);
    e: newloc (eloc);
    w: newloc (wloc);
    u: newloc (uloc);
    d: newloc (dloc);

END (* CASE whichway OF *);
```

The travel procedure is a more compact way to handle directional commands. It removes the need for many of the location procedures that were used in Adventure 1. The rule is that if a location has no special case code, there does not need to be a corresponding location procedure for it. A location such as ladder still needs to have a separate case statement to handle travel. This is true because the ability to go in the up direction depends on whether or not the player is carrying the treasure. This conditional travel is not handled by the code

```
u: newloc (uloc);
```

in travel.

The case statement

```
CASE location OF
```

in the main program block of Adventure 2 now invokes travel in most cases (24 out of 33). This makes the program both smaller and easier to understand.

In Adventure 1, the description of a location is repeated as long as the player stays there. This can get annoying, especially if the description is long. Adventure 2 solves this problem. The description of a location is given only when the player enters the room. If the player then issues commands and stays in the room, the description will not be displayed again. This is accomplished by using the Boolean variable chgloc; chgloc is set to false by the procedures noway and docommand. It is set to true by newloc and by various location procedures whenever the players' location has actually changed. The show procedure checks the variable chgloc to determine whether or not to print the description.

The player may explicitly request that the description be repeated by giving the command look. The plook procedure saves the current value of chgloc, and temporarily sets chgloc to true. It then calls show for the current location. After show prints the description, plook sets chgloc back to its old value (which may be either true or false).

THE USE OF FILE VARIABLES

Most of the descriptions of locations used in Adventure 2 come from a disk file. This saves space in the program allowing more locations and more problems. It also causes the printing of descriptions to be slower. However, this seems to be a reasonable tradeoff.

Placing descriptions in a file requires the use of a subsidiary program that I call MAKEDESC (short for MAKE DESCriptions). MAKEDESC reads a text file of descriptions and creates a *database* of descriptions for use by an adventure. The database consists of two files, an index file and a descriptions file.

The construction and use of MAKEDESC are discussed in great detail in several chapters beginning with Chapter 18. Included in those chapters is information on how to use MAKEDESC in writing your own adventures, as well as technical discussions of MAKEDESC and the support code needed for using the output from MAKEDESC.

SCORING YOUR ADVENTURES

People play adventures for many reasons. They want to solve the problems posed, they want to find the treasures, and they want to "win." The definition of win is usually "accumulate the highest possible score."

A player may gain points for a number of accomplishments including

- Solving problems in the adventure.
- Visiting each location in the adventure (a certain number of points for each location visited).
- Visiting all locations in the adventure (bonus).
- Finding the treasure(s).
- Bringing the treasures back to a safe place.

In addition to points awarded for positive actions, there may be points subtracted from the total score for various other reasons:

- Asking for help or hints during the play of the game.
- Not avoiding various dire actions including:

  Waking the ogre (or other monsters).

  Being killed and having to be reincarnated.

In Adventure 2, I have devised a scoring function that takes such various factors into account. Here's the way I have it now:

- 5 points are awarded for each location visited.
- 140 points are scored for getting the treasure back to start.
- 50 points are deducted for being cooked; that is falling into the flames.
- 50 points are deducted for being eaten by the ogre.
- 25 points are deducted for waking the ogre.

THE HELP COMMAND

Adventure 2 contains a help command. If the player asks for help, the guide will respond by giving hints. If the player has already read the message on the island, the guide will tell the player that the treasure is in the maze. Otherwise, the guide will tell the player where hints may be found—namely, near the lake and in the alcove.

The scoring rules in this adventure do not punish the player for asking for help. You might want to modify Adventure 2 so that a few points are deducted if the player ever asks for help. This would require another Boolean, variable (like cooked or quit), which would be false initially, but which would be set to true if the player asks for help. The score function may then examine this variable to see if points should be deducted or not.

THE LAMP AND THE LIGHT COMMAND

Adventure 2 requires that the player carry the lamp found at the start. The lamp must also be lit. Otherwise, the player falls into a pit and is killed after a few turns. One of the first problems the player must solve is how to treat the lamp properly.

The light command checks to make sure that the player has the lamp by using the set relationship IN:

```
lamp IN stash
```

If this is true, the lamp will be lit if the player says

```
light lamp
```

or, simply

```
light
```

The latter is a convenience for the player. Many adventure games have lamps that need to be lit. In other games, it is possible to use a variety of commands in order to light the lamp: lamp on, lamp, light, and so on. I have only provided two: light lamp and light. You might want to modify Adventure 2 to add further commands that cause the lamp to be turned on.

The cklamp procedure is provided to monitor the status of the lamp. It counts the number of turns the player spends underground with the lamp turned off. If this gets too large, the game is ended. It warns the player whenever the lamp is off. It also heavy-handedly turns the lamp off automatically when the number of turns taken gets too large. This forces the player to finish up the game in a certain amount of time in order to win.

THE DIG COMMAND

When the player gets to the right maze location, it is time to dig for the treasure. Provided that the player has located and is carrying the shovel, and has read the message on the island, the command to dig will be obeyed. However, it is not enough to simply dig once—you have to keep on digging. In fact, you must dig at least three times and no more than four times. Each time the dig command is given, a new message is conveyed to the player. This is controlled by the variable hasdug, which counts the number of times the player has used the dig command.

THE EAT COMMAND

The eat command has been added to Adventure 2 strictly for fun. There is a sandwich that may be found. If the player is carrying the sandwich and says "eat," the guide replies, "Oh, yummy!!" Other messages are given, depending on the circumstances. However, the sandwich and the eat command play no role in the scoring of Adventure 2.

THE OGRE

The procedures pogreroom and ogreaction handle the ogre character. The ogre is strictly bad news—nothing good is associated with the ogre. If the player visits the ogreroom (which must be done in order to get the maximum score), there is a chance that the ogre might wake up. If the ogre wakes up, there is a chance that he might catch and eat you. If you should ask to go down while you are in the ogreroom, you find out that you have stumbled into the ogre's cooking pit. All of these undesirable happenings cause you to lose points.

Adventure 2 uses a very crude technique to decide whether any of these things occur. The number of turns is examined. If it is an even multiple of 3 (3, 6, 9, 12, and so on), the ogre is awakened. If the ogre is already awake and if the number of turns is an even multiple of 2, the player is eaten. The Pascal MOD function is used to determine these conditions:

(turns MOD 3) = 0

or

(turns MOD 2) = 0

This technique could be slightly improved by using a random choice. This would depend on the availability of a random number generator.

17

UCSD Pascal Development Techniques

In Chapter 4 I discussed UCSD Pascal and some elementary techniques for its use. In this chapter, I wish to elaborate on those topics. In particular, I discuss how best to use your UCSD system in writing large adventure games and other Pascal programs.

MANAGING YOUR FILES EFFECTIVELY

Most personal computer systems equipped with UCSD Pascal use floppy disks as mass storage devices. Your files all "live" on various floppy disks. As the number and size of the files you have created grows, the problems of managing them grow accordingly. You have to worry about running out of space on a given floppy. You have to worry about sharing space with various UCSD system files. You have to worry about keeping track of various versions of your files. In short, you need to worry about more than just writing Pascal programs.

Organizing Your Source Files

There are a number of problems associated with writing a large program in UCSD Pascal. I have already hinted at some of these. Now it is time to be more specific.

UCSD Editor Limitations. The UCSD Pascal full screen text editor requires that the entire file being edited fit into memory. Unfortunately, Pascal programs tend to exceed this limit. That implies that there will be one of two results:

- You never write Pascal programs whose source files are bigger than what the UCSD editor can handle.
- You use techniques for splitting Pascal programs into more than one source file.

The first alternative needs no comment. The programs in this book necessitate the use of the second alternative.

Each implementation of the UCSD system imposes its own limitation on the size of an editor file. The Apple Pascal limitation is approximately 18,400 bytes, which is about 38 disk blocks. In order to leave room for expansion and for fixing bugs, it is good to impose a smaller maximum size for each source file. 15,000 bytes seems like a reasonable choice: it is easy to remember and it allows for expansion.

When you start writing an adventure game, you should monitor the size of the source file. In the UCSD editor, you discover the current size of your file by using the set environment command. This command gives you a screenful of information about the file you are editing. Among other things, it tells you the number of bytes used and the number of bytes remaining in the file. When the number of bytes used shows about 15,000 (or whatever limit you decide is reasonable on your system), it is time to start a new file. When to start a new file may also be based on the logical divisions of the program. In other words, it is silly to split a source file in the middle of a procedure just to adhere to the size limit.

As an example of this technique, the following summary shows the source files used in Adventure 2 and the sizes of each:

File Name	Size
a2.data.text	2671 bytes
a2.u1.text	5836 bytes
a2.u2.text	10662 bytes
a2.m2.text	4096 bytes
a2.maze.text	2749 bytes
a2.main.text	3499 bytes

As you can see, none of these files comes close to our self-imposed limit. The division of the source code for Adventure 2 into these files was determined more by the logical structure of the code than by size. However, in the case of a2.u1.text and a2.u2.text, size was the determining factor. These were originally a single file. They were split when the total size exceeded 15,000 bytes. The following summary shows the list of files again, this time with the parts of Adventure 2 included in each file shown instead of the file sizes:

File Name	Contents
a2.data.text	The const, type, and var sections of the program, together with the simple procedure **wipe**.
a2.u1.text	The **introduction** procedure through the **ckobject** function.
a2.u2.text	The **pcarry** procedure through the **travel** procedure.
a2.m2.text	The **ogreaction** procedure through the **pogreroom** procedure.
a2.maze.text	The **pmaze** procedure.
a2.main.text	The **ppit** procedure through the end of the main program.

Compiling Multiple Source File Programs

The UCSD Pascal compiler allows you to compile a single program that exists in more than a single source file. This is accomplished by the use of the include option. The include option tells the compiler to read more source code from another file. The form of the option is as follows:

```
(*$Ixyz.text*)
```

This is similar to other UCSD Pascal compiler options. Options are initiated by an open comment bracket, followed by a dollar sign:

```
(*$
```

Then comes a single letter indicating which option is being used and any other information needed by the option itself. In the case of the include option, the other information is the name of the source file to be "included." For example, in Adventure 2 at the end of the first source file, **a2.data.text**, the following sequence of include options appears:

```
(*$Ia2.u1.text*)
(*$Ia2.u2.text*)
(*$Ia2.m2.text*)
(*$Ia2.maze.text*)
(*$Ia2.main.text*)
```

The result is that the Pascal compiler reads through the source files **a2.u1.text**, **a2.u2.text**, **a2.m2.text**, a2.maze.text, and a2.main.text in that order, after it reads through the file a2.main.text. The net effect is just as if all six source files had been contained in a single file. When you invoke the Pascal compiler to compile a2.data.text, the compiler will automatically find all the other files needed. You don't need to learn any special commands in addition to the include option itself.

Giving the Compiler a Chance

There is another option that should almost always be used when compiling large UCSD Pascal programs. That is the (*$S+*) option. This causes the compiler to go into "swapping" mode. Instead of having all of the code for the compiler in memory at the same time, various parts of the compiler code are swapped in and out. Only part of the compiler code is present in memory at any given time. The rest of the code stays on the floppy disk.

Let us examine the consequences of either using or not using the swapping option. What is affected by the swapping option is the amount of memory that is available to the compiler for its symbol table. When the swapping option is not used, there is a limited amount of symbol table memory. This means that only a medium sized program can be compiled before this memory is exhausted. When the swapping option is used, the amount of symbol table memory increases dramatically and with it the size of program that may be compiled. It is possible to increase the amount of symbol table memory even more. This is done by using the "double swapping" option (*$S++*). This slows down the compiler, because it must do more juggling of code into and out of memory. It increases the symbol table space to its maximum amount and therefore provides for the largest possible source program.

UCSD SYSTEM TRICKS AND PITFALLS

The UCSD system includes some commands that make dealings with your files and disks easier. These, however, should be used with caution.

The Prefix #5 Trick

The prefix command in the UCSD filer allows you to abbreviate file names when communicating with the UCSD system. The system automatically uses the prefix to decide which disk volume to search for a given file. If you set the prefix to #5, the system will read the volume name of the disk currently in the drive corresponding to #5. This means that if later you wish to change the disk in that drive, you must reenter the filer and reset the prefix to #5 again because the name of the physical disk has changed. Either that, or you have to type the volume name explicitly, the very task that the prefix command was designed to allow you to skip.

Some implementations of UCSD Pascal, Apple Pascal in particular, allow you to use the following trick. First enter the filer program. Then open the door on the disk drive corresponding to unit #5. While the door is open, issue the prefix #5 command. The disk will spin, a clicking or buzzing noise may eventually be heard, and the filer will eventually respond by saying:

```
Prefix is #5:
```

This means that no matter what disk is in #5, the filer will use its name as the prefix. Thus, you don't have to reissue the prefix command if you change the disk in #5. The system will automatically detect the change and use the new disk's volume name as the prefix.

The K(runch Command

As you develop a large program, the disk containing its source files may need space maintenance. The available space on the disk tends to become fragmented because of the way the system moves files around during editing and compiling. The UCSD system provides the K(runch command to allow files to be rearranged. This command moves files around in order to create a single large block of unused space. It is a good idea to examine your disks occasionally and if necessary do a K(runch. The question is, when should you K(runch?

There is no hard and fast rule about when to K(runch. However, sooner rather than later is the best idea. To start with, you should use the

```
TAB3:
FORMAT.CODE          20   6-Feb-82     6 Code
CMDNAMES.TEXT         4   7-Feb-82    26 Text
< UNUSED >            8               30
TABCH12.TEXT          4  27-Apr-83    38 Text
TABCH13.TEXT          4  27-Apr-83    42 Text
< UNUSED >           20               46
TABCH11.TEXT         16   7-Aug-83    66 Text
TABCH14A.TEXT        34  24-Aug-83    82 Text
TABCH15.TEXT         34  29-Aug-83   116 Text
< UNUSED >           30              150
TABCH14.TEXT         22  24-Aug-83   180 Text
TABCH14B.TEXT        10  24-Aug-83   202 Text
FAKE.TEXT             4  25-Aug-83   212 Text
HDR.TEXT              4  26-Aug-83   216 Text
< UNUSED >           60              220
11/11 files, 118 unused, 60 in largest
```

Fig. 17-1. A typical output from an E(xtended directory list command.

E(xtended directory list command to get a picture of the current state of your disk. A typical output from such a command is shown in Fig. 17-1.

Each line beginning with < UNUSED > accounts for a block of unused space on the disk. If the largest such blocks is not big enough to hold the largest file on the disk, you probably should K(runch. In the above display, the biggest available space is 60 blocks (this information is always given in the last line of the display: 11/11 files, 118 unused, 60 in largest). The largest files on this disk are both 34 blocks in size. Either will fit comfortably in the 60 block space.

What are the consequences of not K(runching soon enough? It may become impossible to write out a new version of the file from the editor; or it may be impossible to perform a compile, because the compiler may run out of space for its output files. In the former case, there is a way out. In the latter case, you will have to abort the compile, do the K(runch, and recompile. So what should you do if the editor says

ERROR: WRITING OUT THE FILE. PLEASE PRESS <SPACEBAR> TO CONTINUE

At this point, you should remove the offending disk from its drive and insert another that you know has enough room (it is a good idea to have at least one "scratch" disk available for this purpose). Write the file to this new disk using the write command. Then put the old disk back in, K(runch it, and use the filer to move the saved copy on the scratch disk back to your working disk. This is greatly facilitated if you have used the prefix #5 command as described earlier in this chapter.

Losing Source Files Accidentally

There are many ways that source files can get lost. Everyone hopes that such a disaster never happens to them. However, there are only two kinds of programmers: those who have lost their source code, and those who are going to. So it is wise to have some methods for combating lost source files.

You should always have a copy of your programs on paper. If you own a printer, this is easy enough to accomplish. If you don't, you should save your pennies and get one, or you will wind up in the second category of programmers. When you make a listing of your program, write the date on it. Then as you make changes, write them on the listing until you run out of space (or you get tired). Then print a new listing. With an up to date listing, the worst that can happen is that you have to reenter all your code by hand. That fate is bad enough, but the alternative—having to write your code over again from scratch—is far worse.

Backups on Disk. If you have the time, energy, and the money to afford extra disks, keeping *backup* copies of your source code is an alternative solution. Simply copy the entire disk using the filer. Then put it in a disk box and put it away in a cool, dark place. If you lose your primary copy, or the cat tears it to shreds, your backup copy will save the day.

Accidental Loss of Files. Occasionally, you might use the write command in the editor and type the wrong file name. If it is a new file name, there is no problem—simply use the filer to change it to what you originally intended. On the other hand, if it is the name of an already existing file, you have trouble. The file you just overwrote is destroyed by the copy of the new file you are editing. There may or may not be a way to recover a copy of the file that was overwritten.

It may be that the reason you typed that particular wrong name was that you just finished editing that file. If you edit many different files in a row, you may get names confused. This is especially true if the names are similar: source1.text, source2.-text, source3.text, and so on. For the sake of argument, assume that you are editing and saved a file named source2.text. Then you edited source3.text, but instead of saving it as source3.text, you write it to the disk using source2.text as the file name. What actually happens is this: the editor finds a block of space on the disk big enough to hold the new file; the editor writes out the new file; and finally the editor deletes the previous copy of the file. This last action creates a new block of <UNUSED> space on the disk, which actually contains the file you just "overwrote."

How do you recover from this mistake? If you realize the mistake right away, you have a good chance at recovery. Enter the filer immediately. Then use the M(ake command to create files that will occupy the blocks of space currently marked as < UNUSED >. For example, in the display shown earlier, you could issue the following sequence of commands:

```
MAKE WHAT FILE? TMP1.TEXT[8]
MAKE WHAT FILE? TMP2.TEXT[20]
MAKE WHAT FILE? TMP3.TEXT[30]
MAKE WHAT FILE? TMP4.TEXT[60]
```

This will create the four files shown, each filling in one of the "holes" in the disk. Now edit the four files in turn, and see if any of them happens to be the file you just lost. If so, simply delete the remaining files, delete the new copy of the file you lost (which contains the wrong information), and finally rename the tmp file to the name of the file you lost. All this is complicated, but desperate situations call for drastic measures.

Once you have created a file with the editor, it already has a file name that is known to the system. When you edit it again, use the S(ave command to write it back out to disk, instead of the W(rite command. This will avoid the pitfall I have just mentioned in 99 cases out of 100.

The #*%%!!? ESCAPE Key

In the editor there is one particularly nasty pitfall that you should know about. By realizing what can happen, you can work to avoid disaster. When you go into insert mode in the UCSD editor, it is possible at any time to cancel the entire text inserted by simple pressing the ESCAPE key. This action is absolute: there is no escape from this escape! Once you press the ESCAPE key, all that beautiful text you have just typed is wiped off the screen, thrown in the proverbial bit bucket, and gone forever. The system does not give you a second chance to decide if you really want to cancel your insert or not; it just does what you "tell" it.

Notice that on the Apple II family of computers the ESCAPE key is located on the top left corner of the keyboard, right next to the key with the characters ! and 1 on it. (This is on Apple II and Apple *II*e keyboards.) It is disgustingly easy to reach for the 1–! key and accidentally hit the ESCAPE key instead. The moral of this story is this:

don't stay in insert mode for very long before typing ^C to accept the insert. Sooner or later you are going to hit the ESCAPE key by mistake. When you do, if it has been two hours since you started your insert, the only alternative left to you is to have a good cry.

18

Preview of MAKEDESC and BROWSE

Adventure 2 differs radically from Adventure 1 in its treatment of descriptions. All textual matter was embedded directly in the code of Adventure 1. In Adventure 2, most of the descriptions have been moved out of the program and into a disk file. The disk file containing the text of the descriptions, along with another file used as an index for the first file are collectively referred to as the *descriptions database* for Adventure 2. The next six chapters present the program used to generate this kind of database and describe the creation and use of similar databases in adventure games.

DATABASE CONCEPTS

The term *database* is a very general one. It is used in many different contexts, not always in connection with computers. A database can be defined as any collection of information. More often than not the term implies that the information itself is organized for convenient retrieval. Subsidiary information that is not part of the collection of information but is used solely to facilitate retrieval is often referred to as the database *index.*

The databases for Adventure 2 and beyond are textual databases. The text consists of descriptions. In Adventure 2 they are descriptions of adventure game locations. In future adventures they may be descriptions of other things as well, including descriptions of events and speeches of characters in the game.

PREVIEWS OF CHAPTERS 19 THROUGH 24

Chapter 19 contains the listings of two Pascal programs that I call MAKEDESC and BROWSE. The first of these is the program used to generate the descriptions databases. The second is used to examine descriptions databases outside adventure games. It may be used to preview your descriptions databases before you incorporate them into your own games. It also serves as an introduction to the techniques of retrieving data from databases.

Chapter 20 is called "Creating a Database of Descriptions" and tells how to use the MAKEDESC program. MAKEDESC processes a text file that contains a mixture of two kinds of information:

- The actual text lines of the descriptions.
- Instructions to the MAKEDESC program itself.

Chapter 20 tells you more about the nature of the instructions to MAKEDESC. It also describes the process of running the MAKEDESC program on a UCSD Pascal system and the information to provide to the program in response to various prompts.

The title of Chapter 21 is "Random Access Files in UCSD Pascal." It deals with the specific nature of file access. Both random and sequential files are defined and discussed in some detail. The extensions to Pascal needed to support random access files are described in the context of the UCSD system. The use of the BROWSE program for previewing descriptions databases is described. Finally, a discussion of how to incorporate descriptions databases into your own adventure games is given. In particular, the show procedure is described. The show procedure is used both by BROWSE and Adventure 2 to retrieve descriptions from the database and show them to the user.

Chapter 22 describes the structure of the descriptions databases in detail. It is entitled "The Structure of Adventure Databases" and begins with a discussion of index files in general and the descriptions database index file in particular. The contents of the index entries are described in detail and revealed to consist of a collection of *records*. Each record in turn consists of a number of entries: name, id, dbegin, dend, and link. The function of these entries, called *fields*, is described.

The use of the database in an adventure game requires that the game declare and manipulate the database as a collection of files. The second part of Chapter 22 describes this process in detail. Finally, a discussion of the show procedure in the context of adventure games wraps up the chapter.

Chapter 23 delves into the programming techniques used in MAKEDESC. It discusses concepts from the realm of computer language translators including symbol tables, hash functions and hashing techniques, and lookup in symbol tables (linear search and hash lookup). Each of these techniques is discussed in general and in the context of adventure games and MAKEDESC. The advantages of hashing and hash table lookup are explained in comparison with linear sarch techniques.

The manipulation of symbol tables is explained with the MAKEDESC code as an example. The operations of adding entries to the table and looking up entries in the table are both delved into. Chapter 23 merely scratches the surface. If you find yourself fascinated by its concepts and techniques, a book on data structures, computer language translators, or compiler construction might be of interest to you.

The section on MAKEDESC concludes with Chapter 24 which is entitled, "What Else Can You Put on Disk?" It is a short and speculative chapter. Several suggestions for extending the usefulness of adventure game databases are given. Some of the suggestions will be followed up in Adventure 3. Others are offered for your enjoyment and imagination.

19

MAKEDESC and BROWSE

LISTING 19-1. MAKE80 DATABASE GENERATOR

```
{-----------------------------------------------}
{                                               }
{    m    a    k    e    d    e    s    c      }
{                                               }
{  This program reads a file of text            }
{ containing a mixture of descrip-              }
{ tions and commands.  It creates               }
{ output files which may be used as             }
{ a database of textual passages.               }
{ An index file contains information            }
{ about each passage: start and stop            }
{ indices in the data file (which is            }
{ a file of strings of fixed length             }
{ 80), an identifier which may be               }
{ used if desired to retrieve the               }
{ passage by name - say using a hash            }
{ scheme, etc.  A data file is also             }
{ created containing all the text               }
{ lines from the input, either padded}
{ with blanks if the original line              }
{ was less than 80 characters long,             }
```

```
{ or truncated to 80 characters if    }
{ original line was too long.         }
{                                     }
{-----------------------------------*}

PROGRAM makedescriptions;
CONST

  hashmax      =        30;
  blank40      =
    '                                        ';

TYPE

  whichsect     =        (indexsection,descsection);
  pname         =        STRING[40];
  storyline     =        STRING[80];

  byte          =        0..255;

  procs         =        (pnamelookup, pentername,
                          pdescribe, pmakename,
                          pfindrec);
  placerec      =

    RECORD

      CASE section:whichsection OF

        indexsection:   ( tableentry: INTEGER );
        descsection:    ( name:   pname;
                          id:     INTEGER;
                          dbegin: INTEGER;
                          dend:   INTEGER;
                          link:   byte    );

    END;

 VAR

  infile:          text;
  narrate:         FILE OF STRING[80];
  indexfile:       FILE OF placerec;
```

```
   hash:               ARRAY[0..hashmax] OF byte;
   symhash:            INTEGER;

   where:              INTEGER;
   { index TO symbol table }

   places:             ARRAY[0..255] OF placerec;
   dumprec:            placerec;
   lastrec:            placerec;

   nextplace:          byte;         { init=31 }
   outrec:             INTEGER;
   { index TO descriptions.  init=0 }

   placename:          pname;
   line:               storyline;
   blank80:            storyline;

   iname,
   nname,
   xname:              STRING;

   i:                  INTEGER;
   ditto:              BOOLEAN;
   { was last data line a ditto line? }

   tracing:            BOOLEAN;

   ch:                 CHAR;
   warnset:            SET OF CHAR;
   { init = ['$','"','>'] }

{----------------------------------------}
{       t    r    a    c    e            }
{                                        }
{ This procedure allows a trace of       }
{ all procedure calls made by the        }
{ program.  This is most useful in       }
{ the program debugging phase.           }
{----------------------------------------}

PROCEDURE trace (who:procs);
BEGIN

  CASE who OF
```

```
      pnamelookup:  writeln ('namelookup');
      pentername:   writeln ('entername');
      pdescribe:    writeln ('describe');
      pmakename:    writeln ('makename');
      pfindrec:     writeln ('findrec');

    END { CASE who };

  END { PROCEDURE trace };

  {------------------------------------------}
  {          i   n   t   o                   }
  {                                          }
  { Called by procedures on entry - it       }
  { checks to see if tracing is in           }
  { effect and if so, calls the trace        }
  { procedure to print the name of the       }
  { procedure or function which is           }
  { being entered.                           }
  {------------------------------------------}

  PROCEDURE into (who: procs);
  BEGIN

    IF tracing
    THEN
    BEGIN

      write ('entering ');
      trace (who);

    END;

  END { PROCEDURE into };

  {------------------------------------------}
  {   n   a   m   e   l   o   o   k   u   p  }
  {                                          }
  { Called by entername.  Its job is         }
  { to determine if a given name has         }
  { already been entered into the name       }
  { table.  The technique used is to         }
  { traverse a linked list of name           }
  { entries, all of which have the           }
  { same hashvalue.  The hashvalue is        }
```

```
{ computed by the caller and left in }
{ the global variable 'symhash'.      }
{-------------------------------------}

FUNCTION namelookup ( thisname: pname ): BOOLEAN;
BEGIN

  into (pnamelookup);
  places[0].name := thisname;
  where          := hash[symhash];

  WHILE places[where].name <> thisname
  DO
    where := places[where].link
  { enddo };

  namelookup := ( where <> 0 );

END { FUNCTION namelookup };

{-------------------------------------}
{     e  n  t  e  r  n  a  m  e       }
{                                     }
{ This procedure is called in order   }
{ to enter a placename in the symbol }
{ table.  It is called whenever a     }
{ placename instruction line (line    }
{ beginning with a '$') is scanned    }
{ in the make80 source file.  It      }
{ calls namelookup to determine if    }
{ the placename has been used before.}
{-------------------------------------}

PROCEDURE entername;
VAR
  i:     INTEGER;

BEGIN

  into (pentername);
  symhash := 0;
  FOR i := 1 TO length (placename)
  DO
    symhash :=
      (symhash + ord (placename[i])) MOD (hashmax+1)
```

```
  { enddo };

  writeln ('placename: ',placename);
  writeln ('hashvalue: ',symhash);

  IF namelookup (placename)
  THEN
  BEGIN

    writeln ('*** duplicate place:');
    writeln (placename);

  END
  ELSE
  BEGIN

    IF NOT ditto
    THEN
      places[nextplace].dend := outrec - 1
    { endif };

    IF nextplace > 0
    THEN
      lastrec := places[nextplace]
    { END IF };

    nextplace := nextplace + 1;

    WITH places[nextplace] DO
    BEGIN

      id              := nextplace;
      link            := hash[symhash];
      dbegin          := outrec;
      name            := placename;
      hash[symhash] := nextplace;

    END;

  END { IF namelookup };
  ditto := false;

END { PROCEDURE entername };

{-------------------------------------------------}
{     d  e  s  c  r  i  b  e                      }
```

```
{                                        }
{ Adds a line of text to the des-        }
{ criptions file.  It first adjusts      }
{ the input line to be exactly 80        }
{ characters long.  It accomplishes      }
{ this by padding the line with          }
{ blanks.                                }
{----------------------------------------}

PROCEDURE describe ( thisline: storyline );
BEGIN

  into (pdescribe);
  IF length (thisline) < 80
  THEN

    thisline :=
      concat (thisline,
              copy (blank80, 1, 80 - length (thisline)))

  { endif };

  narrate^ := thisline;
  seek (narrate, outrec);
  put (narrate);

  outrec := outrec + 1;

END { PROCEDURE describe };

{----------------------------------------}
{     m  a  k  e  n  a  m  e             }
{----------------------------------------}

PROCEDURE makename ( VAR thisname: pname);
BEGIN

  into (pmakename);
  IF length(thisname) < 40
  THEN

    thisname :=
      concat (thisname,
              copy (blank40, 1, 40-length (thisname)))

  { endif };
```

```
  writeln ('placename: ',thisname);

END { PROCEDURE makename };

{----------------------------------------}
{     f   i   n   d   r   e   c         }
{                                        }
{ Handles the ditto instruction lines}
{ from the make80 source file.  It     }
{ must distinguish between the case    }
{ where a name is specified and the    }
{ case in which only a ditto was       }
{ used.                                 }
{----------------------------------------}

PROCEDURE findrec;
BEGIN

  into (pfindrec);
  IF length (line) = 1
  THEN
  BEGIN

    places[nextplace].dbegin := lastrec.dbegin;
    places[nextplace].dend   := lastrec.dend;
    lastrec := places[nextplace];

  END
  ELSE
  BEGIN

    line := copy (line, 2, length (line) - 1);
    makename(line);
    symhash := 0;
    FOR i := 1 TO length (line)
    DO
      symhash :=
        (symhash + ord (line[i])) MOD (hashmax+1)
    { enddo };

    IF NOT namelookup (line)
    THEN
    BEGIN

      writeln ('error: ditto name does not exist');
      writeln (line);
```

```
    END
    ELSE
    BEGIN

      places[nextplace].dbegin :=
        places[where].dbegin;

      places[nextplace].dend   :=
        places[where].dend;

      lastrec := places[where];

    END { IF NOT namelookup };

  END { IF length(line)>1 };

  ditto := true;

END { PROCEDURE findrec };

{-------------------------------------------------}
{                                                 }
{  m   m  aaaaa  k   k  eeeee  88888  00000       }
{  mm mm  a   a  k  k   e      8   8  0   0       }
{  m m m  a   a  k k    e       8 8   0   0       }
{  m   m  aaaaa  kk     eee      8    0   0       }
{  m   m  a   a  k k    e       8 8   0   0       }
{  m   m  a   a  k  k   e      8   8  0   0       }
{  m   m  a   a  k   k  eeeee  88888  00000       }
{                                                 }
{  Here begins the main program block of make80 }
{  The processing loop scans each line and        }
{  decides whether to add it to the text part     }
{  of the descriptions database, or whether to   }
{  interpret it as a makedesc instruction line.  }
{  The instruction lines are handled by a case   }
{  statement which uses the special character    }
{  at the beginning of the line to determine     }
{  which makedesc instruction to carry out.      }
{-------------------------------------------------}

BEGIN

  blank80 := concat (blank40, blank40);
  nextplace := 0;
  outrec    := 0;
```

```
   warnset    := ['$','"','>'];
   ditto      := false;

   FOR i := 0 TO hashmax
   DO
     hash[i] := 0
   { enddo };

   write ('tracing? ===>');
   readln (ch);
   IF ch='y'
   THEN
     tracing := true
   ELSE
     tracing := false
   { endif };

   iname := '';

   WHILE length (iname)=0
   DO
   BEGIN

     write ('input file===>');
     readln (iname);

END { DO };

nname := '';

WHILE length (nname) = 0
DO
BEGIN

  write ('description file===>');
  readln (nname);

END { DO };

xname := concat (nname,'.x');

reset (infile, iname);
rewrite (narrate, nname);

{-----------------------------------}
{  main processing loop }
{-----------------------------------}
```

```
REPEAT

  readln (infile, line);

  IF length (line) > 0
  THEN
  BEGIN

    ch := line[1];

    CASE ch OF

      '$':

      BEGIN

        line := copy (line, 2, length (line) - 1);
        IF length (line) > 40
        THEN
        BEGIN

          writeln ('placename too long');
          write ('chopping to: ');
          line := copy (line, 1, 40);
          writeln (line);

        END { IF };
        IF length (line) < 40
        THEN
          line :=

            concat (line,
              copy (blank40, 1, 40 - length (line)))
        { endif };
        placename := line;
        entername;

      END;

      '"':     findrec;

      '>':

        BEGIN
```

```
          close (infile);
          iname := copy (line, 2, length (line)-1);
          reset (infile, iname);

        END;

      END { CASE ch OF };

      IF NOT (ch IN warnset)
      THEN

        describe(line)

      { endif };

      { note: this takes advantage of the u.c.s.d.
              "fall through" semantics of the case
              statement and in general will not
              be transportable code.            }

    END { IF length (line)>0 };

  UNTIL eof(infile);

  places[nextplace].dend := outrec - 1;
  { finish last placerec }

  nextplace := nextplace + 1;
  places[nextplace].name := 'nowhere';

  {-----------------------}
  {  write out index file }
  {-----------------------}

  close (narrate, lock);

  rewrite (indexfile, xname);

  dumprec.section := indexsection;
    { SET variant TO accept hash table entries      }

    FOR i := 0 TO hashmax DO
    BEGIN

      dumprec.tableentry := hash[i];
```

```
    seek (indexfile, i);
    indexfile^ := dumprec;
    put (indexfile);

  END { DO };

  dumprec.section := descsection;
  { SET variant TO accept place table entries    }

  FOR i := 1 TO nextplace DO
  BEGIN

    dumprec := places[i];
    seek (indexfile, i + hashmax);
    indexfile^ := dumprec;
    put (indexfile);

  END { DO };

  close (indexfile, lock);

END.
```

LISTING 19-2. BROWSE80 DATABASE SNOOPER

```
}

{-----------------------------------------------------}
{                                                     }
{        b   r   o   w   s   e   8   0                }
{                                                     }
{  Program for previewing makedesc databases          }
{  which have been generated by make80.               }
{                                                     }
{-----------------------------------------------------}

PROGRAM browse80;
CONST

  hashsize      =        31;
  blank40       =
    '                                         ';

TYPE

  whichsect     =        (indexsection,descsection);
```

```
  pname            =        STRING[40];
  storyline        =        STRING[80];

  byte             =        0..255;

  procs            =        (pnamelookup, pentername,
                             pdescribe, pmakename,
                             pfindrec);
  placerec         =

    RECORD

      CASE section:whichsection OF

        indexsection:   ( tableentry: INTEGER );

        descsection:    ( name:   pname;
                          id:     INTEGER;
                          dbegin: INTEGER;
                          dend:   INTEGER;
                          link:   byte    );

    END;


VAR

  infile:          text;
  narrate:         FILE OF storyline;
  xfile:           FILE OF placerec;

  hash:            ARRAY[0..hashsize] OF byte;
  symhash:         INTEGER;

  where:           INTEGER;
  { index TO symbol table }

  places:          ARRAY[0..255] OF placerec;
  dumprec:         placerec;
  lastrec:         placerec;

  start:           INTEGER;
  stop:            INTEGER;

  nextplace:       byte;         { init= 0 }
```

```
  outrec:               INTEGER;
  { index TO descriptions.  init=0 }

  placename:            pname;
  line:                 storyline;
  blank80:              storyline;

  iname,
  nname,
  xname:                STRING;

  i:                    INTEGER;
  ditto:                BOOLEAN;
  { was last data line a ditto line? }

  tracing:              BOOLEAN;

  ch:                   CHAR;
  warnset:              SET OF CHAR;
  { init = ['$','"','>'] }

{----------------------------------------}
{       t    r    a    c    e           }
{----------------------------------------}

PROCEDURE trace (who:procs);
BEGIN

  CASE who OF

    pnamelookup:  writeln('namelookup');
    pentername:   writeln('entername');
    pdescribe:    writeln('describe');
    pmakename:    writeln('makename');
    pfindrec:     writeln('findrec');

  END { CASE who };

END { PROCEDURE trace };

{----------------------------------------}
{           i   n   t   o               }
{----------------------------------------}

PROCEDURE into (who: procs);
BEGIN
```

```
  IF tracing
  THEN
  BEGIN

    write ('entering ');
    trace (who);

  END;

END { PROCEDURE into };

{-------------------------------------------}
{   n   a   m   e   l   o   o   k   u   p   }
{-------------------------------------------}

FUNCTION namelookup ( thisname: pname ): BOOLEAN;
BEGIN

  into (pnamelookup);
  places[0].name := thisname;
  where          := hash[symhash];

  WHILE places[where].name <> thisname
  DO
    where := places[where].link
  { enddo };

  namelookup := ( where <> 0 );

END { FUNCTION namelookup };

{-------------------------------------------}
{      d   e   s   c   r   i   b   e        }
{-------------------------------------------}

PROCEDURE describe;
BEGIN

  into (pdescribe);

  start := places[where].dbegin;
  stop  := places[where].dend;

  FOR i := start TO stop
  DO
  BEGIN
```

```
    seek (narrate, i);
    get (narrate);
    write (narrate^);

  END { DO };

END { PROCEDURE describe };

{-----------------------------------------------------------}
{      m   a   k   e   n   a   m   e                        }
{-----------------------------------------------------------}

PROCEDURE makename (VAR thisname: pname);
BEGIN

  into (pmakename);
  IF length (thisname) < 40
  THEN

    thisname :=
     concat (thisname,
       copy (blank40, 1, 40 - length (thisname)))

  { endif };
  writeln ('placename: ',thisname);

END { PROCEDURE makename };


BEGIN

  blank80 := concat (blank40, blank40);
  nextplace := 1;

  write ('tracing? ===>');
  readln (ch);
  IF ch='y'
  THEN
    tracing := true
  ELSE
    tracing := false
  { endif };

  nname := '';

  WHILE length (nname) = 0
```

```
  DO
  BEGIN

    write ('description file===>');
    readln (nname);

END { DO };

xname := concat (nname, '.x');

reset (xfile, xname);
reset (narrate, nname);

FOR i := 0 TO hashsize DO
BEGIN

  hash[i] := xfile^.tableentry;
  get (xfile);

END;

i := 1;

REPEAT

  places[i] := xfile^;
  get (xfile);
  i := i + 1;

UNTIL eof (xfile);

close (xfile, lock);

{------------------------}
{  main processing loop  }
{------------------------}

REPEAT

  write ('describe what place===>');
  readln (placename);

  IF placename[1] = '?'
  THEN
  BEGIN
```

```
    FOR i := 0 TO hashsize
    DO
    BEGIN

      where := hash[i];
      WHILE where <> 0
      DO
      BEGIN

        writeln (places[where].name);
        where := places[where].link

      END { WHILE where <> 0 DO };

      END { FOR i := 1 TO hashsize DO };

    END
    ELSE
    BEGIN

      makename (placename);

      symhash := 0;
      FOR i := 1 TO length (placename)
      DO
        symhash :=
          (symhash + ord (placename[i])) MOD (hashsize+1)
      { enddo };

      IF NOT namelookup (placename)
      THEN

        writeln ('no such place')

      ELSE

        describe

      { endif };
    END;

  UNTIL placename = 'quit                    ';

END.
```

20

Creating a Database of Descriptions

You may have noticed in Adventure 1 how much of the program consisted of writeln statements. Putting all that creative prose straight into the program takes up an enormous amount of space. The space could be used for other Pascal code; code that could make the game more complex, devious, creative, and challenging. It would be better if most (if not all) of the text of adventure descriptions were stored outside the program code. The natural place for such storage would be on the disk. The adventure program could then refer to the disk whenever it needed to describe a particular location. The program space freed by removing descriptions can then be used to add more problems, locations, and challenges to the game itself.

How can this idea be put into practice? There are some new problems to solve!

1. How to create a file containing the text of adventure game descriptions.
2. How to make sure the file is structured so that the description of any location can be quickly retrieved.
3. How to write Pascal procedures in adventure games(s) that read the descriptions from the file created in step 1.

In this and the next few chapters, I shall attempt to help you solve these problems. In this chapter, I describe a utility program which solves problem 1.

The utility program or "tool" is called MAKEDESC. A listing of MAKEDESC was included in Chapter 19. You can type it into your system and use it. MAKEDESC generates or creates a database of location descriptions for use in your adventure game. What, you may ask again, is a database? A database is any collection of information. Your kitchen recipe file is a database. The files in the office of any business form a database. Your income tax records form a database. However, when computer people use the word *database* to refer to a collection of information, they usually have another requirement in mind:

> The information in a database is structured for easy retrieval.

MAKEDESC creates a database of descriptions of adventure game locations. It is made so that you can easily retrieve the descriptions using a simple Pascal procedure. I will show you how to do that in Chapters 21-23. In the remainder of this chapter, I discuss how to use MAKEDESC to create the descriptions database in the first place.

MAKEDESC: THE DESCRIPTIONS GENERATOR

MAKEDESC has the following inputs and outputs:

>> Input: one or more text files telling MAKEDESC what the descriptions are and how to divide them up into different locations.

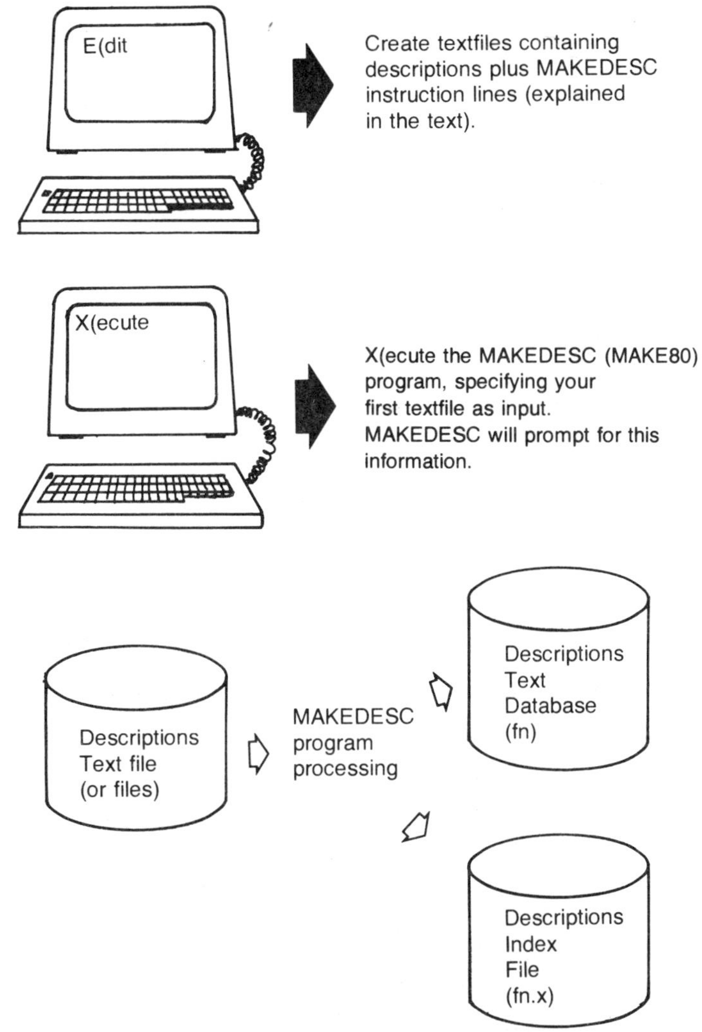

Fig. 20-1. A schematic diagram of the usage of the MAKEDESC program.

>> Output: two files—an index and a descriptions file.

The process of using MAKEDESC is illustrated schematically in Fig. 20-1. The input file to MAKEDESC will consist of ordinary text, which forms descriptions of locations, interspersed with MAKEDESC *instruction lines.* Here is part of a typical MAKEDESC input file:

```
$At the end of a dusty road
You are standing at the end of a dusty road.
In the distance I can see a brick building with
a well in front of it.
$In a maze of confusing tunnels
You are in a maze of twisting, confusing
tunnels. Everything looks alike in here. I am
having great difficulty finding my way.
$maze2
"
$Near a volcano
You are near an active volcano. I can hear
rumbling and I smell a sulfurous odor in the
air. Even though it is dark here, a faint red
glow shatters the darkness and suffuses the
air with light.
```

Any lines beginning with one of the MAKEDESC instruction characters shown in Fig. 20-2 will be processed by MAKEDESC as special instructions to itself and not as part of the descriptions.

All other lines will be taken as textual descriptions of a particular location. I will refer to such lines as *description lines.* Description lines must be 40 characters or less in length. This restriction is there because MAKEDESC was originally written on an Apple II without an 80 column display card. The text display of the Apple II is only 40 characters wide. If you want to modify MAKEDESC to allow longer description lines, you may. Later on, I'll show you how.

HOW TO USE MAKEDESC INSTRUCTION LINES

There are three types of instruction lines:

$ " >

Fig. 20-2. The MAKEDESC instruction characters.

1. Placename lines—instruction lines beginning with a $.
2. Ditto lines—instruction lines beginning with a ".
3. Append file lines—instruction lines beginning with a >.

Placename Instruction Lines

MAKEDESC requires that the description of each location, which may be many lines long, be immediately preceded by a *placename instruction line.* Each placename instruction line tells MAKEDESC two things:

1. Stop collecting the description of the last location.
2. Create a new location with the name provided in the placename instruction line and prepare to start collecting its description.

Suppose the input contained the instruction line:

```
$Pit of Darkness
```

At this point MAKEDESC would close off its current description. It would create a new location whose name would be "Pit of Darkness" and associate subsequent description lines with that location. The description of the Pit of Darkness would encompass all description lines in the input up to (but not including, of course) the next placename instruction line:

```
$Pit of Darkness
You are in a Pit. It is pitch black.
The darkness is so great you cannot see the brightly burning lantern you hold at arm's length. The light from the lantern is quickly absorbed by the greedy, all encompassing blackness. You can almost feel the darkness, like a sinister, oily, choking, substance. You are very close to panic.
$A long narrow tunnel
```

The description of the Pit of Darkness will be taken as all the text lines between the two placename instruction lines.

```
$Pit of Darkness
```

and

```
$A long narrow tunnel
```

There are some restrictions on the use of placename instruction lines:

- You may not have duplicate placenames in your input. In the previous example, if MAKEDESC encountered a second placename instruction line

  ```
  $Pit of Darkness
  ```

  it would complain, and tell you:

  ```
  *** duplicate placename: Pit of Darkness
  ```

The way MAKEDESC is currently written, it will also mess up the old description of Pit of Darkness in such a situation—so my advice is—Don't do it!

- Placenames themselves, such as "Pit of Darkness" or "A long narrow tunnel" must be 40 characters or less in length. If you put in a placename that is longer than that, for example

```
$The Brobdignagian gold, silver, diamond,
  and platinum mines
```

MAKEDESC will chop off everything after the fortieth character and issue the message

```
Placename too long.
Chopping to: The Brobdignagian gold,
  silver, diamond,
```

This will not do any harm to the subsequent descriptions of the place. However, the placename, if used in an adventure game program will be permanently "stunted."

This restriction is more or less arbitrary. Later we will show you how to get longer placenames (they just take up more space).

- There may be no more than 255 placenames in a given MAKEDESC database. This is a limitation imposed by the way that the internal MAKEDESC data structures were designed.

DITTO LINES

Instruction lines that begin with quotation marks (") are known as ditto instruction lines. They are provided mainly for convenience, and may be used to repeat a previous description. They are to MAKEDESC as ditto marks are to handwritten manuscripts.

There are two ways to use ":

- Without a placename.
- With a placename.

If you use " all by themselves, MAKEDESC will repeat the description of the last placename (this includes the possibility that the last placename was itself described using a ditto instruction line). For example, suppose you want to put a maze of "twisty little passages, all alike," as in the original adventure, into your own adventure database. Study the following:

```
$maze1
You are in a maze of little
twisty passages. They all look
alike.
```

```
$maze2
"
$maze3
"
$maze4
"
$maze5
"
```

Notice first the ditto lines. Each of them will cause the corresponding placename instruction to use the description given under the place **maze1**. Notice also that for each new place that uses a ditto instruction line, a separate placename instruction line is required. So it is useless to try saying

```
$maze
You are in a maze of little
twisty passages. They all look
alike.
"
"
"
"
"
```

This doesn't work because MAKEDESC is too dumb to create a place without a name. When it sees a ditto instruction line, it assumes that you have already created a new place that has been described by a placename instruction line.

If anything follows the " on a ditto instruction line, MAKEDESC does something different. It will try to interpret whatever follows the " as the placename of an already existing place. If it succeeds in doing so, it will use the description of that place as the description of the place to which the ditto applies. You really need an example to understand this one!

```
$maze1
You are in a maze of twisty little
tunnels, all alike.
$maze2
You are at a dead end in the maze.
$maze3
" maze1
$maze4
" maze2
$maze5
" maze1
```

In this example, you have created 5 places: **maze1**, **maze2**, **maze3**, **maze4** and **maze5**. There are two descriptions: the first applies to **maze1**, **maze3**, and **maze5**; the second applies to **maze2** and **maze4**.

Caution. The name (if any) used in a ditto instruction line must be the name of an already described place. The name following " is not used to create a new place. You must create the place first by including a placename instruction line. Study the above carefully to help clarify these points in your mind.

CONTINUATION FILE LINES

Textual material takes up lots of space, even on disk. On many systems, if you are writing a really big adventure game, you won't be able to fit all the input to MAKEDESC into a single UCSD Pascal text file. Because I don't want to limit your ability to create lots of exciting descriptions, I have given you a way to "chain" text files together when you are using MAKEDESC. Lines beginning with the > character are called *continuation file instruction lines*.

If the last line of a MAKEDESC input file is

```
>advent2.text
```

MAKEDESC will stop processing that file and continue with the file named **advent2.text**. Any lines that follow a continuation file instruction line will be ignored by MAKEDESC. That is, when it goes to a continuation file for further input, it never returns to the original file.

On the other hand, there is no limit to the number of continuation files that MAKEDESC can process in a given run. Well, that's not quite true—there is always the limit imposed by the total amount of disk space available! Think of continuation files as being "in line" to be processed by MAKEDESC. This is illustrated schematically in Fig. 20-3.

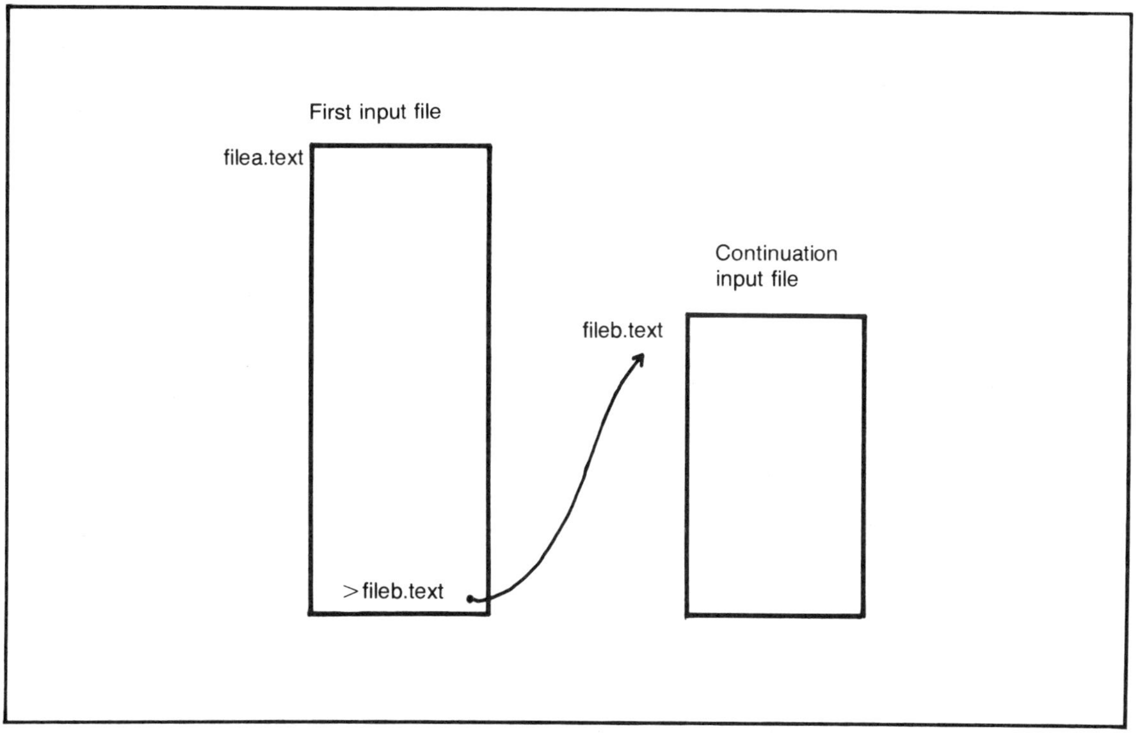

Fig. 20-3. The effect of the use of a continuation instruction line.

RUNNING MAKEDESC

Now, how do you actually use the MAKEDESC program on your own computer? First, of course, you must obtain an executable version of MAKEDESC. To do this, perform the following steps:

1. Enter the source code of MAKEDESC as given in Chapter 19 into a .text file, using the UCSD Pascal editor.
2. Compile MAKEDESC.TEXT to produce MAKEDESC.CODE.

Details on these steps will be found in the documentation for the UCSD Pascal system on your particular computer.

Once you have compiled MAKEDESC.TEXT to obtain MAKEDESC.CODE, you need to construct input for MAKEDESC to "chew" on. This will be constructed, again using the UCSD Pascal editor. It will consist of a mixture of place descriptions and MAKEDESC instruction lines, as described in the first part of this chapter. You will create one or more .text files containing this input. If you have more than one file, make sure to include the appropriate continuation file instruction lines needed for MAKEDESC to link them together.

To execute MAKEDESC, simply type **X** in answer to the UCSD system level prompt. Then when the system asks:

```
Execute what file?
```

respond with

```
MAKEDESC
```

One word of caution is in order here. If you have more than one disk drive attached to your system, you may have to answer the prompt differently. For example, if you have two drives, and MAKEDESC is on the "nonboot" drive, you may have to type:

#5:MAKEDESC

What you type will depend on whether or not you have entered the Filer program and issued a prefix command. For details on the concepts of volumes, file names, prefixes, and so on, consult your "local" UCSD manual.

After you succeed in answering the prompt correctly, MAKEDESC will be loaded and it in turn will prompt you as follows:

TRACING?===>

This prompt asks whether or not you would like to see a dynamic trace of all the procedure names in the program as they are invoked. It was built into MAKEDESC as a debugging aid. Unless you are curious and insist on seeing this information, you may safely "answer" this prompt by pressing the RETURN key.

The next prompt will be:

INPUT FILE===>

Here you should respond with the file name of your first input .text file; for example

INPUT FILE===> #[5:ADVENT1.TEXT

Notice that a volume number may be necessary, as before.

Next you will see

DESCRIPTION FILE===>

This is the last prompt from MAKEDESC and the name you type in response will be used by MAKEDESC as the name of the output file that it creates. There is one slight restriction here: the description file name may be at most 13 characters in length. The reason for this is as follows. MAKEDESC actually creates two output files: the descriptions data file and the descriptions index file.

The descriptions index file is used by your adventure game to quickly locate the part of the descriptions data file containing a given description. How all this works will be explained in subsequent chapters. For now, however, all you need to know is that the descriptions index file name is obtained from the descriptions data file name by appending the string **.x** (the X is for indeX). All file names in the UCSD system must be at most 15 characters in length. Therefore, the descriptions data file name, which by definition is two characters shorter in length than the descriptions index file name, must be at most 13 characters in length.

After you answer the prompts, MAKEDESC will chug away building your descriptions database. As each new placename instruction line is encountered by MAKEDESC, it will echo the placename to the terminal screen:

placename: Above ground
placename: In a pit
placename: Up a tree
.

and so on. This will give you feedback on the progress of MAKEDESC. It will also let you know where MAKEDESC was should anything go seriously wrong during processing.

When MAKEDESC finishes processing, it will have built two files, as described earlier. These files may then be used in your own adventure game programs. How this is done will be described later.

21

Random Access Files in UCSD Pascal

The program MAKEDESC described in Chapter 20 produces a database of adventure game descriptions. This database is stored in two UCSD Pascal files: an index file and a data file. The index file is a sequential file, but the data file is a *random* file. This chapter will explain the concept of random file and discuss its implementation in the UCSD Pascal language.

WHAT ARE RANDOM AND SEQUENTAL FILES?

All files contain records. A file all by itself is not sequential or random, although people sometimes use the term *random file*. It is the *access* to the records in a file that may be either sequential or random. So when I say "sequential file," I mean "file accessed sequentially." When I say "random file," I mean "file accessed randomly."

Sequential Access

When you are using sequential access to a file, the records must be retrieved in the order in which they are stored. Access usually begins with the first record in the file. Therefore, in order to access the last record in a file, using sequential access, you must first access all the records in the file that come before it. A file that is accessed sequentially is like a roll of candy or breath mints as shown in Fig. 21-1: in order to get to the last candy, you must first remove all the ones before it.

This is fine and dandy—when it comes to candy! Database files are a different story. Consider an adventure game descriptions database. Suppose you accessed the place descriptions sequentially. To reach the description of the last place, you would have to read through (but not display) all the place descriptions preceding the last one. In general, you would have to read through any descriptions preceding the one you wished to show to the player. You would be sitting around waiting most of the time! You say you don't believe that—let's do some calculations.

Suppose your adventure game has 100 locations and the descriptions of these locations average five lines apiece. The file of these descriptions would contain approximately 500 lines, each being

Fig. 21-1. An example of sequential access in real life.

readable as a Pascal string variable. Then, on the average, you would have to read 250 strings in order to reach the specific one that begins a particular description. Now I hear you saying to yourself: "Wait! Computers are fast. They can read those strings in no time at all." But consider that a typical minifloppy disk access takes 50 milliseconds—that is 50/1000 seconds or one-twentieth of a second. Then in order to read 250 strings, it will take 250×1/20=12.5 seconds. This means that on the average, you will wait twelve seconds before you see the description of the next place. Most players will probably want responses to be displayed more quickly than this. You can try this experiment on your own system to see how far off my estimates are. Here are two short programs to use. The first creates a file of 500 strings. The second reads through the file sequentially until it gets to the 250th string in the file. Try them out and use your stopwatch!

THE FILE CREATING PROGRAM

```
PROGRAM wrtxt;
VAR

rec: STRING[80];
f: FILE OF STRING[80];
i: INTEGER;

BEGIN

rec :=
'You are in mountains.  To
see all the snow-capped
monsters hereabouts,';
rewrite (f, 'junk.text');

FOR i := 1 TO 500 DO
BEGIN

f^ := rec;
put (f);

END;
close (f, lock);

END.
```

THE FILE READING PROGRAM

```
PROGRAM rdtxt;
VAR

rec: STRING[80];
f: FILE OF STRING[80];
i: INTEGER;

BEGIN

reset (f, 'junk.text');
writeln ('Commencing
reading...');

FOR i := 1 TO 250 DO
BEGIN

f^ := rec;
get (f);

END;

writeln ('Got it');
writeln (f^);
close (f, lock);

END.
```

RANDOM ACCESS

Random access to a file means that any particular record in the file may be retrieved directly. No other records must be read first. A randomly accessed file is like the same roll of candy—but with the wrapper removed! You can grab any of the candies you like at any time.

There is a price to be paid for the ability to access a file randomly:

> All records in a random access file must be of the same fixed size in order for random access to be practical.

In order to understand this limitation, you must delve into the workings of random access files. Here is roughly how they "work."

Each record in the file is a certain "distance" from the beginning of the file. This distance is easy to calculate from two pieces of information:

1. The size of the records in the file (which I have assumed is the same for all records in the file).
2. The number of the record sought. Records are assigned numbers, beginning with the number 0, according to their position in the file.

Once the position of a given record is calculated, the computer hardware can be given instructions to seek to that position in the file. This means that the disk drive's read mechanism is moved in such a way that the record in question will pass under the read head. Then, simply reading a record from the file will produce the desired result. It is almost as if each record were its own tiny, separate file. Of course, all this depends on the ability to calculate the position of the record.

Limitations of Random Access

The concept of a random access file is not part of Standard Pascal. It was added to the UCSD Pascal language and must be considered an *extension.* Actually, that is not quite true—you may declare files of fixed size records in Standard Pascal. In fact, because every file consists of records of some predeclared Pascal type, they are automatically of fixed size. (The exception to this is the text file: FILE OF CHAR. A "record" may be thought of as a line of text that is terminated by an anonymous internal EOL.)

UCSD Pascal and Random Access

The UCSD Pascal language has added support for accessing files randomly. This support is surprisingly simple. It consists of a single new intrinsic procedure called seek:

```
seek (fileid, recnumber);
```

This procedure can be called to position the file to the correct record, according to the value contained in recnumber. Following a call to the seek procedure, a call to get or put may be made, just as if the file were being read or written sequentially.

There are some rules to remember when using seek:

- Don't do two seeks in a row without an intervening get or put.
- Remember that the get or put that follows a seek moves the file window. This is just the same as if no seek had first been performed.
- EOF (f) is always false after a seek has been performed.

You may ignore all this if you don't plan to use seek in your own programs. The use of seek in the adventure games in this book is always the same. The code is already written and works—you may simply imitate it and you won't go wrong.

THE BROWSE PROGRAM

In Chapter 19, I presented the listings of two Pascal programs. One is the MAKEDESC adventure database generator program. The use of MAKEDESC was described in Chapter 20. The other is BROWSE, a program that may be used to review the output of MAKEDESC before including that output in one of your adventures.

BROWSE uses all the same declarations as MAKEDESC. It starts out by prompting you for the file name of your descriptions. This is read by

BROWSE and used to open the descriptions file for reading. The name of the description file is used to derive the name of the index file, as described in Chapter 20. The index file is also opened for reading. BROWSE uses the index file and the descriptions file in the same way that adventure games do.

The BROWSE program prompts the user for a placename. You may respond with one of the placenames used in generating the descriptions database. In this case, BROWSE will look up the place by name and print its description on your terminal. If you don't have a list of the placenames handy, you may also type ? in response to the prompt for a placename. In this case, BROWSE will print a list of all the placenames in the database you are reviewing.

USING DESCRIPTIONS DATABASES IN YOUR ADVENTURES

If you read Adventure 2 carefully, you will see how to incorporate the databases generated by MAKEDESC into your own adventures. There are several key points to remember:

- Declare the relevant types and variables. These are discussed in more detail in the next chapter.
- Make sure to open the descriptions data and index files in the initialization procedure in your adventure.
- Incorporate the **show** procedure, used to retrieve and display each description from the database. The **show** procedure is almost identical to **describe** procedure in the BROWSE program. More detail on how **describe** and **show** operate will be given in the next chapters, which discuss the details of the structure and programming techniques associated with the descriptions database generated by MAKEDESC.

22

The Structure of Adventure Databases

In Chapter 21 I briefly described the files comprising an adventure database. In this chapter I shall delve into the detailed makeup of those files. In the process, I shall elaborate on several topics:

- Index files in general and the descriptions index in particular.
- The use of Pascal variant records in building the index file.
- The incorporation of the database in Adventure 2—the use of the show procedure for retrieving the description of a place and so on.
- The BROWSE program for previewing your database after creating them.

INDEX FILES AND THE DESCRIPTIONS INDEX

An index file is analogous to an index in a book. It contains information about where in the data file(s) of a database specific entries may be found. In the adventure database, the data consists of descriptions of places or locations, in the adventure. The index file consists of entries, each of which has information about a specific location.

The adventure database index file actually has two sections, as shown in Fig. 22-1. The first section is an array of numbers known as ***hash values***. The techniques of hashing and hash table lookup are discussed in the next chapter. They are mainly of interest to the MAKEDESC program, which creates the database, and the BROWSE program, which may be used to preview the database. Adventure 2 does not use the hash table part of the index itself. The use of the hash table is a key to being able to retrieve the description of a location given its name. This information is quite vital to the operation of MAKEDESC in particular, because MAKEDESC checks for the presence of duplicate placenames.

The second part of the index file is a collection of records that I shall call *description information entries*. Each of the records contains the information needed to locate the description of one particular adventure location. The Pascal type declaration that is in MAKEDESC, BROWSE, and Adventure 2 reveals the nature of the information contained in these records.

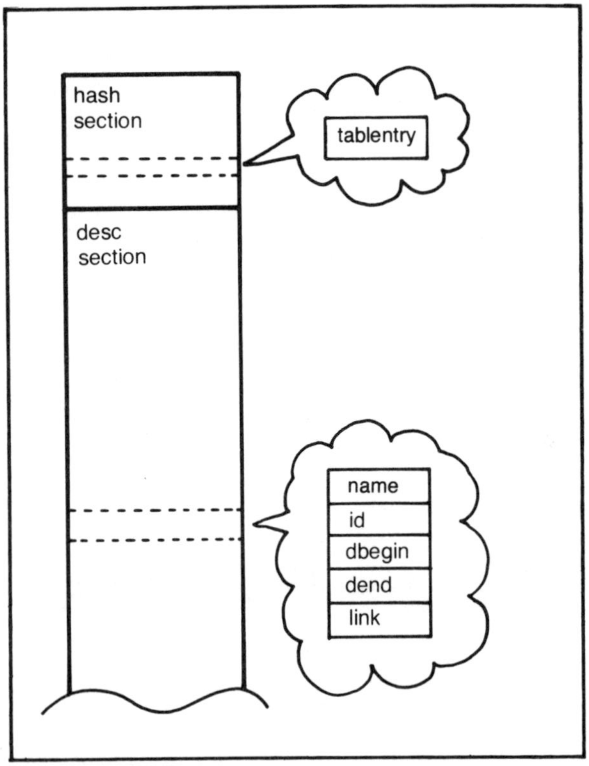

Fig. 22-1. The format of the index file of a descriptions database.

```
placerec =
  RECORD
    CASE section: whichsection OF
        hashsection: (tableentry: INTEGER);
        descsection: ( name: pname;
                        id: INTEGER;
                        dbegin: INTEGER;
                        dend: INTEGER;
                        link: byte );
  END;
```

This declaration is an example of what is known in Pascal as a *variant record* type. It enables the information stored in variables of that type to be nonhomogeneous. The case statement in the record declaration introduces the variants. Each case label in the declaration represents one of the possible variations that the record can take on. In this example, the record type **placerec** has exactly two variants—hash section and descsection. The first variant accounts for the records in the hash-table section of the index file. The second variant accounts for the remainder of the file, which consists of one record for each description in the data portion of the database.

All three programs, MAKEDESC, BROWSE, and Adventure 2, use the **placerec** data type in the declaration of a file:

```
VAR
    xfile:              FILE OF placerec;
```

The file window **xfile ^** always contains a record from **xfile**. The structure of that record may match the hash section record or the descsection record. This depends on which variant of the record type has been selected by the program. The **section** variable declared in the case statement of the record type declaration is used to control and remember this at run time. I will touch on this again in Chapter 23 when I discuss the operation of the BROWSE program.

Contents of the Descriptions Index Entries

The descsection record structure shows several fields in the corresponding records. Each of these fields is present in a descriptions index entry for a location. The fields are described as follows:

- name
  This is a string containing the name of the location as it was present in the "source" file that MAKEDESC used to process this entry when the database was generated. The user-defined type pname is used to limit the size of the string in order to conserve file space. The value 20 was chosen as the maximum length for values of this string. The names of locations could be used as shorter descriptions, in which case it might be desirable to allow for a slightly longer string.

- id
  This is an integer that records the positional value of the individual location in the list of locations. It is a redundant piece of information that was used in debugging MAKEDESC originally and was never removed from the declaration of placerec. It "wastes" two bytes of disk space per index entry. If you feel that this is an intolerable misuse of disk space, you can easily remedy the situation. Simply remove the id: field from all declarations of the placerec data type.

- dbegin
  This is an integer that gives a record number in the data file of descriptions. It is the first record number for the description of the location to which a given index entry corresponds. It tells the show procedure or other retrieval code how to get to the right place on the disk in order to start reading the location's description.

- dend
  This is an integer that gives another record number in the data file of descriptions. It is the record number of the last line in the description of the corresponding location. It tells the show procedure when to stop reading description lines from the data file.

- link
  This is a value between 0 and 255 that is used in the hash table lookup algorithm. It determines another index entry to examine should this one not correspond to the specific name being sought. The details of how this works will be revealed in the next chapter.

The structure of the descriptions database files and their relationships are in some detail shown in Fig. 22-2.

USING THE DESCRIPTIONS DATABASES IN ADVENTURE GAMES

Once a descriptions database for a given adventure has been generated using MAKEDESC, there still remains the question of how to access that database in an adventure game. Adventure 2 presents a model for accomplishing this.

Initialization of the Database

There are two files that need to be made accessible to the adventure game:

```
xfile:          FILE OF placerec;
narrate:        FILE OF storyline;
```

The narrate file is the descriptions data file. It only needs to be opened in order to be accessible for reading later on. This is accomplished in the initialization procedure in Adventure 2 via the statement:

```
reset (narrate, "a2.data");
```

The xfile file is the index file and has been discussed in detail above. It must be read into memory by the adventure game in order to be used for retrieval purposes. The xfile file is opened by the statement:

```
reset (xfile, "a2.data.x");
```

Then the following code reads in the index file and stores the descsection records in the array called places:

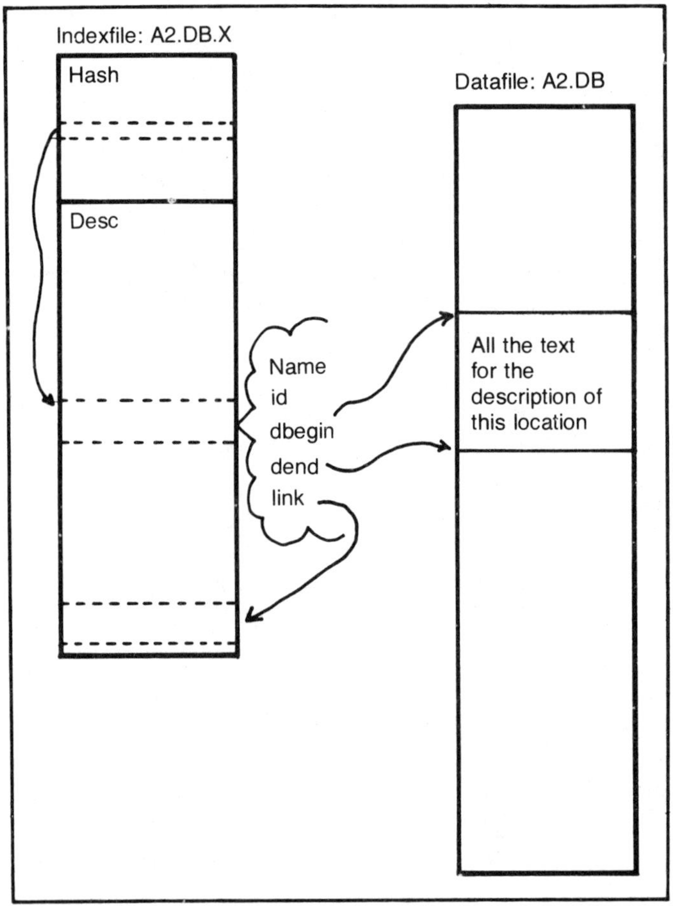

Fig. 22-2. The file structure of the entire descriptions database.

```
FOR i := dbegin TO dend DO
BEGIN
   seek (narrate, i)
   get (narrate);
   write (narrate^);
END;
```

The seek command in this code accounts for the fact that none of the has section records stored in the index file are actually used by the adventure game program. The records numbered 0 to 31 in the index file are all hash section records. Therefore, in order to skip over them, the initialization code first "seeks" to position 32 in the index file. After that, each call to the I/O **get** procedure will advance the record pointer one position in the index file. That is why no further calls to **seek** are necessary inside the repeat loop.

The Operation of the show Procedure

Once the index file has been read into the **places** array, the procedure called **show** is used to retrieve various descriptions and show them to the player. The key to the operation of **show** is the following loop:

```
loc := start;
seek (xfile, 32);
```

```
get (xfile);
places [loc] := xfile^;
REPEAT
    loc := succ (loc);
    get (xfile);
    places[loc] := xfile^;
UNTIL loc = flames;
```

The interpretation of this is simple, given what you know about the descsection records. The show procedure starts at dbegin for a given location and goes to dend. For each value of i between those two numbers, there is a line of description in narrate. The show procedure calls seek to position itself to the correct place in the narrate file; then it calls get to retrieve the line of description, and finally it calls write to display the line on the screen.

This for loop uses dbegin and dend directly. Actually these are abbreviations for:

places[where].dbegin, and
places[where].dend.

The with statement that surrounds the for loop is a Pascal method for abbreviating references to components of records. If you say

WITH places[where]

you can refer to any of the fields of the record represented by places[where] without repeating the prefix places[where]. This is not only a way of saving the programmer some typing. It also allows the Pascal compiler to generate better code for accessing the corresponding record fields.

THE BROWSE PROGRAM FOR PREVIEWING DATABASES

In Chapter 19 I presented the listing of BROWSE. BROWSE is a simple program, similar to MAKEDESC, which you can use to examine adventure game databases that you have generated with MAKEDESC. BROWSE allows you to ask for locations by placename, then it displays the corresponding description from the data file generated by MAKEDESC. It has a convenience feature for those situations when you can't remember the exact names of the locations in your adventure database. If you type ? as the name of a place to be described, the BROWSE program will display the names of all the locations in the database you are examining.

23

Programming Techniques Used in MAKEDESC

In this chapter I delve into the programming techniques used in MAKEDESC. I discuss the following ideas:

- Symbol tables (information gathering and storage).
- Hashing (hash tables, hash values, and so on).
- Symbol table lookup using both linear search techniques and hashing.

These ideas are taken from computer science. They may be a bit technical for some readers. However, you don't need to understand them in order to use the MAKEDESC program itself. If all you wish to do is use descriptions databases in your own adventures, you can probably skip this chapter entirely. On the other hand, if you make your way through this material, you will have some valuable programming techniques that will serve you in many other situations as well.

SYMBOL TABLES

The term *symbol table* is usually encountered in discussions of programs like assemblers and compilers. Symbol tables keep track of information about source programs that compilers or assemblers process. The UCSD Pascal compiler has a symbol table that, among other things, keeps track of the identifiers declared in a Pascal program. MAKEDESC is a much simpler program than a compiler or assembler, but it nonetheless uses a symbol table. The symbol table in MAKEDESC keeps track of placenames and information associated with placenames that is needed for building the descriptions database.

The information kept in the MAKEDESC symbol table has already been described in the previous chapter. In fact, a large part of the MAKEDESC symbol table is a copy of the database index file. The additional component of the MAKEDESC symbol table is an auxiliary array called the *hash table*. I shall discuss the concept and usage of hash tables in detail below.

The MAKEDESC Symbol Table: Functional Requirements

In order to understand how the symbol table

works, it is useful to know what operations it needs to perform. The operations required can dictate the programming techniques utilized. In MAKEDESC the following tasks must be performed:

- The addition of a placename to the symbol table.
- The addition of information about a placename to the entry for that name; for example, when the description of the placename is completely processed, the dend value is added to its entry. (Recall that dend represents the record number of the last line of description of the placename.)
- The looking up of a placename in the symbol table. This action occurs more than once. It occurs first when the name is placed in the table to begin with. At that time, the lookup operation fails. It occurs again if the same placename is used later. Then the lookup operation will succeed, and MAKEDESC will warn the user that a duplicate placename has been detected. The lookup operation is also part of the add-a-placename-to-the-symbol-table operation. The lookup is performed in order to tell MAKEDESC where to put the new placename entry.

LOOKUP TECHNIQUES: THE LINEAR SEARCH

I have already discussed the technique of linear searching and the variation on that technique that uses a sentinel to simplify the search. The linear search has its advantages and its disadvantages.

Advantages of Linear Searches

Linear searching is a very simple technique. It is easy to understand and easy to implement. Most programmers have used this technique in one fashion or another. The code for a linear search is quite simple and easy to remember.

Disadvantages of Linear Searches

Linear searching is the most inefficient of all possible search techniques. That is its main disadvantage. If there are N items that must be searched through, on the average it will take N/2 attempts to locate what is being searched for. If the item being searched for is not present (which is the case most of the time in MAKEDESC), all N items in the table have to be examined in order to determine that the search has failed.

As the number of items being searched through increases, the disadvantages of linear searching begin to outweigh its advantages. In the case of MAKEDESC, as the number of placenames in the adventure database increase, the inefficiency of searching them linearly increases proportionally. Because the number of placenames allowed by MAKEDESC is limited to 255, this would never be an intolerable burden. However, it was decided when MAKEDESC was implemented to use a more efficient search technique.

HASHING: A MORE EFFICIENT SEARCH TECHNIQUE

What is needed is a way to narrow the search through the symbol table. If you could put a limit on the number of entries that need to be considered during each lookup, this would increase the efficiency of the lookup process. The technique of *hashing* provides just such a method. The hashing technique uses an auxiliary array called the *hash table*. The hash table allows the placenames to be divided into a number of smaller groups. For a given placename, only the placenames in one of the groups need be searched rather than all the placenames present in the table. The smaller groups are organized into what are called *linked lists*. Each linked list consists of only a fraction of all placenames. Each linked list is searched using a linear search with a sentinel. The linear search of the much smaller list of placenames is acceptably efficient compared to a linear search of all the placenames. In order to understand the hashing technique, you need to understand several concepts and techniques:

- The idea of a *hash value*.
- The computation of hash values.
- The use of hash values to determine a smaller list of placenames.
- The organization of the small lists using links.

I shall discuss these ideas in the remainder of this section.

The Idea of a Hash Value

A hash value is a number. It is a number that is associated with a string of characters such as an identifier in a Pascal program or a placename in the source for a MAKEDESC database. Such numbers must satisfy some simple requirements:

1. In a given application, the hash values are limited to a certain set of values.
2. For simplicity, the smallest hash value is usually taken to be 0. This is because hash values are used as index values for the array known as the hash table.
3. The largest hash value is usually taken to be a prime number. This usually means that all the identifiers under consideration will be divided into relatively equal sized lists. This is clearly desirable, because the smaller lists are being searched using linear search. It would be self-defeating if one of the lists was quite large and all the others only one or two elements long.

The Computation of Hash Values

Given a character string, such as a MAKEDESC placename, the hash value of that string must be computed. The technique used in this computation is usually referred to as a ***hash function***. The choice of a good hash function is an entire technical subject in itself and much has been written about it. I shall not dwell on details of that choice, but merely present one common solution. In MAKEDESC hash values are computed using the ORD and MOD functions from Pascal. The method is as follows:

> To form the hash value of placename s, consider the individual characters s[i] of s. Each such character has an internal number that may be computed in Pascal by applying the ORD function:
>
> internal value of s[i] = ORD (s[i])
>
> If you added all those values (for each character in s, that is for i = 1 to LENGTH (s)), you would obtain a number, hv. The possible values for that number would be quite large, however. You want the hash value of s to range from 0 to some fairly small number. In MAKEDESC, the upper limit for hash values is 30. In order to produce such a value from the sum, hv, just described, you would use the Pascal MOD function. The MOD function produces the remainder of one number when it is divided by another number. The two numbers in question here are the sum described above and the number 31 (a prime number, as mentioned above). Thus, the final algorithm is as follows:

```
symhash := 0;
FOR i := 1 TO length (placename)
DO
symhash := (symhash + ORD
(placename[i])) MOD (hashmax + 1)
{ END DO };
```

The Use of Hash Values to Determine a Smaller List of Placenames

Once the hash value of a given placename has been computed, how is it used? The hash value is used as an index into the array known as the hash table. Each entry in the hash table determines the beginning of one of the smaller lists of placenames. The characteristics of that list are as follows:

- Every placename on the list has the same hash value.
- The list is arranged in reverse order, that is, the first name on the list was the last name added to the list.

The numbers stored in the hash table array are also index values but they index into the places array. The places array is the array that is written out to the descriptions index file. The hashing technique now allows you to think that the descriptions index file consists of a number of short lists. Each hash table entry "points" to the beginning of one of these lists. This is illustrated in Fig. 23-1.

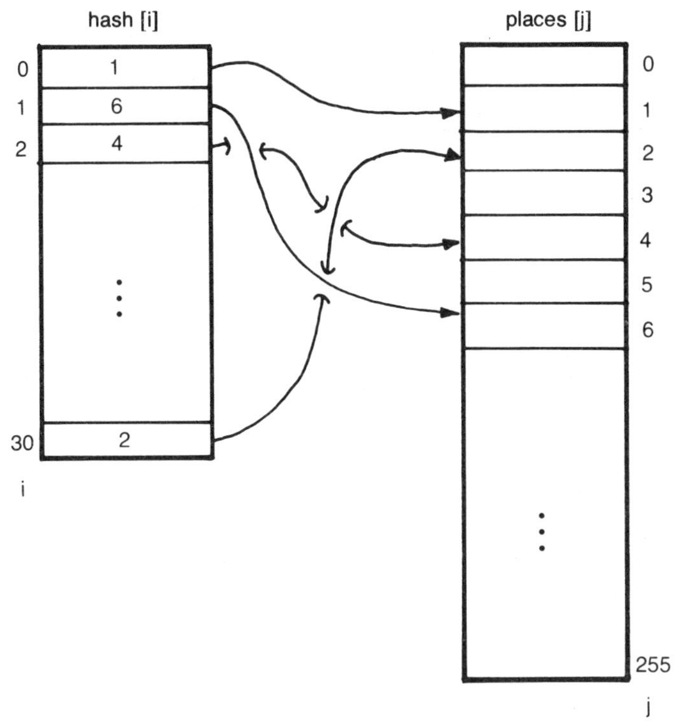

Fig. 23-1. Hash table entries.

The Organization of the Small Lists Using Links

Each entry in the places array is a record containing information about one placename. The last item in each record is called the *link* field. This is the index (in the places array) of the next placename that has the same hash value. This piece of information is called a link, because it determines the next item on a *linked* list of items. That item is located at some possibly remote place in the places array, rather than being the next sequential entry in that array. The link field tells the lookup process how to proceed when it fails to find a given placename at the current entry.

Figure 23-2 shows the concept of the link field pictorially. Within the large array, places, a given placename entry "points" to another by means of its link field.

To summarize the concepts of hashing, let us consider an analogy. Think of the world headquarters of a large corporation. People within this corporation work in certain locations in that building. If you set out to find a certain employee by searching through every office in the building in order, you might be occupied for quite a long time. On the other hand, if you started with the knowledge of what department the employee you sought worked in, your search would be considerably narrowed.

The linked lists of elements all with the same hash value may be thought of as analogous to a department in a large corporation. They all have

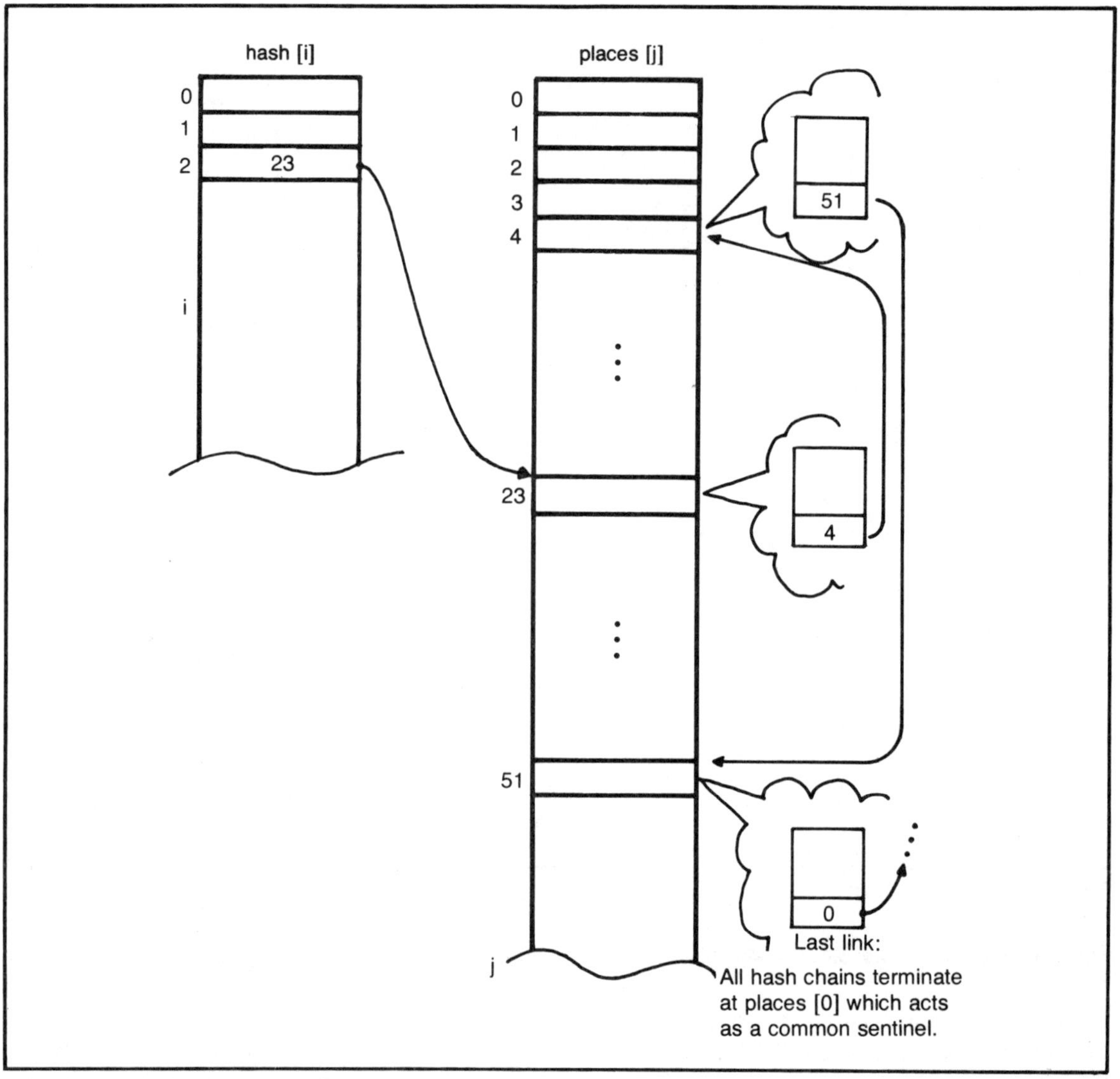

Fig. 23-2. The linked lists or "hash chains" in the **places** array.

something in common: in the corporation it is their department number; in the hash search technique it is their hash value. Searching a linked list of elements is like searching through just the offices within a given department. There are far fewer offices in a single department than in the entire corporation. In the same manner, there are far fewer elements on a single hash list than there are in the entire symbol table (or in our case the entire places array).

THE HASH TABLE LOOKUP TECHNIQUE

I conclude this chapter by reviewing the actual algorithm used in the hash table lookup technique. That is, once a hash value has been determined, how is the linked list of items with that hash value searched?

In MAKEDESC, I have used the entry places[0] as a sentinel to mark the end of every linked list in the hashing scheme. The hash table itself is set up to contain all zeros to begin with.

This means that all the linked lists are empty. This is the situation before any placename descriptions have been read from the MAKEDESC source file. This is illustrated in Fig. 23-3.

Adding Placenames to the MAKEDESC Symbol Table

As MAKEDESC reads placenames from its source file (by reading placename instruction lines—see Chapter 20), it enters them into its hashed symbol table. The process of entering the next name is as follows:

- First the hash value of the new placename is computed.
- The hash value of the placename is used as an index into the **hash** array. The number stored there determines the index of an entry in the **places** array. If the number found is 0, there are no placenames yet with the given hash value, and an entry for the placename is created. How the new entry is created and added to the table is described below.
- If the number found in **hash** is not 0, there are already placenames in the symbol table with the same hash value as the current placename. The linked list of those hash values must be searched to eliminate the possibility that the current placename is a duplicate. Here is the process used:

1. Store the current placename in the name field of **places[0]**. This is the sentinel concept in operation: the record in **places[0]** is at the end of all the linked lists in the symbol table. The lookup process will eventually reach the entry if the placename under consideration is not found earlier. The statement

   ```
   places[0].name = thisname;
   ```

   accomplishes this. The statement

   ```
   where := hash[symhash];
   ```

   takes the value out of the hash table to

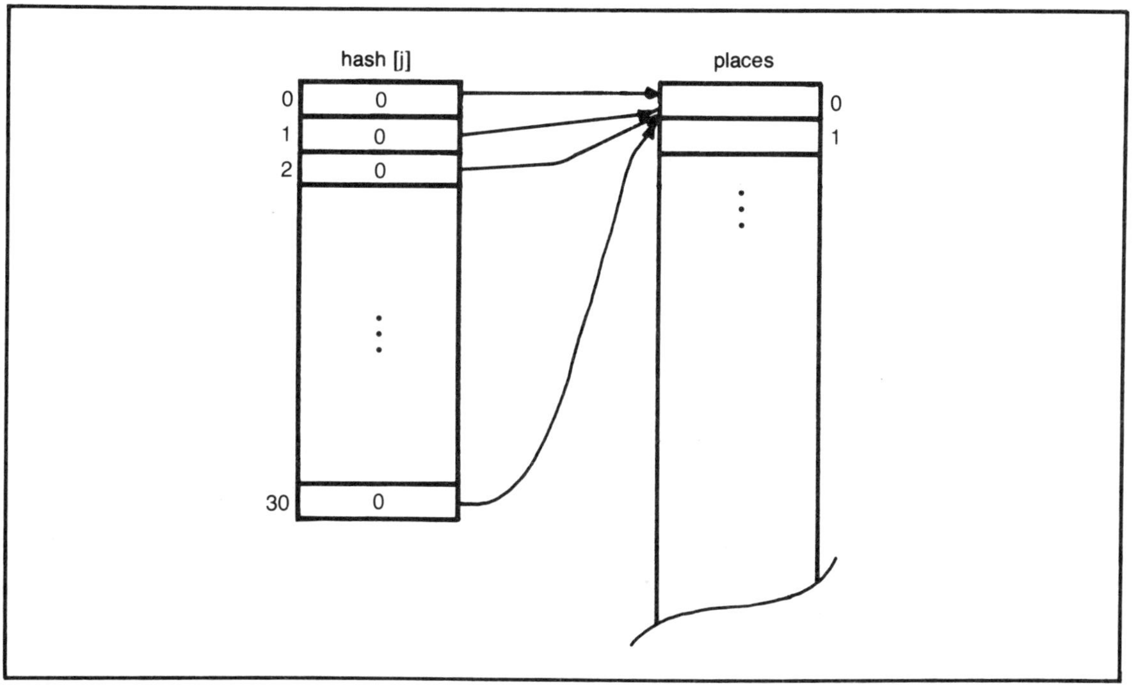

Fig. 23-3. The initial configuration of the hash table: all hash chains consist of only the sentinel location (**places[0]**).

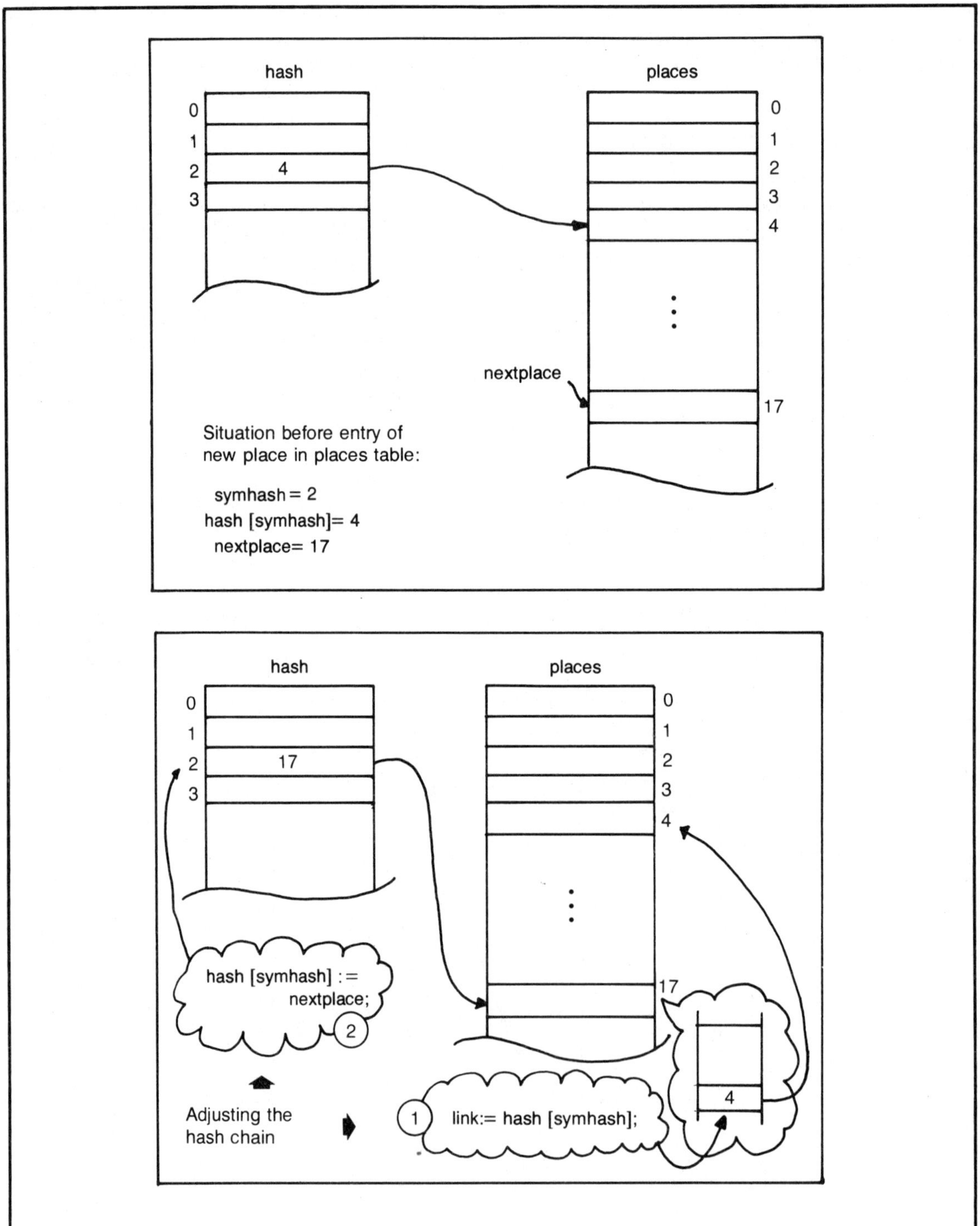

Fig. 23-4. A diagram of the process of making an entry in the **places** array.

determine the head of the linked list to be searched.

2. Use the following Pascal while loop to search the linked list of places with the same hash value as the current placename:

```
WHILE places[where].name <>
    thisname
DO
    where := places[where].link
{ END DO };
```

At the end of this loop, the variable where determines whether or not the search has succeeded. If where contains the value 0, the search proceeded all the way to the sentinel and the lookup failed. Otherwise, the search succeeded and where contains the index of the entry that duplicated thisname.

Adding an Entry to the Places Table

If a given placename is determined not to exist in the places array, it is added by MAKEDESC. The new entry must be placed into the linked list of names with the same hash value. The variable nextplace always contains the index of the next available spot in the places array. This variable is initially set to 0. It is then increased every time a new placename is added to the symbol table. In particular, it is set to 1 before the very first placename is added to the table.

The process of adding the new place to the symbol table is accomplished by the entername procedure in MAKEDESC. Figure 23-4 illustrates the process pictorially.

24

What Else Can You Put on Disk?

In the preceding four chapters I have discussed the MAKEDESC program used for creating a database of place descriptions on disk. In this brief postscript I speculate on what else you might want to or be able to put into disk files.

OTHER DESCRIPTIONS

The descriptions in the databases have so far been limited to those of adventure game locations. These are by far the most extensive kind of textual description that has been used in either of the sample adventures so far. However, there are many other kinds of descriptions that are not descriptions of rooms or locations:

- Descriptions of events that occur during the game. For example, in Adventure 2 the ogre's being awakened is accompanied by some description.
- Descriptions of speech that can be either that of the guide in certain situations or that of other beings that might be encountered during the play of the game.
- Descriptions associated with objects that occur in the game. There might be extra information to convey about an object either by itself or under special circumstances.
- Descriptions of places that are only given conditionally. The descriptions database as described so far is set up so that any time a location is visited, the description is the same. Examples of conditional descriptions in Adventure 2 are the various descriptions given as the player digs for the treasure.

Some of the categories of descriptions in the above list can easily be accommodated within the current implementation of MAKEDESC and its associated databases. I give examples in Adventure 3, which begins in Chapter 25. Other categories are not so easy to accommodate. One of the more difficult is the conditional description idea as it relates to the current method of traveling. Consider the example of the ladder room in Adventure 2, where the response to "up" depends on whether or not the player is carrying the treasure. In order to accommodate that conditionality, some additional arguments to travel might be needed, tied in somehow with the database. I leave it to you to speculate on this further.

PUTTING THE WHOLE PROGRAM ON DISK: ADVENTURE INTERPRETERS

A radical approach to writing adventure games is to first design an adventure machine. This would be an abstract machine whose only purpose was to run adventure games. The machine language of such a machine would be designed specifically for executing adventure games. Programs for the machine would be referred to as *adventure code*.

A Pascal program, which emulated such an adventure machine could be written. The program could be designed in such a way that the entire adventure code program that it interpreted would "live" in various disk files. This would have the following consequences:

- The size of an adventure would be limited only by the size of file(s) that could be fit onto a floppy disk. In fact, given the ability to swap disks in and out at the behest of the emulator, there would be no limit. That would mean you could write very long adventures.
- The play of the game might be slower. The adventure emulator would have to do more disk i/o and that would slow down response time. This might turn out to be tolerable or it might not, depending on the details of the implementation of the adventure emulator.
- In addition to an adventure emulator, you would need another program that translated adventure games in some high-level form into *adventure code*. This would be an adventure compiler, if you will. The adventure compiler would process the specification of an adventure game in the *adventure language*. You would have to design the adventure language, making sure to include all the necessary features to support reasonable and interesting adventures.

While all of this is quite interesting and fun to speculate on, I will not have room to expand upon it in this book. Others before me have already acted upon these ideas: the Scott Adams Adventures were implemented in somewhat this fashion; Zork and other adventures from Infocom, Ltd. were implemented using the adventure language concept.

25

Preview of Adventure 3

Adventure 3 is the most ambitious adventure game in the book. Compared to the original adventure, it would still be rated as intermediate. However, compared to Adventure 1 it is quite advanced. There are more locations, more problems, better descriptions, and more challenges than there were in the previous examples. Much of the code is shared with previous adventures. The newest concept is the organization of the program into "units."

OUTLINES, DIAGRAMS, AND MAPS

Because Adventure 3 is more complex than previous adventures, there are more figures associated with it. Figures 25-1 through 25-6 present the code outlines of Adventure 3. Each UCSD unit used by the program is outlined, as well as the main program, which uses the units. Figure 25-7 shows the units of Adventure 3 and the uses relations between them.

The map for Adventure 3 is large. I have divided it into several parts so that it will fit into the book's page size. Figure 25-8 shows that the map of Adventure 3 has six separate pages and also shows the offpage connections between them. Figures 25-9 through 25-14 provide the map of Adventure 3 and Figure 25-15 presents a summary of the problems of Adventure 3.

CHAPTER PREVIEWS

Adventure 3 is described in Chapters 27 through 29. The listing of Adventure 3 is in Chapter 26. The three chapters do not repeat territory covered in the descriptions of earlier adventures. So if you find code that you think should be explained but isn't, refer back to preceding sections, and perhaps you will find it discussed there.

Chapter 27 is entitled "Larger Programs: Using UCSD Units" and deals with the organizational technique of program units. The UCSD version of Pascal provides a method of structuring called *units*. A unit is a self-contained part of a program containing two parts, an interface and an implementation. The interface of a unit contains all

```
PROGRAM mtadvent:

    USES applestuff.                     List of units used by the
        {$umt1.code} advdata,            program. Those preceded
        {$uprobs.code} probs,            by comments of the form:
        {$ucmds3.code} cmds3,                   {$u . . .
        {$ucmds2.code} cmds2,            are found in the code files
        {$ucmds1.code} cmds1,            specified in the comment.
        {$ulocs.code} locs;              All others must be in the
                                         SYSTEM.LIBRARY file.

    CONST, TYPE. VAR declarations,
    procedures, and functions

BEGIN

    The main program block is invoked first, as in other Pascal
    programs. Procedures and functions declared in the
    interfaces of any unit used by the program may be
    invoked here or in any of the procedures and functions
    declared in the main program.

    Code here handles travel between locations. Because of a
    size limit to UCSD code blocks, it invokes two procedures
    (t1 and t2) to carry out what is logically a single case
    statement.

END.
```

```
Units list:  Applestuff       from SYSTEM.LIBRARY: must provide
                              a function RANDOM (see unit mtad-
                              vent)

                  Advdata     See Figure 25-2
                  Probs       See Figure 25-3
                  Cmds3       See Figure 25-4
                  Cmds2       See Figure 25-5
                  Cmds1       See Figure 25-6
                  Locs        See Figure 25-5
```

Fig. 25-1. The code outline for Adventure 3: the program outline including the units list.

```
UNIT advdata

  INTERFACE

TYPE

  descs
    Enumerated type representing all descriptions used by Adventure 3.
  rooms
    Enumerated type representing the locations in Adventure 3.
    The rooms type is a subrange of the descs type.
  goodies
    Enumerated type representing all objects in Adventure 3.
  fakes, trash, wmmgoody
    Subranges of the goodies type—each represents a different category
    of objects: for example, fakes represents objects that seem like treasures
    but are of no interest to wmm.
  collection - as in Adventure 2

VAR

  location - as in Adventures 1 and 2
  trollocs - set of rooms at which the trolls may appear.
  wmmwants, wmmhas, wmmfakes, stash
    various sets of goodies used during the game.
  whatshere, }
  visited,   }  As in Adventure 2
  objname    }
  trlives, saidwadda, isopen, eaten, killed, done
    Boolean variables representing possible events in Adventure 3.

IMPLEMENTATION

  PROCEDURE init1; }   Initialization procedures used in
  PROCESURE init2; }   order to avoid the "procedure too
                       large" error.

BEGIN

  Init1; }  Initialization code for the variables
  Init2; }  declared in the advdata unit.

END.
```

Fig. 25-2. The code outline for Adventure 3: the outline of UNIT advdata.

UNIT probs;

INTERFACE

TYPE

problems
Enumerated type representing the components of the problems in Adventure 3. Each identifier in the **problems** type corresponds to a Boolean expression that must be true before the problem represented is solved. The unit itself is named probs to avoid conflict with the **problems** type.

FUNCTION solved (which: problems): Boolean;
Function to centralize the evaluation of the Boolean expressions corresponding to problem components. Other parts of the adventure use calls to this function, rather than evaluating the expressions directly.

BEGIN
END. } No initialization required by the probs unit.

Fig. 25-3. The code outline for Adventure 3: the outline of UNIT probs.

UNIT cmds3;

INTERFACE

TYPE

directions
cmds
pname
storyline
placerec
} As in Adventure 2

VAR

xfile
narrate
places
command
head
tail
cmdname
chgloc
} As in Adventure 2

PROCEDURE pinventory;
PROCEDURE plook; } command procedures as in Adventure 2
PROCEDURE show (where: descs);
PROCEDURE show goodies; } As in Adventure 2 (**showgoodies** ↔ **showobjects**)

FUNCTION objlookup:goodies;
FUNCTION ckgoodies(it:goodies):Boolean; } Similar to Adventure 2.

IMPLEMENTATION

VAR

plurals, somes, useans
SET OF goodies variables - used by showgoodies to improve the grammar of object descriptions.

Code implementing the interface procedures and functions.

BEGIN
Initialization code for the varibles in **cmds3**.

END

Fig. 25-4. The code outline for Adventure 3: the outline of UNIT cmds3.

```
UNIT cmds2:

  INTERFACE

PROCEDURE phelp;

  IMPLEMENTATION

VAR

  asked: INTEGER;
  Variable to keep track of how many times the player has asked for help.

BEGIN

  asked := 0;

END.
```

```
UNIT locs;

  INTERFACE

PROCEDURE pwmm;
  Procedure to handle the action at the wise man
  of the mountain's location.

  IMPLEMENTATION

VAR
  atwmm: INTEGER;
  Variable to count the number of times the player has visited the
  wmm's location.

BEGIN
  atwmm := 0;

END.
```

Fig. 25-5. The code outline for Adventure 3: the outline of UNIT cmds2 and UNIT locs.

```
UNIT cmds2:

  INTERFACE

PROCEDURE travel (nloc,sloc,eloc,wloc,uloc,dloc:rooms);
PROCEDURE pcarry;
PROCEDURE pdrop;
PROCEDURE popen;
PROCEDURE pshout;
PROCEDURE pwadda;
  Procedures for command implementation and travel from one
  location to another.

  IMPLEMENTATION

VAR
  dchars: SET OF CHAR; CHAR SET—representing letters that
                       correspond to direction commands.

PROCEDURE ckproblems; }  Private procedure used in support of
PROCEDURE trolmeal;   }  the problems of Adventure 3. In
PROCEDURE trolaction; }  particular, ckproblems monitors the
                         status and actions of the trolls.

FUNCTION cmdlookup: cmds;       }
FUNCTION pscore: integer;       }
PROCEDURE listen;               }  As in Adventure 2
FUNCTION docommand: CHAR;       }
FUNCTION whichway: directions;  }
  Code to implement the interface procedures.

BEGIN

  dchars : = [ 'n', 's', . . .

END.
```

Fig. 25-6. The code outline for Adventure 3: the outline of UNIT cmds1.

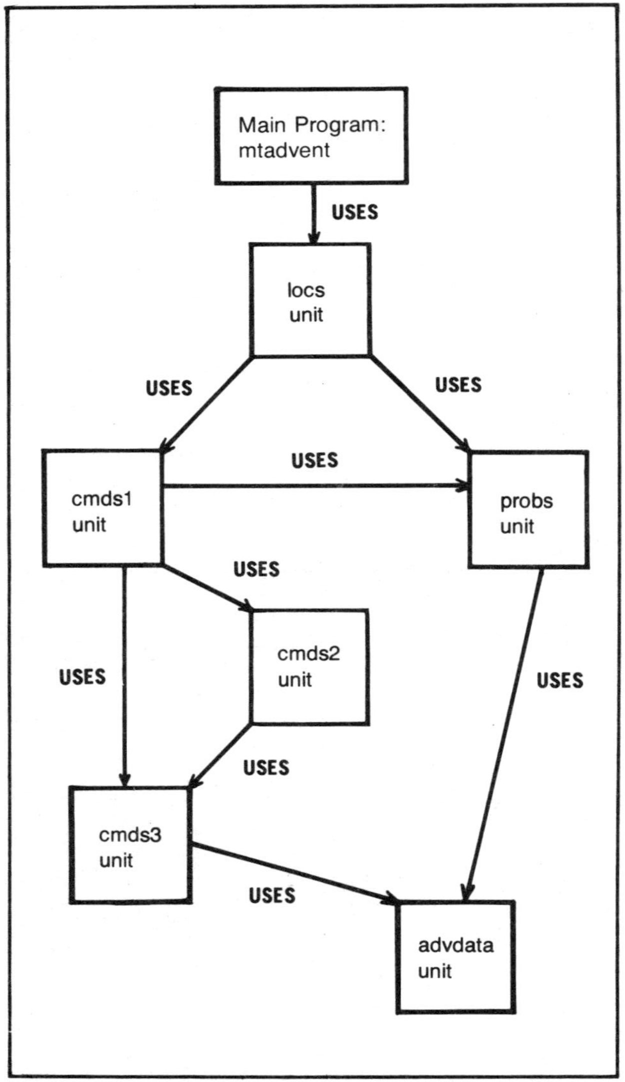

Fig. 25-7. The uses relations for the units of Adventure 3.

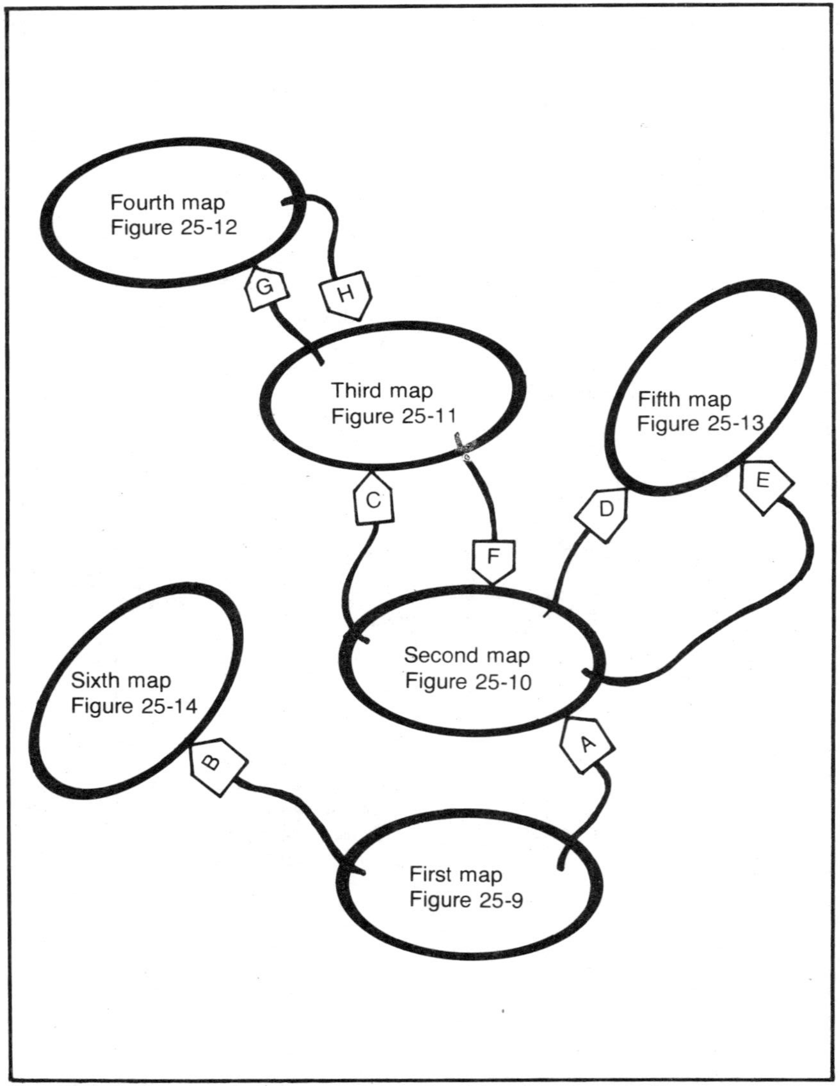

Fig. 25-8. A diagram showing map pages for Adventure 3 and offpage connections between them.

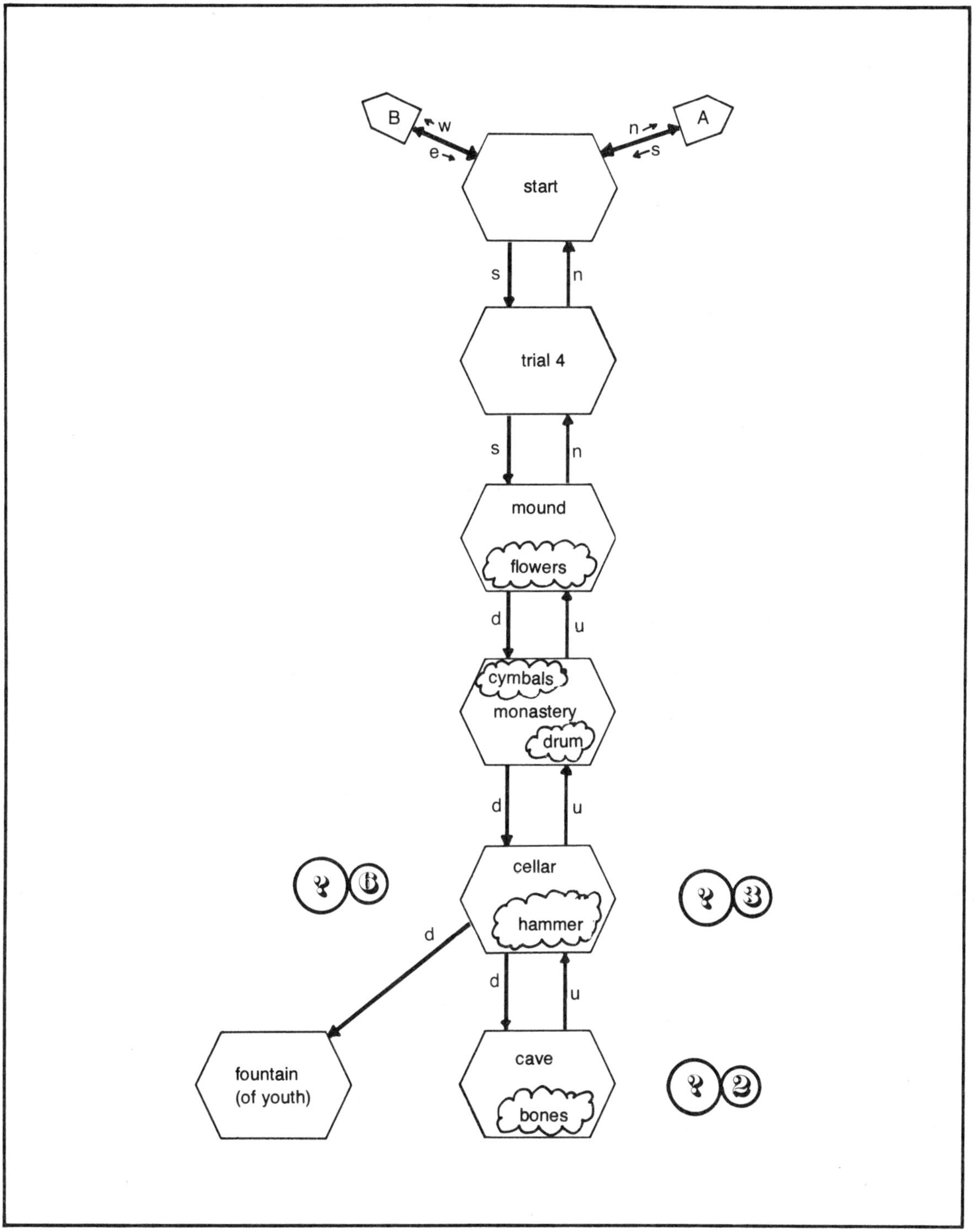

Fig. 25-9. The map of Adventure 3: Page 1.

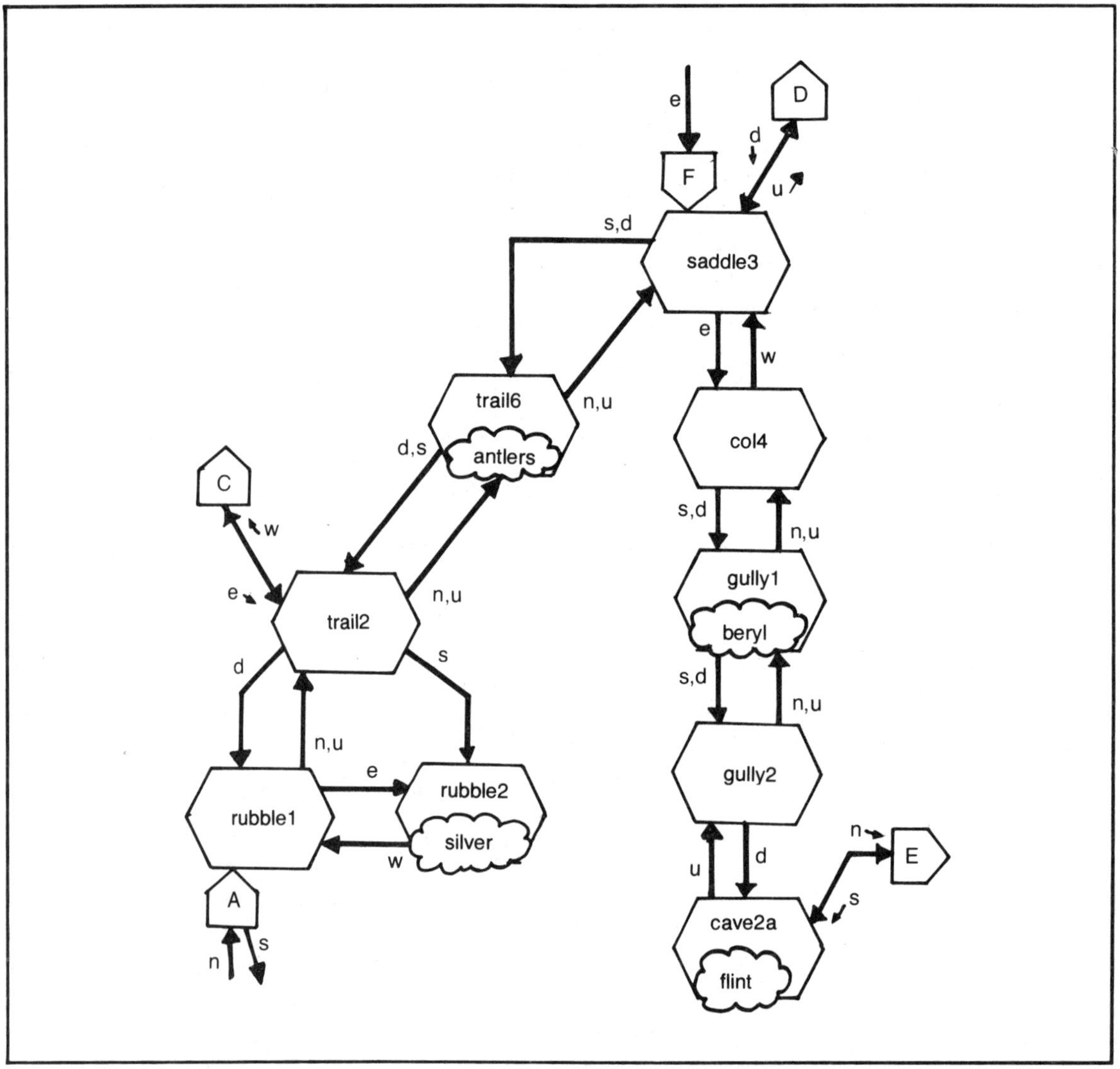

Fig. 25-10. The map of Adventure 3: Page 2.

the information that the unit provides to other parts of the program. The implementation contains the code for all procedures and functions of the unit. The advantage of the unit concept lies in the fact that any part of the implementation may be changed without requiring the remainder of the program to be recompiled. Also, other parts of the program cannot use knowledge of the innards of a unit in order to play programming "tricks." This makes for more robust code and fewer bugs. Chapter 27 explains the syntax of units and how to use them in your adventure game programs. It explains the interface and implementation concepts and talks about *linking* units together to form a program. Units are separately compiled from one another, and so there is an extra step in preparing a program that uses units. This step is called linking.

Chapter 28 delves into the problems implemented in Adventure 3. It explains how a large part of the representation of those problems is en-

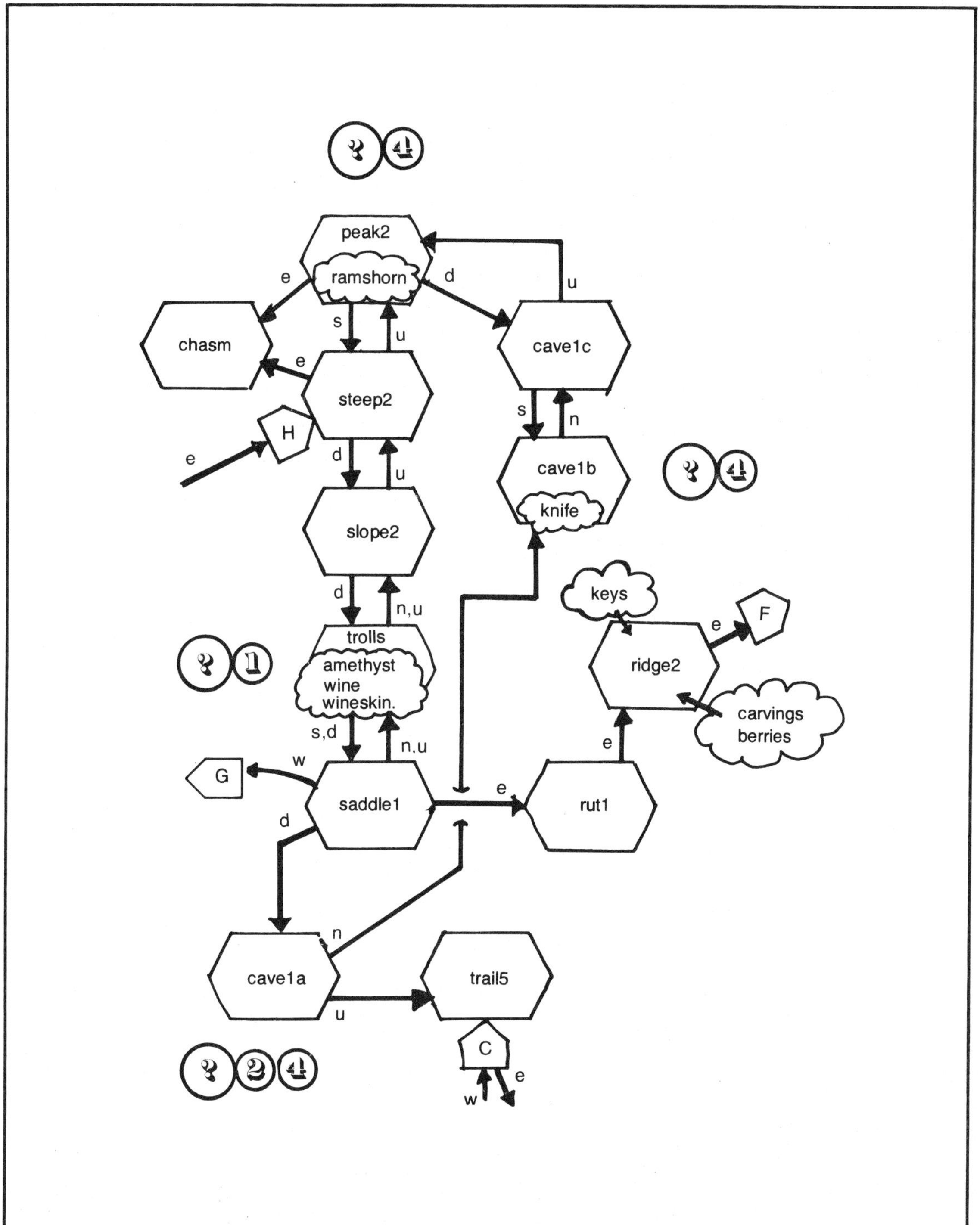

Fig. 25-11. The map of Adventure 3: Page 3.

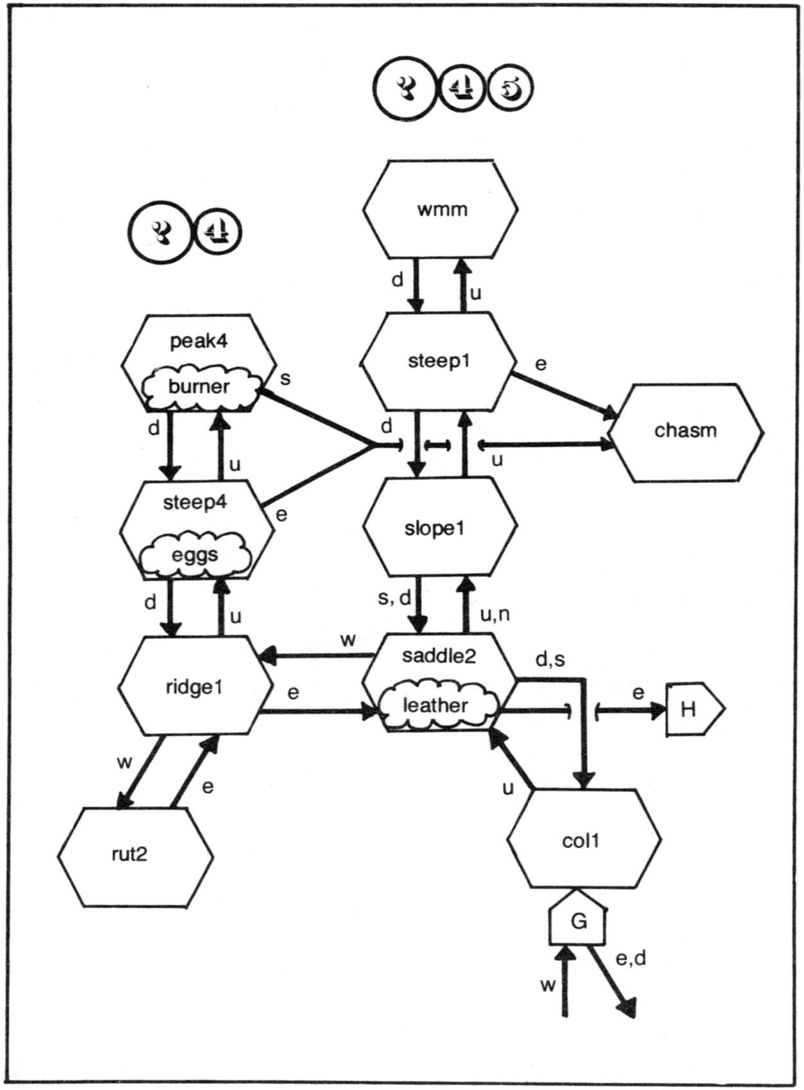

Fig. 25-12. The map of Adventure 3: Page 4.

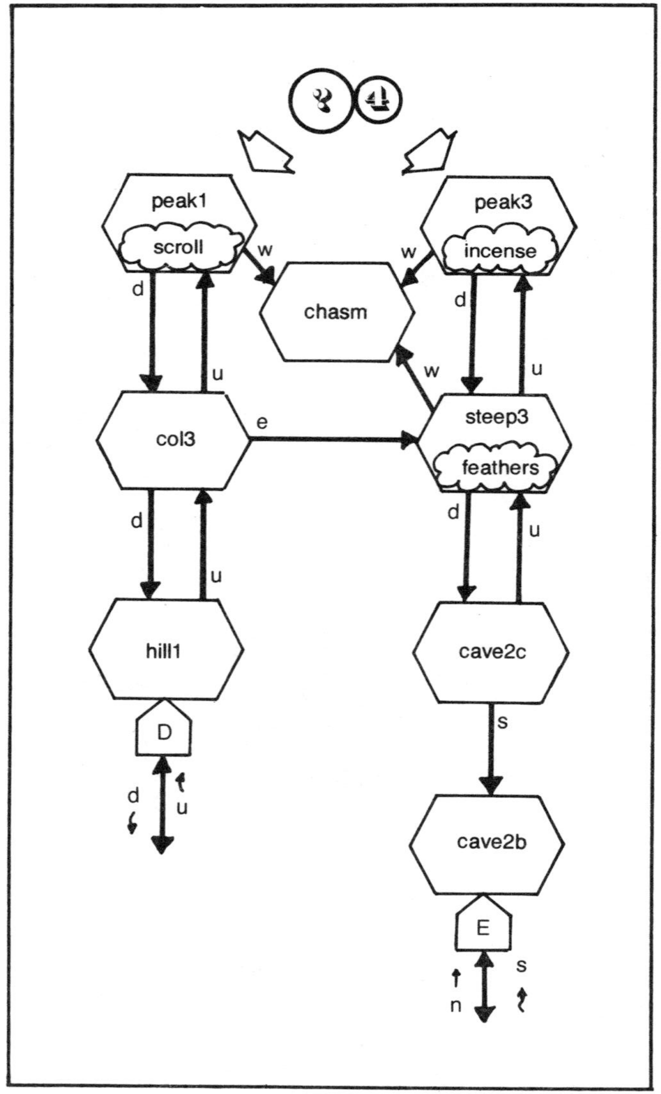

Fig. 25-13. The map of Adventure 3: Page 5.

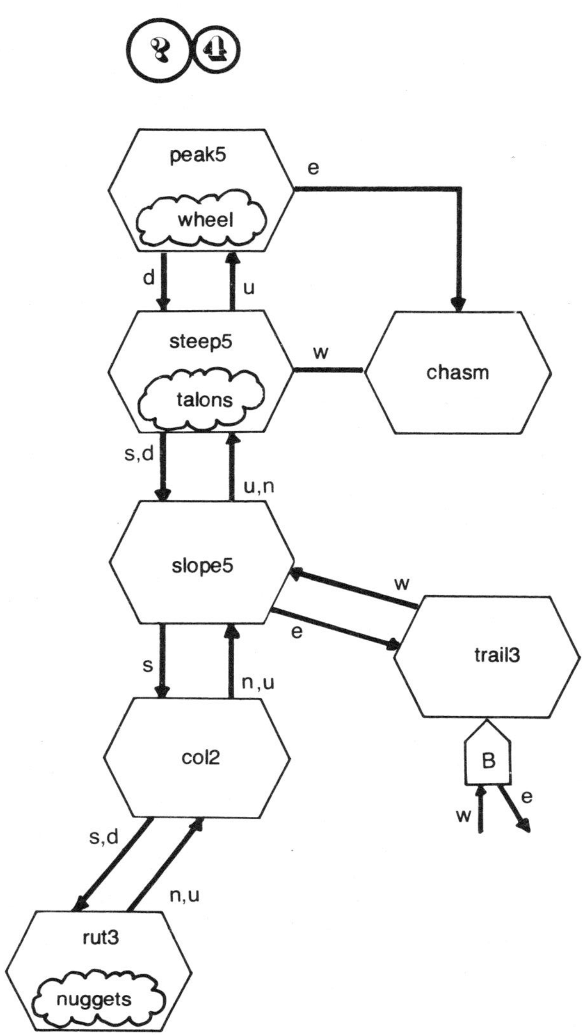

Fig. 25-14. The map of Adventure 3: Page 6.

1. You must avoid being eaten by the trolls. This means that you must be carrying the bones when you arrive at the trolls location.

2. You must find the bones in the cave and carry them. You must use them to lure the trolls to cave1a. Then if you drop the bones, you can be rid of the trolls forever.

3. You must locate the keys and carry them to the cellar in order to open the hatch leading to the cave.

4. You must distinguish "fake" treasures from those objects that the wmm truly desires. You must bring all the "wmmgoodies" to location wmm and leave them. This includes finding the troll's tooth at location cave1a—after solving problem 2.

5. You must remove all "fakes" and all "trash" from the wmm's location after solving problem 4. Then and only then will the wmm reveal the magic word.

6. After the wmm reveals the magic word to you, you must return to the cellar and use it as a command. When you do, the way to the fountain of youth is opened up.

Fig. 25-15. The problems of Adventure 3.

capsulated in the program unit known as the **probs** unit. The use of the **solved** function is discussed in connection with this. The problems posed by the adventure and the Pascal code used to implement them are described. The precondition—postcondition notation is used as it was in the description of Adventure 2.

Chapter 29 discusses the miscellaneous coding techniques used in the implementation of Adventure 3.

26

The Listings of Adventure 3

This chapter presents the listings of Adventure 3. There is a separate listing for each of the Pascal units used in the program, as well as the main program.

LISTING 26-1. ADVENTURE 3 MAIN PROGRAM

```
PROGRAM mtadvent;

{$s+}

    USES   applestuff,
           {$umt1.code} advdata,
           {$uprobs.code} probs,
           {$ucmds3.code} cmds3,
           {$ucmds2.code} cmds2,
           {$ucmds1.code} cmds1,
           {$ulocs.code} locs;

PROCEDURE t1 (l1: rooms);
BEGIN

  CASE l1 OF

    start:     travel (trail1, trail4, nowhere,
```

```
                        trail3, nowhere, nowhere);
trail1:     travel (rubble1, start, nowhere,
                        nowhere, nowhere, nowhere);
trail2:     travel (trail6, rubble2, nowhere,
                        trail5, trail6, rubble1);
trail3:     travel (nowhere, nowhere, start,
                        slope5, nowhere, nowhere);
trail4:     travel (start, mound, nowhere,
                        nowhere, nowhere, nowhere);
trail5:     travel (nowhere, nowhere, trail2,
                        saddle1, saddle1, nowhere);
trail6:     travel (saddle3, trail2, nowhere,
                        nowhere, saddle3, trail2);
col1:       travel (nowhere, nowhere, saddle1,
                        nowhere, saddle2, saddle1);
col2:       travel (slope5, rut3, nowhere,
                        nowhere, slope5, rut3);
col3:       travel (nowhere, nowhere, steep3,
                        nowhere, peak1, hill1);
col4:       travel (nowhere, gully1, nowhere,
                        saddle3, nowhere, gully1);
rubble1:    travel (trail2, trail1, rubble2,
                        nowhere, trail2, nowhere);
rubble2:    travel (nowhere, nowhere, nowhere,
                        rubble1, nowhere, nowhere);
mound:      travel (trail4, nowhere, nowhere,
                        nowhere, nowhere, monastery);
monastery:travel (nowhere, nowhere, nowhere,
                        nowhere, mound, cellar);
cellar:     travel (nowhere, nowhere, nowhere,
                        nowhere, monastery, cave);
cave:       travel (nowhere, nowhere, nowhere,
                        nowhere, cellar, nowhere);
slope1:     travel (nowhere, saddle2, nowhere,
                        nowhere, steep1, saddle2);
slope2:     travel (nowhere, nowhere, nowhere,
                        nowhere, steep2, trolls);
slope5:     travel (steep5, col2, trail3,
                        chasm, steep5, nowhere);
rut1:       travel (nowhere, nowhere, ridge2,
                        trolls, nowhere, nowhere);
rut2:       travel (nowhere, nowhere, ridge1,
                        nowhere, nowhere, nowhere);
rut3:       travel (col2, nowhere, nowhere,
                        nowhere, col2, nowhere);
```

```
  END { CASE ll OF };

END { PROCEDURE t1 };

PROCEDURE t2 (ll: rooms);
BEGIN

  CASE ll OF

    steep1:   travel (nowhere, nowhere, chasm,
                      nowhere, wmm, slope1);
    steep2:   travel (nowhere, nowhere, chasm,
                      nowhere, peak2, slope2);
    steep3:   travel (nowhere, nowhere, nowhere,
                      chasm, peak3, mtcave2c);
    steep4:   travel (nowhere, nowhere, chasm,
                      nowhere, peak4, ridge1);
    steep5:   travel (peak5, slope5, nowhere,
                      chasm, peak5, slope5);
    peak1:    travel (nowhere, nowhere, nowhere,
                      chasm, nowhere, col3);
    peak2:    travel (nowhere, steep2, chasm,
                      nowhere, nowhere, mtcave1c);
    peak3:    travel (nowhere, nowhere, nowhere,
                      chasm, nowhere, steep3);
    peak4:    travel (nowhere, chasm, nowhere,
                      nowhere, nowhere, steep4);
    peak5:    travel (nowhere, nowhere, chasm,
                      nowhere, nowhere, steep5);
    saddle1:  travel (trolls, nowhere, rut1,
                      col1, trolls, mtcave1a);
    saddle2:  travel (slope1, col1, steep2,
                      ridge1, slope1, col1);
    saddle3:  travel (nowhere, trail6, col4,
                      nowhere, hill1, trail6);
    mtcave1a: travel (mtcave1b, nowhere, nowhere,
                      nowhere, trail5, nowhere);
    mtcave1b: travel (mtcave1c, nowhere, nowhere,
                      nowhere, nowhere, nowhere);
    mtcave1c: travel (nowhere, mtcave1b, nowhere,
                      nowhere, peak2, nowhere);
    mtcave2a: travel (mtcave2b, nowhere, nowhere,
                      nowhere, gully2, nowhere);
    mtcave2b: travel (mtcave2c, mtcave2a, nowhere,
                      nowhere, nowhere, nowhere);
```

```
    mtcave2c: travel (nowhere, mtcave2b, nowhere,
                      nowhere, steep3, nowhere);
    gully1:   travel (col4, gully2, nowhere,
                      nowhere, col4, gully2);
    gully2:   travel (gully1, nowhere, nowhere,
                      nowhere, gully1, mtcave2a);
    hill1:    travel (nowhere, nowhere, nowhere,
                      nowhere, col3, saddle3);
    trolls:   travel (slope2, saddle1, chasm,
                      nowhere, slope2, saddle1);
    ridge1:   travel (nowhere, nowhere, saddle2,
                      rut2, steep4, nowhere);
    ridge2:   travel (nowhere, nowhere, saddle3,
                      nowhere, nowhere, nowhere);
    wmm:      BEGIN
                pwmm;
                travel (nowhere, nowhere, nowhere,
                        nowhere, nowhere, steep1);
              END;
    chasm:    BEGIN
                done := true;
                killed := true;
              END;

  END { CASE location OF };

END { PROCEDURE t2 };

BEGIN

  writeln ('adventure 3 begins...');
  writeln ('there are ', memavail, ' bytes of memory left.');

  repeat

    visited[location] := visited[location] + 1;
    show (location);

    IF ord (location) < ord (steep1)
    THEN
      t1 (location)
    ELSE
      t2 (location)
    { END IF ord ... };

  UNTIL done;
```

```
END.
```

LISTING 26-2. LOCATION PROCEDURE UNIT

```
{------------------------------------------------------------}
{                                                            }
{         l   o   c   s          u   n   i   t               }
{                                                            }
{ the locs unit contains procedures needed for               }
{ handling special situations at certain game                }
{ locations.  in mtadvent the only such place                }
{ is 'wmm'.  therefore, this implementation of               }
{ locs contains only the procedure pwmm.                     }
{                                                            }
{------------------------------------------------------------}

{$s+}

UNIT locs;

  INTERFACE

    USES  applestuff,
          {$umt1.code} advdata,
          {$uprobs.code} probs,
          {$ucmds3.code} cmds3,
          {$ucmds2.code} cmds2,
          {$ucmds1.code} cmds1;

PROCEDURE pwmm;

  IMPLEMENTATION

VAR

  atwmm:          INTEGER;

{----------------------------------------}
{         p    w    m    m               }
{                                        }
{ handle special occurrences at the      }
{ location wmm.                          }
{----------------------------------------}

PROCEDURE pwmm;
VAR
  r:     INTEGER;
```

```
BEGIN

  atwmm := atwmm + 1;

  IF solved (wmmhappy)
  THEN
    show (wmmblab)
  { END IF };

  IF wmmcount >= 3
  THEN
    show (wmmharp)
  { END IF };

  IF atwmm > 1
  THEN
  BEGIN

    r := rand (1,5);

    CASE r OF

     1:   show (wmmsp1);
     2:   show (wmmsp2);
     3:   show (wmmsp3);
     4:   show (wmmsp4);
     5:   show (wmmsp5);

    END { CASE r OF };

  END { IF atwmm > 1 };

  IF atwmm = 1
  THEN
    show (wmmhello)
  { END IF };

END { PROCEDURE pwmm };

BEGIN

  atwmm := 0;

END.
```

LISTING 26-3. COMMANDS 1 UNIT

```
{----------------------------}
{ source file: cmds1.text }
{----------------------------}

{-----------------------------------------------------}
{                                                     }
{   c  m  d  s  1        u  n  i  t                   }
{                                                     }
{ this unit contains all command processing          }
{ support procedures and functions.  each            }
{ command in the adventure is carried out by a       }
{ procedure called p<cmd>, where <cmd> stands        }
{ for the name of the command, as typed by the       }
{ player: e.g. pcarry <===> carry command.           }
{ some of the p<cmd> procedures are located in       }
{ this unit, the others are in cmds2 and cmds3.      }
{ procedures and functions like travel, noway,       }
{ docommand, listen, and cmdlookup which are         }
{ invoked in order to recognize the command are      }
{ all located in this unit.                          }
{                                                     }
{ the procedures ckproblems, trolmeal, and           }
{ trolaction are also located here in order to       }
{ be accessible to the appropriate command           }
{ processing code.  none of these procedures is      }
{ in the interface to cmds1.                         }
{                                                     }
{-----------------------------------------------------}

{$s+}
UNIT cmds1;

  INTERFACE

    USES  applestuff,
          {$umt1.code} advdata,
          {$uprobs.code} probs,
          {$ucmds2.code} cmds2,
          {$ucmds3.code} cmds3;

PROCEDURE travel (

           nloc,
```

```
          sloc,
          eloc,
          wloc,
          uloc,
          dloc:   rooms);

PROCEDURE pcarry;
PROCEDURE pdrop;
PROCEDURE pshout;
PROCEDURE popen;
PROCEDURE pwadda;

  IMPLEMENTATION

VAR

  dchars:       SET OF char;

{-----------------------------------------------}
{     c   k   p   r   o   b   l   e   m   s    }
{                                               }
{ see if the player has solved any problems    }
{ because of the command just executed.         }
{-----------------------------------------------}

PROCEDURE ckproblems;
BEGIN

  IF (solved (bonetrolls)) AND (solved (luretrolls))
  THEN
  BEGIN

    show (tgabbones);
    trlives := false;    { make 'em disappear    }
    whatshere[mtcave1a] :=
        whatshere[mtcave1a] - [bones];

  END { IF (solved (bonetrolls) ... };

  IF (NOT trlives) AND (location <> mtcave1a)
  THEN
    whatshere[mtcave1a] :=
        whatshere[mtcave1a] + [tooth];

END { PROCEDURE ckproblems };
```

```
{----------------------------------------}
{    t   r   o   l   m   e   a   l       }
{                                        }
{ print the description of the player    }
{ being done in by the trolls and        }
{ exit the program.                      }
{----------------------------------------}

PROCEDURE trolmeal;
BEGIN

  show (trtalk);
  exit (PROGRAM);

END { PROCEDURE trolmeal };

{--------------------------------------------------}
{     t   r   o   l   a   c   t   i   o   n        }
{                                                  }
{ handle the trolls and associated problems.       }
{ detect the first encounter with the trolls,      }
{ monitor the trolls following the player when     }
{ the player is carrying the bones.  check for     }
{ luring the trolls to mtcave1a.                   }
{--------------------------------------------------}

PROCEDURE trolaction;
BEGIN

  IF (location = trolls) AND (troltime = 0)
          { first encounter }
  THEN
  BEGIN

    IF bones IN stash
    THEN
    BEGIN
      troltime := turns;
      { solve luretrolls problem }
      show (trhungry);
    END
    ELSE
      trolmeal
    { END IF bones IN stash };

  END { IF (location ... };
```

```
  IF solved (luretrolls)
  THEN
    IF (location <> trolls) AND
       (bones IN stash)
    THEN
      show (trfollow)
    ELSE
      trolmeal
    { END IF (location .. }
  { END IF solved (luretrolls) };

  IF (location = mtcave1a) AND
     solved (luretrolls) AND
     (bones IN stash)
  THEN
    show (tgablure)
  { END IF };

END { PROCEDURE trolaction };

{-----------------------------------------------------------}
{       c    m    d    l    o    o    k    u    p          }
{                                                           }
{ determine which command the player has typed }
{ and dissect the command string into 'head'   }
{ and 'tail' for command verbs with objects.   }
{-----------------------------------------------------------}

FUNCTION cmdlookup : cmds;
VAR
  p:     INTEGER;
  lcmd: cmds;
BEGIN

  writeln;
  write ('your wish is my command> ');
  readln (command);

  p := pos (' ', command);
  { check for verb-object }

  IF p = 0
  THEN
  BEGIN

    head := command;
```

```
    tail := '';

  END
  ELSE
  BEGIN

    head := copy (command, 1, p-1);
    tail := copy (command, p+1, length(command)-p);

  END { IF p = 0 };

  cmdname[nocmd] := head;
  lcmd           := carry;

  WHILE head <> cmdname[lcmd] DO
    lcmd := succ (lcmd)
  { END DO };

  cmdlookup := lcmd;

END { FUNCTION cmdlookup };

{-----------------------------------------------}
{          p   s   c   o   r   e               }
{                                              }
{ calculate the number of points scored by the }
{ up to this point in the game.                }
{-----------------------------------------------}

FUNCTION pscore : INTEGER;
VAR
  r:    rooms;
  keepscore:    INTEGER;

BEGIN

  keepscore := 0;

  FOR r := start TO wmm
  DO
    IF visited[r] > 0
    THEN
      keepscore := keepscore + 5;

  IF saidwadda
  THEN
```

```
    keepscore := keepscore +
                  (350 - ord (fountain) - 24);

  IF location = fountain
  THEN
    keepscore := keepscore + 25;

  pscore := keepscore;

END { FUNCTION score };

{-----------------------------------------------------}
{            l   i   s   t   e   n                    }
{                                                     }
{ dispatch calls to the command execution             }
{ procedures ( p<cmd> as described in the             }
{ header comment for this unit.)                      }
{-----------------------------------------------------}

PROCEDURE listen;
VAR
  lcmd: cmds;

  PROCEDURE lscore;
  BEGIN
    writeln ('if you should quit now, your score would be ');
    writeln (pscore, ' points of a possible 350.');
  END { PROCEDURE lscore };

  PROCEDURE lquit;
  VAR
    ch:   CHAR;
    {hold response for quit confirmation}
  BEGIN
    writeln ('are you sure you want to quit?');
    readln (ch);
    IF (ch = 'y') OR (ch = 'y')
    THEN
    BEGIN
      writeln ('you would have scored ', pscore, ' points.');
      exit (PROGRAM);
    END {IF (ch = 'y') ...};
  END { PROCEDURE lquit };

BEGIN
```

```
  REPEAT

    turns := turns + 1;
    lcmd  := cmdlookup;

    CASE lcmd OF

      take,
      carry:     pcarry;
      drop:      pdrop;
      help:      phelp;
      invent:    pinventory;
      score,
      tally:     lscore;
      look:      plook;
      shout:     pshout;
      open:      popen;
      unlock:    popen;
      wadda:     pwadda;
      quit:      lquit;
      nocmd:     ;

    END { CASE lcmd OF };

    ckproblems;
    {see if any problems were solved by the }
    { command issued by the player.         }

  UNTIL lcmd = nocmd;

END { PROCEDURE listen };

{--------------------------------------------------}
{     d   o   c   o   m   m   a   n   d            }
{                                                  }
{ call listen in a loop.  when the length of       }
{ head is greater than zero, the user has given}
{ a travel command so return the first letter      }
{ of 'head' to the caller.                         }
{--------------------------------------------------}

FUNCTION docommand : CHAR;

 BEGIN
```

```
  head   := '';
  tail   := '';
  chgloc := false;

  REPEAT

    listen;

  UNTIL length (head) > 0;
  docommand := head[1];

END { FUNCTION docommand };

{---------------------------------------------------}
{       w   h   i   c   h   w   a   y               }
{                                                   }
{ determine which way the player wishes to go.      }
{---------------------------------------------------}

FUNCTION whichway : directions;
VAR
  ch: CHAR;
  ww: directions;
BEGIN

  REPEAT

    ch       := docommand;
    whichway := x;

    CASE ch OF

      'n':      IF (head = 'n') OR (head = 'north')
                THEN
                  whichway := n;

      's':      IF (head = 's') OR (head = 'south')
                THEN
                  whichway := s;

      'e':      IF (head = 'e') OR (head = 'east')
                THEN
                  whichway := e;

      'w':      IF (head = 'w') OR (head = 'west')
                THEN
```

```
                 whichway := w;

     'u':       IF (head = 'u') OR (head = 'up')
                THEN
                  whichway := u;
     'd':       IF (head = 'd') OR (head = 'down')
                THEN
                  whichway := d;

     'q':       { empty for now };

    END { CASE ch OF };

  UNTIL ch IN dchars;

  writeln;

END { FUNCTION whichway };

{-------------------------------------------------}
{             n    o    w    a    y              }
{-------------------------------------------------}

PROCEDURE noway;
BEGIN

  writeln;
  writeln ('it is impossible to go in that direction.');
  chgloc := false;

END { PROCEDURE noway };

{-------------------------------------------------}
{            t    r    a    v    e    l          }
{                                                }
{ handle travel to the next location.  the       }
{ possible destinations from the current room    }
{ or adventure location are passed to travel     }
{ parameters.  the value 'nowhere' means that    }
{ there is no way to go in the corresponding     }
{ direction.  there is special case code for     }
{ direction 'd' or 'down'.  the location         }
{ 'cellar' has two possible destinations in      }
{ that direction, one of which is the winning    }
{ location.                                      }
{-------------------------------------------------}
```

```
PROCEDURE travel;

  PROCEDURE newloc (loc:descs);
  BEGIN

    IF loc = nowhere
    THEN
      noway
    ELSE
    BEGIN


      location := loc;
      chgloc   := true;
    END { IF loc = nowhere };

  END { PROCEDURE newloc };


  PROCEDURE wingame;
  BEGIN

    show (fountain);
    writeln ('you scored a total of ', pscore);
    writeln (' points out of a possible 350.');
    exit (PROGRAM);

  END { PROCEDURE wingame };

BEGIN     {***** t  r  a  v  e  l   ****}

  IF (location IN trollocs) AND trlives
  THEN
    trolaction;

  CASE whichway OF

    n:  newloc (nloc);
    s:  newloc (sloc);
    e:  newloc (eloc);
    w:  newloc (wloc);
    u:  newloc (uloc);
    d:  BEGIN
          IF location = cellar
          THEN
          BEGIN
```

```
          IF saidwadda
          THEN
            wingame
          ELSE
            IF isopen
            THEN
              newloc (cave)
            ELSE
              noway
            { END IF isopen}
          { END IF saidwadda }
        END
        ELSE
          newloc (dloc)
        { END IF location = cellar };
      END { case d: };
   x:  BEGIN
        writeln ('i do not understand that.');
        writeln ('please try another command');
      END;

  END { CASE whichway OF };

END { PROCEDURE travel };

{--------------------------------------------------}
{         p    c    a    r    r    y               }
{                                                  }
{ implement the carry command.  call the           }
{ function 'objlookup' to determine which          }
{ object (if any) has been requested.  then        }
{ call 'ckgoodies' to see if that object is        }
{ present in the current location.  if so, the     }
{ object is added to the set 'stash' and also      }
{ removed from the set 'whatshere[location]'.      }
{--------------------------------------------------}

PROCEDURE pcarry;
VAR
  it: goodies;
BEGIN

  it := objlookup;

  IF NOT ckgoodies (it)
  THEN
```

```
  BEGIN

    write ('i don''t see any ');
    write (tail);
    writeln (' here.');

  END
  ELSE
  BEGIN

    writeln ('ok');

    stash := stash + [it];
    whatshere[location] :=
        whatshere[location] - [it];

    IF (location = wmm) AND (it IN wmmfakes)
    THEN
      wmmcount := wmmcount - 1
    { END IF };

  END { IF NOT it IN ... };

END { PROCEDURE pcarry };

{---------------------------------------------------}
{          p   d   r   o   p                         }
{                                                    }
{ implement the drop command.  similar in            }
{ action to the carry command (q.v.).                }
{---------------------------------------------------}

PROCEDURE pdrop;
VAR
  it: goodies;
BEGIN

  it := objlookup;

  IF NOT (it IN stash)
  THEN
  BEGIN

    write ('you are not carrying any ');
    writeln (tail);
```

```
  END
  ELSE
  BEGIN

    writeln ('ok');
    stash := stash - [it];
    IF (location = wmm)
    THEN
    BEGIN

      IF it IN wmmwants
      THEN
        wmmhas := wmmhas + [it]
      ELSE
        whatshere[wmm] := whatshere[wmm] + [it]
      { END IF it IN wmmwants };

      IF it IN wmmfakes
      THEN
        wmmcount := wmmcount + 1
      { END IF it IN wmmfakes};

    END
    ELSE
      whatshere[location] :=
          whatshere[location] + [it]
    { END IF (location = wmm) };

  END { IF NOT it IN stash };

END { PROCEDURE pdrop };

{-----------------------------------------------}
{            p    o    p    e    n              }
{                                               }
{ handle the open command.  the player can      }
{ open the hatch to the cave under the cellar   }
{ provided the keys are being carried.          }
{-----------------------------------------------}

PROCEDURE popen;
BEGIN

  IF NOT solved (canopen)
  THEN
```

```
    writeln ('you can''t open anything here!')
  ELSE
  BEGIN

    writeln ('ok.');
    isopen := true;
    writeln ('one of the hatches is now open.');

  END { IF NOT solved ... };

END { PROCEDURE popen };

{-----------------------------------------------}
{          p   w   a   d   d   a               }
{                                               }
{ handle the wadda command.  in order to win,  }
{ the player must say 'wadda' at location      }
{ cellar.  this can only happen after the wmm  }
{ problem has been solved.                     }
{-----------------------------------------------}

PROCEDURE pwadda;
BEGIN

  IF NOT solved (ftofyouth)
  THEN
    writeln ('i don''t understand baby talk.')
  ELSE
  BEGIN

    saidwadda := true;
    writeln ('you are close to the secret.');

  END { IF NOT solved ... };

END { PROCEDURE pwadda };

{-----------------------------------------------}
{        p   s   h   o   u   t                 }
{-----------------------------------------------}

PROCEDURE pshout;

VAR
  i:     INTEGER;
  j:     INTEGER;
```

```
BEGIN

  writeln ('ok.');
  FOR i := 1 TO 500 DO
    ;
  write ('a');
  FOR i := 1 TO 75 DO
  BEGIN
    write ('a');
    FOR j := 1 TO 100 DO
      ;
  END;
  writeln;
  FOR i := 1 to 15 DO
  BEGIN
    write ('g');
    FOR j := 1 TO 100 DO
      ;
  END;
  write ('h!');
  FOR i := 1 TO 58 DO
  BEGIN
    write ('!');
    FOR j := 1 TO 100 DO
      ;
  END;
  writeln;
  FOR i := 1 TO 500 DO
    ;
  writeln ('there - now i feel much better.');

END { PROCEDURE pshout };

BEGIN

  dchars :=
    ['q', 'n', 's', 'e', 'w', 'u', 'd', 'x'];

END.
```

LISTING 26-4. COMMANDS 2 UNIT

```
{----------------------------------------------------}
{                                                    }
{       c  m  d  s  2     u  n  i  t                 }
{                                                    }
```

```
{ this unit contains the procedure phelp.  the  }
{ help command needs no access to data in unit  }
{ 'advdata'.  it does use procedure 'show',      }
{ however, and hence USES unit cmds3.            }
{-----------------------------------------------}

{$s+}

UNIT cmds2;

  INTERFACE

    USES applestuff,
         {$umt1.code} advdata,
         {$ucmds3.code} cmds3;

PROCEDURE phelp;

  IMPLEMENTATION

VAR

  asked:          INTEGER;

PROCEDURE phelp;
BEGIN

  IF asked > 2
  THEN
    show (helpspiel)
  ELSE
  BEGIN

    writeln ('help is on the way');
    asked := asked + 1;

  END;

END { PROCEDURE phelp };

BEGIN

  asked := 0;

END.
```

LISTING 26-5. COMMANDS 3 UNIT

```
{-----------------------------}
{ source file: cmds3.text     }
{-----------------------------}


{-------------------------------------------------}
{                                                 }
{  c  m  d  s  3    u  n  i  t                    }
{                                                 }
{ This unit contains procedures implementing      }
{ commands.  The particular commands implemented}
{ herein need access to the unit advdata, but     }
{ not to the unit 'probs'.                        }
{                                                 }
{-------------------------------------------------}

{$s+}

UNIT cmds3;

  INTERFACE

    USES  applestuff,
          {$umt1.code} advdata;

TYPE

  directions     = (n,s,e,w,u,d,x);
  cmds           = (carry, drop, help, score, invent,
                    take, tally, look, shout, open,
                    unlock, wadda, quit, nocmd);

  pname          = STRING[40];
  storyline      = STRING[80];
  byte           = 0..255;

  whichsect      = (indexsection, descsection);

  placerec       =

    RECORD

      CASE section: whichsection OF
```

```
        indexsection:    (  tableentry:    INTEGER);
        descsection:     (  name:         pname;
                            id:           INTEGER;
                            dbegin:       INTEGER;
                            dend:         INTEGER;
                            link:         byte);
    END;

VAR

  xfile:           FILE OF placerec;
  narrate:         FILE OF storyline;

  places:          ARRAY [descs] OF placerec;

  command:         STRING;
  head:            STRING;
  tail:            STRING;

  cmdname:         ARRAY[cmds] OF STRING;

  chgloc:          BOOLEAN;
  { has player moved since last cmd? }

PROCEDURE pinventory;
PROCEDURE plook;
PROCEDURE show (where:descs);
PROCEDURE showgoodies;
FUNCTION  objlookup: goodies;
FUNCTION  ckgoodies (it: goodies) : BOOLEAN;

   IMPLEMENTATION

VAR

  r:               descs;
  plurals:         SET OF goodies;
  somes:           SET OF goodies;
  useans:          SET OF goodies;
  { for benefit of showgoodies }

{----------------------------------------------}
{             s   h   o   w                    }
{                                              }
{ Retrieve descriptions from the database      }
{ and display them on the player's console.    }
```

```
{ The argument to show is of type 'descs'     }
{ which includes descriptions of situations }
{ and spoken words as well as descriptions  }
{ of locations.  Show uses the ord function }
{ to detect what kind of description is     }
{ involved.  The description of locations   }
{ suppressed if the player has not changed  }
{ locations or if the location has been     }
{ visited recently.  If the player has not  }
{ changed location, then nothing happens.   }
{ If the player has visited the same place  }
{ recently, then just the short description }
{ is displayed.                             }
{-------------------------------------------}

PROCEDURE show;

VAR
  i: INTEGER;
BEGIN

  IF (chgloc) OR
     (ord (where) > ord (nowhere))
  THEN
  BEGIN

    IF (visited[location] = 1) OR
       ((visited[location] MOD 4) = 0) OR
       (ord (where) > ord (nowhere))
    THEN
    BEGIN

      WITH places[where] DO
      BEGIN

        FOR i := dbegin TO dend DO
        BEGIN

          seek (narrate, i);
          get (narrate);
          write (narrate^);

        END { FOR i := ... };
      END { WITH places[where] };

    END
```

```
    ELSE
    BEGIN

      write ('you are ');
      writeln (places[where].name);

    END { IF visited[location] = 1 ... };

  END { IF chgloc };

  IF ord (where) < ord (nowhere)
  THEN
    showgoodies;

END { PROCEDURE show };

{-----------------------------------------------------}
{       s  h  o  w  g  o  o  d  i  e  s              }
{                                                     }
{ Print a list of the objects present at the}
{ current adventure game location.                   }
{-----------------------------------------------------}

PROCEDURE showgoodies;

VAR
  lobj: goodies;
BEGIN

  FOR lobj := nuggets TO noobj DO
    IF lobj IN whatshere[location]
    THEN
    BEGIN

      IF lobj IN plurals
      THEN
        write ('There are some ')
      ELSE
        IF lobj IN somes
        THEN
          write ('There is some ')
        ELSE
          IF lobj IN useans
          THEN
            write ('There is an ')
          ELSE
```

```
          write ('There is a ')
        { END IF lobj IN useans }
      { END IF lobj IN somes }
    { END IF lobj IN plurals };

    write (objname[lobj]);
    writeln (' here.');

  END { IF lobj IN whatshere... }
{ END FOR lobj := ... };

END { PROCEDURE showgoodies };

{--------------------------------------------}
{     o   b   j   l   o   o   k   u   p      }
{                                            }
{ Determine if the name typed by the player }
{ in a carry or drop command is the name of }
{ any object actually part of the game.  If }
{ so, return the internal value of the      }
{ object in question.                       }
{--------------------------------------------}

FUNCTION objlookup;
VAR
  lobj: goodies;
BEGIN

  objname[noobj] := tail;
  lobj := nuggets;

  WHILE tail <> objname[lobj] DO

    lobj := succ (lobj);

  objlookup := lobj;

END { FUNCTION objlookup };

{--------------------------------------------}
{     c   k   g   o   o   d   i   e   s      }
{                                            }
{ See if an object is present.              }
{--------------------------------------------}

FUNCTION ckgoodies;
```

```
BEGIN

  IF it IN whatshere[location]
  THEN
    ckgoodies := true
  ELSE
    ckgoodies := false
  { END IF it IN ... };

END { FUNCTION ckobject };

{-----------------------------------------------------}
{           p    l    o    o    k                   }
{                                                     }
{ Implement the look command.  This forces           }
{ out the full description of the current            }
{ location.  The variables chgloc and                }
{ visited[location] must be temporarily              }
{ reset in order to accomplish this goal.            }
{-----------------------------------------------------}

PROCEDURE plook;
VAR
  savchg:        BOOLEAN;
  savisit:       INTEGER;
BEGIN

  savchg  := chgloc;
  chgloc  := true;
  savisit := visited[location];
  visited[location] := 1;

  show (location);

  visited[location] := savisit;
  chgloc            := savchg;

END { PROCEDURE plook };

{-----------------------------------------------------}
{   p   i   n   v   e   n   t   o   r   y            }
{                                                     }
{ Implement the inventory command.  Print            }
{ the names of all objects carried by the            }
{ player.                                             }
{-----------------------------------------------------}
```

```
PROCEDURE pinventory;
VAR
  lobj: goodies;
BEGIN

  IF stash <> []
  THEN
  BEGIN
    writeln ('You currently hold: ');
    FOR lobj := nuggets TO noobj DO
    BEGIN

      IF lobj IN stash
      THEN
        writeln (objname[lobj])
      { END IF };

    END { FOR lobj := ... };
  END { IF stash <> [] };

END { PROCEDURE pinventory };

BEGIN

  plurals := [nuggets, diamonds, carvings,
              wineskins, flowers, keys,
              antlers, talons, feathers,
              eggs, cymbals, bones, berries];
  somes   := [wine, amethyst, flint,
              incense, silver, leather];
  useans  := [axe];

  cmdname[carry]        := 'carry';
  cmdname[drop]         := 'drop';
  cmdname[help]         := 'help';
  cmdname[invent]       := 'inventory';
  cmdname[tally]        := 'tally';
  cmdname[take]         := 'take';
  cmdname[score]        := 'score';
  cmdname[look]         := 'look';
  cmdname[shout]        := 'shout';
  cmdname[open]         := 'open';
  cmdname[unlock]       := 'unlock';
  cmdname[wadda]        := 'wadda';
  cmdname[quit]         := 'quit';
  cmdname[nocmd]        := 'sentinel';
```

```
  reset (xfile, 'mtadv.x');
  reset (narrate, 'mtadv');

  r := start;
  seek (xfile, 31);
  get (xfile);
  places[r] := xfile^;

  REPEAT

    r := succ (r);
    get (xfile);
    places[r] := xfile^;

  UNTIL r = helpspiel;

  close (xfile);
  chgloc := true;
  { Force out description of start }

END.
```

LISTING 26-6. PROBLEMS UNIT

```
{-----------------------------------------------------}
{                                                     }
{     p  r  o  b  s        u  n  i  t                 }
{                                                     }
{ this unit contains the single function:             }
{ solved.  solved is passed an argument of type }
{ 'problems'.  the argument corresponds to one   }
{ of the boolean expressions used to detect the }
{ solution of problems and components of         }
{ problems.  the rest of the adventure code      }
{ uses code like:                                 }
{                                                     }
{       IF NOT solved (luretrolls)                 }
{       THEN                                          }
{                                                     }
{ instead of using the complex expressions.       }
{ the details of the problem expressions are      }
{ contained here and may be changed without       }
{ forcing the rest of the adventure game code    }
{ change as well.                                   }
{                                                     }
{-----------------------------------------------------}
```

```
{$s+}

UNIT probs;

  INTERFACE

    USES  applestuff,
          {$umt1.code} advdata;

TYPE

  problems = (wmmhappy, luretrolls,
              bonetrolls, canopen, ftofyouth);

FUNCTION solved (which: problems) : BOOLEAN;

  IMPLEMENTATION

FUNCTION solved;
BEGIN

  solved := false;

  CASE which OF

    wmmhappy:    solved :=
                   (wmmhas = wmmwants) AND
                   (whatshere[wmm] * wmmfakes = []);


    luretrolls: solved :=
                   (troltime > 0 ) AND
                   ((turns - troltime) > 0) AND
                   ((turns - troltime) < 25);

    bonetrolls: solved :=
                  bones IN whatshere[mtcave1a];

    canopen:     solved :=
                   (location = cellar) AND
                   (keys IN stash);

    ftofyouth:   solved :=
                   (wmmhas = wmmwants) AND
                   (whatshere[wmm] * wmmfakes = []) AND
                   (location = cellar);
```

```
   END { CASE which OF };

END { FUNCTION solved };

BEGIN
END.
```

LISTING 26-7. ADVENTURE 3 DATA

```
{----------------------------------}
{ source file: mt1.text           }
{----------------------------------}

{-------------------------------------------------------}
{                                                       }
{  r  o  o  m  s        u  n  i  t                      }
{                                                       }
{  types and variables used by all other units          }
{  in mountain  adventure.  this includes the           }
{  descs enumerated type, extended to account           }
{  for some descriptions that are not actual            }
{  game locations.  the goodies type accounts           }
{  for all objects in the adventure and the             }
{  objname array contains names for all of              }
{  them (for use in descriptions and in                 }
{   commands).                                          }
{                                                       }
{-------------------------------------------------------}

{$s+}

UNIT advdata;

  INTERFACE

    USES applestuff;

TYPE

  descs = (start, trail1, trail2, trail3, trail4,
           trail5, trail6, col1, col2, col3, col4,
           rubble1, rubble2, mound, monastery,
           cellar, cave, slope1, slope2, slope3,
           slope4, slope5, rut1, rut2, rut3,
           steep1, steep2, steep3, steep4, steep5,
           peak1, peak2, peak3, peak4, peak5,
```

```
          saddle1, saddle2, saddle3, mtcave1a,
          mtcave1b, mtcave1c, mtcave2a, mtcave2b,
          mtcave2c, gully1, gully2, hill1,
          trolls, ridge1, ridge2, wmm, chasm,
          nowhere, cellardown, fountain, trtalk,
          wmmblab, wmmharp, wmmhello, wmmsp1,
          wmmsp2, wmmsp3, wmmsp4, wmmsp5,
          tgablure, tgabbones, trhungry,
          trfollow, helpspiel);

  rooms = start..nowhere;

  goodies = (nuggets, silver, diamonds, beryl,
             amethyst, carvings, wine, wineskins,
             flowers, axe, hammer, flint, keys,
             antlers, talons, feathers, eggs,
             walkstick, leather, cymbals, drum,
             bones, scroll, wheel, ramshorn,
             berries, knife, burner, incense,
             tooth, noobj);

  fakes      = nuggets..wineskins;
  trash      = flowers..bones;
  wmmgoody   = scroll..tooth;
  collection = SET OF goodies;

VAR

  location:     rooms;
  trollocs:     SET OF rooms;

  wmmwants:     collection;
  wmmhas:       collection;
  wmmfakes:     collection;
  stash:        collection;

  whatshere:    ARRAY[rooms] OF collection;
  visited:      ARRAY[rooms] OF INTEGER;
  objname:      ARRAY[goodies] OF STRING[15];

  turns:        INTEGER;
  troltime:     INTEGER;
  wmmcount:     INTEGER;
  trlives:      BOOLEAN;
                {true when trolls still around}
  saidwadda:    BOOLEAN;
```

```
   isopen:         BOOLEAN;
   eaten:          BOOLEAN;
   killed:         BOOLEAN;
   done:           BOOLEAN;

FUNCTION rand (low, high: INTEGER) : INTEGER;

   IMPLEMENTATION

VAR

   r:    rooms;
   { loop control for initialization }

FUNCTION rand;
VAR
   mx, c, d: INTEGER;
BEGIN
   rand := 0;
   IF low = high
   THEN
     rand := low

   ELSE
   BEGIN

     c := high - low + 1;
     mx := (maxint - high + low) DIV c + 1;
     mx := mx * (high - low) + (mx - 1);

     REPEAT
       d := random
     UNTIL d <= mx;
     rand := low + d MOD c;

   END { IF low = high };

END { FUNCTION rand };

PROCEDURE init1;
BEGIN

   location := start;

   objname[nuggets]        := 'nuggets';
   objname[silver]         := 'silver';
```

```
  objname[diamonds]       := 'diamonds';
  objname[beryl]          := 'beryl';
  objname[amethyst]       := 'amethyst';
  objname[carvings]       := 'carvings';
  objname[wine]           := 'wine';
  objname[wineskins]      := 'wineskins';
  objname[flowers]        := 'flowers';
  objname[axe]            := 'axe';
  objname[hammer]         := 'hammer';
  objname[flint]          := 'flint';
  objname[keys]           := 'keys';
  objname[antlers]        := 'antlers';
  objname[talons]         := 'talons';
  objname[feathers]       := 'feathers';
  objname[eggs]           := 'eagle-eggs';
  objname[walkstick]      := 'walking-stick';
  objname[leather]        := 'leather';
  objname[cymbals]        := 'cymbals';
  objname[drum]           := 'drum';
  objname[bones]          := 'bones';
  objname[scroll]         := 'scroll';
  objname[wheel]          := 'prayer-wheel';
  objname[ramshorn]       := 'ramshorn';
  objname[berries]        := 'berries';
  objname[knife]          := 'knife';
  objname[burner]         := 'incense-burner';
  objname[incense]        := 'incense';
  objname[tooth]          := 'tooth';

  FOR r := start TO chasm DO

  BEGIN

    whatshere[r] := [];
    visited[r]   := 0;

  END { FOR r := start ... };

END { PROCEDURE init1 };

PROCEDURE init2;
BEGIN

  whatshere[peak1]       := [scroll];
  whatshere[peak2]       := [ramshorn];
  whatshere[peak3]       := [incense];
```

```
  whatshere[peak4]         := [burner];
  whatshere[peak5]         := [wheel];
  whatshere[trail3]        := [walkstick, axe];
  whatshere[cave]          := [bones];
  whatshere[mound]         := [flowers];
  whatshere[mtcave1b]      := [knife];
  whatshere[rut3]          := [nuggets];
  whatshere[rubble2]       := [silver];
  whatshere[trolls]        := [amethyst,
                               wine,
                               wineskin];

  whatshere[gully1]        := [beryl];
  whatshere[ridge2]        := [carvings,
                               keys,
                               berries];

  whatshere[mtcave2a]      := [flint];
  whatshere[trail6]        := [antlers];
  whatshere[steep5]        := [talons];
  whatshere[saddle2]       := [leather];
  whatshere[steep4]        := [eggs];
  whatshere[monastery]     := [drum, cymbals];
  whatshere[cellar]        := [hammer];
  whatshere[steep3]        := [feathers];

  trollocs := [trolls, slope2, steep2, peak2
               saddle1, col1, saddle2,
               mtcave1a, mtcave1b, trail5,
               trail2, rut1, ridge2];
  wmmwants  := [scroll..tooth];
  wmmhas    := [];
  wmmfakes  := [nuggets..wineskins];
  stash     := [];
  turns     := 0;
  troltime  := 0;
  wmmcount  := 0;
  trlives   := true;
  saidwadda := false;
  isopen    := false;
  eaten     := false;
  done      := false;

END { PROCEDURE init2 };

BEGIN

  init1;
  init2;

END.
```

27

Larger Programs: Using UCSD Units

As your adventure game programs grow larger and larger, it will become more and more difficult to work with them. Even with the include option of the Pascal compiler, the program itself is still one large, monolithic piece of code. Using lots of procedures and functions helps to organize it, but it would be convenient to break it into pieces. The UCSD Pascal extension known as a unit is a way to break large programs into smaller ones. In this chapter I shall discuss UCSD units and show how to use them in adventure games.

WHY UNITS?

You may question the usefulness of units. As with other techniques, there are both advantages and disadvantages to using units in writing Pascal programs. I will emphasize the positive and discuss the advantages.

- Each UCSD Pascal unit is separately compiled. This can mean shorter compilation times if you have enough units: instead of having to recompile the entire program, you only have to recompile one unit. This is not the whole story, as you shall see later on. In general, however, units, when properly used, can save you time.
- Each unit is a self-contained piece of the larger program. You can treat it like a small program itself. This reduces the amount of code you have to deal with at a single time and simplifies your design and programming effort. It is possible to misuse units and throw away this advantage. However, if you keep logically related code together in a single unit or in several related units, you will simplify your programs.
- Units can be used to "hide" certain information from the programs that use the units. This is a subtle concept that takes awhile to absorb. I shall try to elucidate further as I elaborate on units and their use.

THE UNITS IN ADVENTURE 3

The following pages describe the units used in Adventure 3 and how they interact with each other.

The Main Program

Every Pascal program must have a main program, whether it uses units or not. The main program is not itself a unit, but it must contain a uses statement that requests all the units that the program requires. I explain the uses statement when I go into the details of unit syntax and semantics. There are seven units used in Adventure 3, one of which comes from the SYSTEM.LIBRARY. The remaining six units are part of the code of Adventure 3 itself.

The Locations Unit

Units are arranged in a hierarchical fashion, as noted in the diagram in Chapter 25. The top level units contain uses statements for the lower level units that they rely upon. The locations unit is the highest level unit in the Adventure 3 hierarchy. It contains the locations procedures pwmm and pcellar. Any other location procedures that might be needed in further developing Adventure 3 should be placed into the locations unit.

The cmds1 Unit

The cmds1 unit contains the general support procedures for command processing: cmdlookup, listen, docommand, whichway, noway, and travel. In addition, it contains three of the specific command procedures: pcarry, pdrop, and pshout. Finally, it contains the code for dealing with the problem surrounding the trolls: ckproblems, trolmeal and trolaction.

If a procedure or function needs to call the solved function, which is in the probs unit, it must be included in cmds1. Otherwise, it may be placed in one of the other cmds units.

The cmds2 Unit

This is a very small unit—it contains only the phelp procedure. The procedures that go into the cmds2 unit are those specific command procedures that do not need access to any data declared in the advdata unit. Because most commands do need access to some sort of data, very few procedures will wind up here. Commands that could be added, whose implementation procedures could be placed in cmds2, are those that cause no change to the status of the adventure; instead they cause some sort of reaction from the guide in the form of dialogue. The help command is a good example. The only side effect of the use of the help command is an increase in the count of how many times help has been requested. This total is used in the scoring at the end of the game.

The cmds3 Unit

The cmds3 unit contains two other command implementation procedures; pinventory, and plook. It also contains procedures used in displaying descriptions of locations and objects: show, showgoodies, objlookup, and ckgoodies. None of the functions or procedures in cmds3 need access to the probs unit. That is the general rule for putting them in cmds3 as opposed to cmds1. They do need access to various pieces of adventure game data, however, and that is the criterion used to decide that a procedure should go into cmds3 instead of cmds2.

The probs Unit

I use the abbreviation for the probs unit, because the full name, problems, is used inside the unit for the name of an enumerated type. Probs contains a single function called solved, which evaluates whether various problems in the adventure have been solved or not. It is not the sole arbiter of problem solution. However, it is a convenient way to centralize and organize the approach to parts of problems that depend on complicated Boolean expressions.

The advdata Unit

This unit contains the bulk of the types and variables needed in more than one place elsewhere in the adventure. It is at the bottom of the uses hierarchy so that all those units above it can "see" the data that it declares.

UNITS: SYNTAX AND SEMANTICS

A unit is a self-contained UCSD Pascal compilation entity. That rather pompous statement simply means that you can compile a unit by itself. Several units can be compiled separately as part of a single larger program. When you compile a unit, a *code* file is produced, just as when you compile a program. The difference is that the resulting code file may not be X(ecuted. It must be linked with other code files, including at least one from a program that uses the unit. There is a relationship between the code files for different units of a single program. It mirrors the relationship dictated by the uses statements in the various units and program itself. I discuss these relationships further when I delve into uses in detail below.

Every unit has three parts: a unit heading, an interface part, and an implementation part. The interface part declares what in the unit is public, that is, available to those units and programs that use the unit. The implementation part implements the functions and procedures declared in the interface part and may contain other Pascal code whose scope is limited strictly to the implementation part.

The Unit Heading

The unit heading is analogous to the program heading. It appears at the start of the unit and gives a name to the unit. The syntax is trivial:

```
UNIT unitname;
```

The only other requirement for units is that the compiler swapping option must be turned on before the unit heading:

```
{$S+}
```

The Interface Part of a Unit

The interface part of a unit is initiated by the key word INTERFACE. The interface part therefore may contain CONST, TYPE, and VAR declarations as does a normal Pascal program. All constants, types, and variables declared in the interface part behave as if they were declared in the main program's outermost part. This is another way of saying that these declarations are ***public***. People also describe the situation by saying that the interface declarations are *exported* to the rest of the program (actually to any program or unit that uses the unit in question).

After the CONST, TYPE, and VAR parts of the interface, there may be declarations of procedures and functions. That is, the procedures and functions whose code will appear in the implementation part have their headings in the interface part. The idea here is that the interface part tells you what procedures and functions are available in the unit and how to call them. It does not reveal any details of how the procedures and functions are actually implemented. This allows the implementation to change without requiring the users to recompile their own code. This may seem trivial on first glance, but it is actually one of the important ideas in modern programming language design.

The interface part of the unit ends with the last procedure or function declaration. The interface may contain no code. It must declare at least one procedure or function; that is, you cannot have a unit that contains only data.

The Implementation Part of a Unit

The implementation part of a unit is started with the key word IMPLEMENTATION. It is the private part of the unit and may be changed without requiring the users of the unit to recompile their code. This statement is only true if no change is made to the interface part. The following things that cannot change are

- The specific constants, types, and variables declared cannot change. Any additions or subtractions here will cause a need for recompilation.
- The headings of functions and procedures cannot change: the number and types of parameters and the return types of functions must be untouched.

The implementation part of a unit may have its own CONST, TYPE, and VAR declarations. Anything declared there is strictly private to the unit and cannot be referred to anywhere else in any program that uses the unit. The implementation part must contain code for all the functions and procedures declared in the interface part. It may also contain its own private procedures and functions (which may be called from within the public procedures and functions inside the unit, but may not be called from outside the unit). The code for the implementation of the interface procedures and functions must not repeat the entire heading of the procedure or function. Only the key word PROCEDURE or the key word FUNCTION must appear, followed by the name used in the interface declaration. For example, in the probs unit of Adventure 3 you find the declaration

```
FUNCTION solved (which: problems) :
  BOOLEAN;
```

In the implementation part of probs, the code for solved begins with

```
FUNCTION solved;
```

Any repetition of the heading other than the parts indicated will cause a syntax error to be generated by the compiler.

The Uses Statements

Units are used by other units and by Pascal programs. The UCSD Pascal language provides the uses statement for telling the compiler which units are being used. Uses statements immediately follow the program heading in Pascal main programs. Units may also use other units and the uses statements in units immediately follows the INTERFACE key word.

Each unit that is used in a program or other unit must be located by the compiler in a library code file. I shall not go into all the details of libraries in UCSD Pascal. The compiler is nice enough to provide a way to avoid the hassle of having to install units in libraries before using them. The compiler option U may be used to specify a code file to search for a unit at compile time. This is best illustrated with examples. In the main program of Adventure 3 you see

```
PROGRAM mtadvent;
{$S+}
    USES applestuff,
{$Umt1.code}      advdata,
{$Uprobs.code}    probs,
{$Ucmds3.code}    cmds3,
{$Ucmds2.code}    cmds2,
{$Ucmds1.code}    cmds1,
{$uloc.code}      locs;
```

The first item to note is that the uses statement allows a list of units to be specified. The total number of units allowed is limited by the number of Pascal segments available. This may vary from system to system. I never exceed it, so I say no more. You should be aware that there is a limit.

In the above example, each unit except the first has a {$U . . . compiler option preceding the name of the unit. If no {$U . . . appears, the compiler will search SYSTEM.LIBRARY for the unit. In Apple Pascal, SYSTEM.LIBRARY happens to contain a unit called *applestuff*. This unit provides the random function used in the advdata unit of Adventure 3. If you enter Adventure 3 in your system, you should replace the reference to applestuff to the equivalent unit (or provide random in some other way).

When a unit in the uses statement list is preceded by a {$U . . . option, the file name specified there is used by the compiler. This file must be a code file and must contain the code generated by the Pascal compiler when that unit was compiled. For example, mtl.code must contain the code for the advdata unit. If no such file exists, or if the file does not contain code, the compiler will issue an appropriate error message and will no doubt have great difficulty continuing.

You can now see that if a unit is to be compiled, all the units that it uses must be compiled first. This means that the uses statements in all the units of a program cannot contain any circularities. For example if Unit A said USES B, Unit B said USES C, and Unit C said USES A, you could never compile A! Why? Because in order to compile A you would first have to compile B because A uses B. In order to compile B, you would first have to compile C because B uses C. But in order to compile C, you would first have to compile A, because C uses A! Therefore, in order to compile A, you would first have to compile A—but that is impossible: you can't compile A before you compile A.

In Adventure 3, mt1.text must be compiled first to provide a code file containing the advdata unit. Then cmds3 and probs can be compiled in any order (they both use advdata). cmds2 can be compiled at any time because it does not use any other unit, but it must be compiled before cmds1, which uses it. cmds1 may be compiled after advdata, probs, and cmds2 are available. locs is the last unit of Adventure 3 to be compiled: it uses all the others. Finally, the program of Adventure 3 cannot be compiled until all the units of Adventure 3 (including locs) have been compiled.

LINKING PROGRAMS THAT HAVE UNITS

When you compile the main program of Adventure 3, the resulting code file may not be X(ecuted. If you try, the system will tell you:

```
Must L(ink first
```

The process of linking combines the separately compiled main program code file with all the code files for the units that it uses. The result is another code file, which is X(ecutable. In the UCSD system, linking is accomplished by using the L(ink command. This requires that the SYSTEM .LINKER program be on line.

Using the UCSD linker is relatively simple. It will engage you in a dialogue. It wants to know the names of all the files it needs in order to perform the linking process. It starts out by requesting

```
HOST FILE?
```

This file will always be the code file of the main program for our adventure games. Thus, respond with

```
HOST FILE? mtadvent
```

assuming that the main program has been compiled into mtadvent.code.

The linker continues by asking:

```
LIB FILE?
```

The response here should be the name of a .code file containing one of your units. The question will be repeated and you should respond by giving the names of all the .code files for the units required by the program:

```
LIB FILE?  mt1
LIB FILE?  probs
LIB FILE?  cmds3
LIB FILE?  cmds2
LIB FILE?  cmds1
LIB FILE?  locs
LIB FILE?
```

When you are finished, simply pressing RETURN will cause the linker to stop prompting for lib files. It then requests:

```
MAP FILE?
```

It is safe to answer this by again pressing RETURN. The map file is a file of technical information generated by the linker. You won't need this file in the ordinary course of linking adventure games.

At this point in the dialogue, the linker will read in all the code for the program being linked and finally will ask:

```
OUTPUT FILE?
```

For Adventure 3, respond with

```
OUTPUT FILE?  advent
```

The linked program will be placed in the advent.code file. You may then execute the adventure game by commanding the system to X(ecute and answering with advent when it asks Execute what program?

MAINTAINING A PROGRAM WRITTEN WITH UNITS

One of the advantages of using units is that you have less compiling to do than with large, monolithic programs. Whenever you change a unit, you do not necessarily have to recompile all the units in the entire program. The general rules are as follows:

- If you make a change in a unit that does not involve changing the interface part of the unit, all you need to do to incorporate the change is

    1. Recompile the unit
    2. Relink the program

- If you change the interface to a unit, you must recompile all other parts of the program that use the unit. In order to know which parts are involved, it is good to keep a diagram of the uses relations between all the units in your program. I showed such a diagram for Adventure 3 in Chapter 25, Fig. 25-7.

Starting from the top of the uses diagram, work downwards until you find the unit whose interface has changed. Then recompile that unit and all the units (including the main program) above that unit. Then relink the program in order to incorporate the change. If you are careful, this rule is not difficult to follow. On the other hand, if you don't keep a good uses diagram and are careless about recompiling all the units that can "see" a change to an interface, your program will start behaving very strangely. When you have "weird" bugs that you simply do not understand, one good idea is to just recompile everything.

To illustrate the above rule, consider the probs unit of Adventure 3. If the interface to probs is changed, all units above probs must be recompiled. This consists of the units probs itself, cmds1, locs, and the main program.

A unit is considered to be *above* another unit if there is an arrow or sequence of arrows in the uses diagram leading from the other unit to the unit in question. For example, if we start at locs, there is an arrow pointing directly to probs. Thus, locs is above probs. Starting at main, we can reach any other unit by a sequence or arrows. Thus, main is above all units in the program. In other words, main must always be recompiled if the interface to any unit changes.

28

Problems in Adventure 3

The problems in Adventure 3 are more complex than those in earlier adventures. They pose their own special implementation difficulties. In this chapter I dwell on the techniques used to implement the problems in Adventure 3.

THE PROBS UNIT

In the introduction to Adventure 3 and again in the last chapter, I touched on the probs unit. The probs unit exemplifies a new approach to problems in general. The solved function in the probs unit is used to centralize the evaluation of complicated Boolean expressions that are part of the problem-solving process. This makes the representation of problems in general both simpler and more systematic.

Solved is a Boolean function, that is, it returns either true or false. It takes a single parameter, which of type problems. The enumerated type

```
problems= (wmmhappy, luretrolls,
           bonetrolls, canopen, ftofyouth);
```

is declared in the interface of the probs unit. Its values represent the individual Boolean expressions needed for the problems in Adventure 3. The units that use the probs unit can "see" the declaration of problems and can pass those values to solved.

The solved function consists of a simple case statement controlled by the parameter which:

```
CASE which OF
     wmmhappy: solved :=
    (wmmhas= wmmwants) AND
     etc.
```

solved simplifies the approach to problem representation. Take for example the problems value luretrolls and its appearance in solved:

```
luretrolls:      (troltime > 0) AND
                 ((turns – troltime)> 0) AND
                 ((turns – troltime) < 25);
```

The complicated expression for luretrolls is

evaluated once and for all in **solved**. The rest of the code for the adventure can use statements like

```
IF solved (luretrolls)
THEN
```

or

```
IF NOT solved (luretrolls)
THEN
```

which are simple and easy to understand. The adventure game writer may think in terms of **solved** rather than in terms of the more complicated expressions hidden inside **solved**.

Hiding complicated problem expressions inside **solved** can be a debugging aid as well. Suppose there are many different references to a given Boolean expression (like the one corresponding to **luretrolls**). Suppose the formulation of the expression was incorrect. With **solved** you only have to fix one place in the program. The calls to **solved** don't need to change. Without **solved**, you would have to fix all the places where the expression is used, making sure that the expressions in all those places were identical. Once you found all the places and edited in the change, you would have to recompile all the units or programs involved. With **solved** you only have to recompile the probs unit (assuming that the fix did not change the interface to the unit). In the course of debugging a long and complicated adventure, this simplification can be a great advantage.

THE PROBLEMS IN ADVENTURE 3

This part of the chapter describes the various problems that must be solved in order to successfully complete Adventure 3.

The Trolls

Adventure 3 presents the trolls, a hairy, hungry bunch of monsters who will eat you if you are not careful. The trolls start out at the **trolls** location (where else?) and there are several facets to their behavior in the adventure:

- The first time you see them is the first time you visit the trolls location.

    1. If you arrive at the trolls location empty handed, you will be promptly dispatched. In short, the trolls will eat you!
    2. If you are carrying the bones with you when you arrive at **trolls** the first time, the trolls will follow you. You may thus lure the trolls away from their mountain lair. This turns out to be the only way to get past their location.

- The trolls will follow you (as long as you are carrying the bones) to any of the locations in the collection **trollocs**:

    trolls, slope2, steep2, peak2, saddle1, col1, saddle2, mtcave1a, mtcave1b, trail5, rut1, ridge2

    If you drop the bones at any time before solving the trolls problem and subsequently visit one of these locations, the trolls will materialize there and promptly eat you.
- The trolls may be pacified by luring them to **mtcave1a** and dropping the bones there.
- If you do succeed in pacifying the trolls, their troll teeth will forever after be located in **mtcave1a**. You can pick them up and carry them elsewhere, drop them, return to **mtcave1a** and there will be another tooth there! The trolls break their teeth crunching away on the bones you drop in **mtcave1a** and their teeth then litter the floor of said cave.
- Once the trolls have been pacified, they no longer bother you. They are removed from the adventure forever after.

Finding the Bones

The bones are initially located in the cave beneath the cellar beneath the monastery. In order to get into the cave, a hatch must be opened. This requires that you have the keys with you. You must find the keys (located elsewhere in the adventure) and return to the cellar in order to get into the cave.

Of course, just finding the bones is not enough. You must also carry them with you back to the trolls location in order to solve the trolls problem. There are various subtle hints to this effect in the descriptions that accompany being eaten by the trolls when you fail to have the bones. After a few failures, you will figure out what to do.

Making the Wise Man of the Mountain Happy

Strewn about the map of Adventure 3 are many seeming treasures. These treasures are fakes as far as the wise man of the mountain is concerned. He is more interested in "spiritual" things. If you bring the fakes to him and drop them at the wmm location, you eventually get reprimanded for your efforts. The problem of making the wise man of the mountain happy involves:

- Realizing that the conventional treasures are of no interest to the wmm.
- Figuring out which items in the adventure will make the wmm happy.
- Bringing all the wmm treasures to the wmm location and dropping them there.

There is a subtle way to figure out which items the wmm values. If you bring something to the wmm location that the wmm considers to be of true value and drop it there, it disappears completely. In other words if you say drop x and then try to carry x, you will get "I don't see any x here" in reply. This will seem strange at first, but the idea is that the wmm is immediately and silently spiriting those items away to his own private collection.

Opening the Doorway to the Fountain of Youth

There is a secret word that the wise man of the mountain will reveal after you have brought him all his true treasures. This word, if uttered in the cellar beneath the monastery, has the effect of opening the door to the fountain of youth. If you then go down you will win the game.

IMPLEMENTING ADVENTURE 3 PROBLEMS

I now delve into the Pascal details of Adventure 3 problems. I shall occasionally use the precondition—postcondition terminology of Chapter 15. If you skipped that chapter earlier, now would be a good time to read it.

The Trolls: First Encounter

The first implementation headache involves the trolls. The problem is how do you prevent the trolls from "following" the player before the first encounter with them? If you look at the map of Adventure 3, you will see that it is impossible to reach the trolls location without first passing through at least two or three other locations in the trollocs set. The solution to this implementation problem is implicit in the use of the variable troltime.

The variable troltime is an integer. It is initialized to 0 in the initialization part of the advdata unit. As long as troltime remains equal to 0, the trolls can only appear at the trolls location. The trolocation procedure, invoked whenever the value of location is one of those in trollocs and the trolls are still "alive" handles this:

```
IF (troltime = 0) AND (location = trolls)
THEN
        . . .
```

The trolocation procedure is responsible for more than just the first encounter with the trolls. The other code in trolocation must be written so that it will not be invoked before the first encounter. The rest of the code consists of two IF statements. In both of these statements the condition

```
solved (luretrolls)
```

must be met before the statements will be executed. In turn, the Boolean expression for the luretrolls problem contains the condition

```
troltime > 0
```

All in all, troltime guards the first encounter and forces it to occur at location = trolls.

What Happens at Trolls the First Time?

The trolls problem as described earlier requires that the player be carrying the bones in order to avoid being eaten. This is easy to express in Pascal:

```
IF bones IN stash
THEN
BEGIN
   troltime := turns; {solve luretrolls
   problem}
   show (trhungry);
END
ELSE
    trolmeal
{END IF bones IN stash};
```

If the player is carrying the bones:

```
bones IN stash
```

the luretrolls problem is solved (for the time being) by setting troltime equal to the value of turns. Of course, by now the value of turns must be > 0. If the player should be unlucky enough not to have the bones, a procedure called trolmeal is invoked. Needless to say, the trolls' meal is not potatoes and gravy!

Here are the preconditions and postconditions for this problem:

Preconditions:

```
(troltime = 0) AND (location = trolls)
bones IN stash
```

Postcondition

```
troltime > 0
```

Of course, if the preconditions are only partially met, the trolls eat the player and the game is ended.

The Trolls: After the First Encounter

The problem expression for luretrolls has the following component:

```
(turns - troltime <= 25)
```

This means that the player must get rid of the trolls within 25 turns after first luring them. This is plenty of time, once you know how. It may take a few games (and troll meals) to learn how to get rid of the trolls. After all, the trolls have to have some fun too.

Getting Rid of the Trolls. In order to get rid of the trolls for good, the player must

1. Lure the trolls to location mtcave1a.
2. Drop the bones and scram.

The trolls will remain in mtcave1a and merrily feast on the bones left behind. Then they will melt away into the mountains, never to appear again. The implementation problem this poses is how to detect the successful completion of 1 and 2 above. In particular, how do you detect when the player has left the cave after dropping the bones there in the presence of the trolls?

There is a special procedure in Adventure 3, called ckproblems. It is silently invoked after every command. It is called in order to see if the execution of a command has caused any problems to be solved. The current implementation of Adventure 3 caters to two situations:

1. The player has successfully lured the trolls to mtcave1a and dropped the bones. This situation may be detected while the player is still in location mtcave1a.
2. The trolls have been disposed of and the player has left mtcave1a. It is at this juncture that the tooth is made to materialize in the cave: part of the problem solution is to return to the cave and find the tooth. This takes courage on the player's part because he knows the trolls were there when he last visited the cave. The wmm must be given the tooth (among other objects) in order for the player to win the game.

The first situation is detected as follows:

Precondition

```
solved (luretrolls) AND solved (bonetrolls)
```

Postcondition

trlives = FALSE
NOT (bones IN whatshere[mtcave1a])

The second situation is detected as follows:

Precondition

(NOT trlives) AND (location <> mtcave1a)

Postcondition

tooth IN whatshere[mtcave1a]

The first clause of the second situation is only made true by successfully achieving the first situation as you can see in the postconditions for the first situation.

The Wise Man of the Mountain

The wise man of the mountain sits on the grandest peak in the mountain range and dispenses "wisdom." The player must bring the wmm (abbreviation for wise man of the mountain) the goodies that he deems valuable. The wmm goodies are not the conventional treasures like gold and silver. Part of the challenge to the player is to determine what objects the wmm might desire.

There is one obvious hint that the player receives: every time the player drops one of the wmm goodies at location wmm, that object will disappear. In other words, if the player says:

drop incense

and then

carry incense

the response will be:

I don't see any incense here.

The object goes directly into the collection owned by the wmm.

In addition the player must remove everything else from the wmm's sight in order to make him happy. That is, whatshere[wmm] must be the empty set of objects. This may be the most difficult part of the problem to solve. The wmm gives only a vague hint. In the descriptions database, the description corresponding to $wmmharp contains an exhortation to take certain items from the wmm's sight.

The Secret Word

When the wmm has all the objects he desires and the wmm location is bare of all other trash, the wmm will reveal the "secret word." The word is wadda. The player must return to the cellar and then say

wadda

in order to open the hatch leading to the fountain of youth. Once that has been accomplished, going down from the cellar brings you to the fountain and wins the game. If you try to say "wadda" before you have made the wmm happy, your guide will refuse to understand. This is controlled by a Boolean variable saidwadda. It may only be set to true when the canopen problem has been solved.

Preconditions

(wmmhas= wmmwants) AND
(whatshere[wmm]= [ ])
(location = cellar)
Command given is: "wadda"

Postcondition

canopen = TRUE

29

Other Techniques Used in Adventure 3

As in the other adventures I have presented, there are a number of ad hoc Pascal coding techniques used in Adventure 3. This chapter is devoted to explaining why they are there and how they work.

PUTTING MORE INTO THE DATABASE

The descriptions database for Adventure 3 contains more than just descriptions of locations. The enumerated type rooms of Adventure 2 has become the type descs in Adventure 3. The identifiers in the declaration of descs fall into two sequences: those before nowhere and those after nowhere. The identifiers before nowhere comprise the locations for Adventure 3. There is a subrange declaration

```
rooms = start . . nowhere;
```

that indicates this. The identifiers that follow nowhere all correspond to special descriptions used in Adventure 3.

Various Descriptions Involving the Trolls

The trolls play an important part in Adventure 3. They and their actions are described in great detail as the game progresses. Rather than embed this description in the game code itself, it has been put into the database. The following "placenames" correspond to troll descriptions:

- trhungry—When you arrive at the trolls' location carrying the bones, you get this message. It tells you that the trolls exist and that they are eager to eat you. It also boldly hints that the bones are connected with their interest. You will know this for sure if you played the game before and managed to get eaten.
- trfollow—This is what the player is told when the trolls are following him or her. It describes the trolls and hints at the solution of the trolls problem by continuing to mention their interest in bones.
- trtalk—The player gets only one chance to read

this message! It describes the player's demise upon reaching the trolls' location without carrying the bones.

- tgablure—When the player lures the trolls to mtcave1a, he or she will still be carrying the bones. This is the big fat hint to drop them there.
- tgabbones—If the player succeeds in luring the trolls to mtcave1 a and is smart enough to drop the bones there, he or she is rewarded with this message. It describes the trolls sudden switch in interest from you to the bones you have dropped. It also hints at the tooth problem by mentioning breaking teeth. The player should connect this hint to the wmm hint later about troll's teeth.

Descriptions Involving the Wise Man of the Mountain (wmm)

There are many entries in the Adventure 3 database that involve the wmm. Most of them are things that the wmm may say to the player at some point during the play of the game. Here is a summary of the wmm related entries:

- wmmsp1, wmmsp2, wmmsp3, wmmsp4, wmmsp5—These are five "spiels" of varying length that the wmm gives the player on second and subsequent visits to his domain. They contain hints, varying in their degree of obviousness, about the objects that the wmm truly desires as treasures.
- wmmhello—This is the initial speech delivered by the wmm when the player first visits the wmm location. It is a general description of the fact that the player should find various treasures and deliver them to the wmm. It deliberately misleads the player (or tries to) into thinking that the treasures desired are of the conventional variety.
- wmmharp—This speech is delivered as soon as the player manages to bring enough bogus treasures to the wmm. The number of fakes delivered so far is recorded in the variable wmmcount. How wmmcount is kept up to date is discussed later in this chapter. If wmmcount is greater than or equal to three, this message is displayed. It gives the player the rude surprise of finding out that what the wmm means by treasures is not the usual meaning. It also contains a hint about the trolls tooth.
- wmmblab—When the player succeeds in gathering all the wmm's true treasures and delivering them to location wmm, the wmm spills his secret. The location of the fountain of youth is dispensed along with a magic word for opening the doorway to that fountain.

The Fountain Description

The desc identifier fountain corresponds to the description of the fountain of youth. This is displayed only at the very end of the game when the player has succeeded in opening the hatch leading to the fountain. It could have been made an ordinary location, but because the game ends as soon as the player arrives, it was easier to handle it as a special description.

Modifications to the Show Procedure

The addition of descriptions not corresponding to adventure game locations could have been accomplished in another way. I could have created a separate database. The disadvantage of this is the requirement for two more open files during the play of the adventure game. Each file opened while the UCSD Pascal program is running causes a permanent requirement for RAM memory. The more RAM used for file, the less RAM there is available for coding features into the adventure. Therefore, I decided to extend rooms to descs as I have already begun to explain. This causes the show procedure to change, as I shall now discuss.

The show procedure simply prints lines from the descriptions database on the player's screen. In Adventure 2, these descriptions were limited to adventure game locations. In Adventure 3 they can include descriptions of troll activity and speeches given by the wmm. Recall from Chapter 16 that show only displays the description of a location when the variable chgloc is true. During the development of Adventure 3 situations arose when chgloc was still false, yet a description other than a location description was needed by the Pascal code. This required that show be changed in order to force out nonlocation descriptions when chgloc was false.

The solution involves the use of the intrinsic function ord. The ord function may be used to compare the position of two identifiers in the declaration of an enumerated type. If one identifier appears after another in the declaration, the ord value for the second identifier will be greater than that for the first identifier. For the descs enumerated type, all identifiers corresponding to special descriptions come after the identifier nowhere. The ord function can detect this as follows:

```
ord (where > ord (nowhere)
```

This is one of the additions to the tests used in show to determine when to print a description and when not to print it.

An unexpected side effect of nonlocation descriptions also turned up in Adventure 3. Part of the act of showing a location to the player is showing all the objects that happen to be there. In Pascal terms, the procedure showgoodies, which describes the objects present, is invoked from inside the procedure show, which describes the unchanging physical appearance of the location. When nonlocation descriptions were added, the listing of objects present in certain locations started to be repeated. Whenever there were objects present in a location and a nonlocation description was printed while the player visited that location, the objects there were described twice. For example, the first time at location trolls, the trolls location description was given; then the objects present were listed; then the trtalk message was printed; then the objects present were listed a second time.

The solution to the multiple showing of objects at a location also involved the use of ord. The idea is—never call showgoodies for a nonlocation description. This is accomplished by placing the call to showgoodies inside an IF test that uses ord:

```
IF ord (where) < ord (nowhere)
THEN
    showgoodies;
```

A Few Pitfalls to Watch Out For

In the process of making rooms into descs some problem areas were noted. Here is a brief list, so you can watch out for them when you start writing your own adventure games.

Value Out of Range Errors. There still exists a rooms type in Adventure 3. It is declared as a subrange of descs:

```
rooms = start . . nowhere;
```

If you declare variables of type rooms—for example, loop control variables for loops that range over the values in rooms—you must be careful not to assign those variables values that are "out of range." For example

```
VAR
    r: rooms;
BEGIN
    FOR r := start TO fountain DO
```

Because ord (fountain) > ord (nowhere), fountain is not a legitimate value of type rooms. The Pascal compiler unfortunately does not check this in the for statement. The check does occur when the program runs, however. The assignment r := fountain causes the program to come to a screeching halt. The moral of the story is—Be careful!

MAKEDESC Considerations. The source for the adventure game database must be handled carefully. The main requirement is that there must be a placename description line for every identifier in the descs enumerated type. Even if an identifier has no description actually associated with it, there must be a placename description line for it. In particular, nowhere must have its own placename description line. If this rule is not followed, the index to the database may get out of whack. That is, the index entry for a given identifier may point to the wrong description in the database.

CODING TECHNIQUES TO GET AROUND UCSD LIMITATIONS

There are two places in the implementation of Adventure 3 where the programming make look arbitrary at first glance. The first is the main program block:

```
IF ord (location) < ord (steep1)
THEN
    t1 (location)
ELSE
    t2 (location)
{ END IF ord . . . }
```

The second occurs in the initialization part of the advdata unit:

```
BEGIN
    init1;
    init2;
END;
```

In both of these places there are two procedures invoked. It might seem that either a single procedure or direct inline code might have been adequate in both cases. The explanation of the two instances of strange coding is that UCSD Pascal places a limit on the size of a procedure. If the amount of code generated by the procedure exceeds this limit, the compiler issues the error message:

```
Error 253: Procedure too long
```

and refuses to create a .CODE file for the program or unit being compiled.

When a procedure becomes too long, the solution is to break it apart. The result may be confusing when the program listing is read by someone later on. When you get Error 253 from the compiler, however, you are much more likely to be frustrated than confused.

TRICKERY IN showgoodies

The showgoodies procedure, which lists the objects present in a given location, has been improved as compared to the similar procedure in Adventure 2. The guide uses good English grammar in the descriptions. This is accomplished by the use of a few extra set variables declared and initialized in the cmds3 unit. The variables are called plurals, somes, and useans and are all of type collection, that is, SET OF objects. The objects in Adventure 3 are divided into these three sets to indicate which pronoun to use when mentioning the corresponding object. For example, the object keys belongs to the set plurals. When keys are present in a given location the guide will say

```
There are some keys here.
```

The object leather is in the set somes. When describing it, the guide will say

```
There is some leather here.
```

The object axe is in the set useans—in fact, it is currently the only object in useans. The guide will say

```
There is an axe here.
```

when describing it. Finally, the object scroll belongs to none of the sets. The guide will describe it with

```
There is a scroll here.
```

This is a little tough, admittedly. However, the existence of Pascal set variables makes it so painless to implement that I couldn't resist.

30

Writing Your Own Adventures

If you have read this book carefully and studied the examples presented, you should now be ready to write your own adventure games. You have all the tools necessary, and the only limit now is your own imagination and perseverance. The purpose of this final chapter is to present several final suggestions. I shall discuss possible extensions to the adventure game programs in this book, especially Adventure 3. Finally, before saying farewell, I present a possible step-by-step approach to the game writing process from start to finish.

EXTENDING ADVENTURE 3

There are several directions you might take if you were interested in extending Adventure 3. You may think of ideas beyond those presented here.

- Adding Locations

  Adventure 3 has no maze. You might add one, starting somewhere in one of the two caves. You might add more mountainpeaks—currently all the peaks contain important objects of interest to the wise man of the mountain. This is somewhat of a giveaway to one of the central problems of the adventure. Adding more peaks and possibly relocating some of the fake or trash objects to those peaks might make the game more interesting. You might also add more nooks and crannies in the general locations of the game. A final possibility would be to add rooms inside the monastery—either as a diversion, or possibly containing one of the wmm treasures.

- Adding Problems

  There are only a few problems in Adventure 3. Adding more would definitely make the game more interesting. It would also be a good opportunity for you to practice your problem inventing and problem implementing skills. There is more on possibilities in this area later in the chapter.

Extending the Map

When you add new locations to an adventure that uses a descriptions database, you have several steps to perform and several things to worry about.

1. The new locations must be given names and added to the descs enumerated types definition. They should be placed in the section of the declaration corresponding to actual locations, that is, before location nowhere.
2. For each new location, a description must be added to the database. To accomplish this, the MAKEDESC source file must be updated to include a placename instruction line for each new location, followed by the text of the descriptions.
3. The added descriptions must be placed in the MAKEDESC source file in the same position and order as the corresponding names were added to the descs enumerated type.
4. The MAKE80 generator must be run on the updated MAKEDESC source in order to generate a new database.
5. All the units and main programs of the adventure must be recompiled. This is because the descs types is in the interface of the lowest level unit in the program—everything else uses that unit.
6. The adventure game must be relinked after all its component parts have been recompiled.

Adding Problems to Adventure 3

There are any number of possibilities for adding problems to Adventure 3. New problems should fit in with the spirit of the game. They should fit with the setting and the feel of the game. Here are a few possibilities:

1. The shout command, so far, is used for atmosphere only. You could extend it in two ways, both of which could pose problems for the player.

   First, you could cover one of the important objects with snow. It would only be revealed if the player asked the guide to shout in its vicinity. Some of the descriptions already used in the game have hints to the effect that shouting might cause an avalanche. The second change to the shout command would, in the wrong places, cause an avalanche that buries the player and ends the game. The two new problems are thus to discover the buried object and to avoid being buried in the process. You might modify some more of the descriptions to insert bolder hints regarding shouting.
2. The only "roadblocks" in the current mountain adventure are the trolls and the locked door leading to the cave under the cellar. You could easily block other important passages. You might have a pile of boulders blocking the pass to an important peak and so on. How such problems would be solved by the player, I leave to your imagination.
3. You could make the tooth problem more difficult by making the tooth appear only once. Then after a certain number of turns, it would go away forever.
4. You could require some sort of toll in order to gain access to the wmm. The first time you visit his location, if you cannot provide the toll, you will be rudely dismissed and unable to regain access to the wmm until you do provide it. If you fail to bring the toll the first time, you will be unable to score the maximum number of points.

   The toll could involve almost anything. For example, you might have to discover some secret documents inside the monastery and decipher them to find a magic phrase that you must intone in the wmm's presence. I again leave to your imagination other possibilities.

USING A SKELETON ADVENTURE

Using the term *skeleton adventure* might bring to mind another game based on Halloween themes. However, in this case I have a different interpretation in mind. A *skeleton program* is a program outline, or partial program, that may serve as the starting point for writing many different incarnations of the same kind of program. By paring down the code for Adventure 3 to just those parts that you are likely to use in every adventure game, you will arrive at a skeleton adventure. When you begin writing a new adventure game, you will copy the skeleton adventure and use it as a starting point. In each new game, the code you add will differ as will the game you create.

Adventure 3 consists of a main program and six units. Each of these components can form the basis of part of a typical skeleton adventure. The main program retains the idea of a repeat statement with a CASE nested inside it. The case statement is based on the rooms enumerated type and invokes either the travel procedure, to cause a change of location, or a location procedure, to handle special action at the location, or a location procedure, to handle special action at the location in question. The form of the code is always the same; only the specifics vary from game to game.

Likewise, many of the procedures and functions of the units cmds1, cmds2, and cmds3 will be used by every adventure game in the process of handling commands. The specific commands implemented will vary, but the general outline of the code that handles them will remain the same. The same sort of reasoning applies to the units locs, probs, and advdata.

A Sample Skeleton Adventure

In Appendix A I present a listing of a skeleton adventure based on Adventure 3 and its division into units. You may use this skeleton as a basis for your own games or you may decide to create your own skeleton based on the techniques presented in this book and others you invent for yourself.

A SYSTEMATIC APPROACH TO WRITING ADVENTURES

Above all else, writing adventure games should be fun. The whole idea is to enjoy yourself. Create interesting games and let your friends and family try to solve the problems they pose. You can add to your enjoyment by having a "system." Approaching the software development process in an organized fashion can help you produce more games in a shorter period of time, with fewer bugs in them.

The following checklist is only a suggestion. You will probably deviate from it when you develop your own approaches to adventure game writing. But when you do, develop your own checklist. Then use it when you write your next game. See if you don't finish sooner and enjoy yourself more.

The Adventure Game Writer's Checklist

1. Draw the adventure map. Use a big sheet of paper and leave room for notations and additions and subtractions. You might create fragments of the map on smaller pieces of paper and transfer them to the larger map when you are satisfied with them. I use artists drawing paper bought in an office supply store for this purpose. Large size computer printout paper is also good.

   Remember to use the tricks I covered earlier. Note places on the map where problems need to be solved. Number the problems and either write brief descriptions of them beside the numbers on the map or somewhere else. Write down enough when you think of the problems so that you won't forget them later on.
2. Write the descriptions. When you have completed the map or at least derived enough of it to have a good idea of the overall flavor of the adventure game, sit down and start writing the descriptions of the game locations. This can be one of the most enjoyable parts of the game writing process. You have a chance here to pretend you are writing an adventure thriller. Exercise your imagination. Pretend you are actually in the adventure game and try to describe the places as you imagine they would be.

   Remember as you write descriptions to include hints. Problems that are difficult to solve may involve the player's discerning these hints and using them to deduce solutions. Try to make the hints substantial without being obvious.
3. Create the problems. I have belabored this aspect of adventure game writing enough. You know what to do and how to do it. Just one last time, I will say, "Be creative!"
4. Decide on the objects for the game. Many objects may be associated with problems, so you have a head start on this step. Decide which objects are essential to the game play and which are merely decorative or misleading. Try to keep a balance between the two categories.

   Think about where you want the various objects to be located at the start of the game. Make notations on your map indicating this information. Decide whether you want any trickery like that associated with the troll's tooth in Adventure 3. If you do, think about how you will implement the tricky parts.

5. Decide which commands the guide will recognize. I have barely scratched the surface of this subject. There are endless possibilities for interesting commands. Make sure that your intended commands won't be too hard for the command handling code to decipher.
6. Write the Pascal code for the adventure. Compile and link it and debug the program. When this step is finished, you will have your completed adventure. Again, you may start with the skeleton source files provided in Appendix A, or you may code "from scratch" if you decide upon a radically different organization for your program. Unless you are a very experienced programmer, the first approach is probably best for your first few games.

FAREWELL

I hope you enjoyed reading this book, and I hope you will enjoy writing your own adventures even more. I enjoy playing adventure games, but I think writing them is much more fun. If you have any comments or further interest in adventure games, feel free to send them along to me. May all your adventure games run the first time.

Appendices

Appendix A
Skeleton Adventure Program

In this Appendix I provide you with the listings of the skeleton adventure game as discussed in Chapter 30. These listings are derived from Adventure 3 and are organized into a main program and several units. The main program and each unit has a separate listing. There are a total of 7 listings in all.

SKELETON ADVENTURE MAIN PROGRAM

```
PROGRAM adventure;

(*$s+*)

    USES   applestuff,
           (*$usk1.code*) advdata,
           (*$uprobs.code*) probs,
           (*$ucmds3.code*) cmds3,
           (*$ucmds2.code*) cmds2,
           (*$ucmds1.code*) cmds1,
           (*$ulocs.code*) locs;

BEGIN

  REPEAT

    visited[location] :=
```

```
      visited[location] + 1;
    show (location);

    { the following CASE statement controls travel }
    { within the adventure.  it contains one case  }
    { label for each place in the adventure game.  }
    { the procedure 'travel' is passed the         }
    { destinations in each of the six directions:  }
    { n,s,e,w,u,d  which are reachable from the    }
    { location represented by the case label.  if  }
    { the location needs "special handling", then  }
    { a location procedure p<xyz> is invoked       }
    { instead (xyz is the location identifier).    }
    { if there are so many locations that this     }
    { CASE causes the procedure to become too      }
    { large, then a trick like that in adventure   }
    { 3 must be used to split the CASE into two   }
    { or more parts.                               }

    CASE location OF

      start:    travel (nowhere, nowhere, nowhere,
                        nowhere, nowhere, nowhere);

    END { CASE location OF};

  UNTIL done;

END.
```

SKELETON LOCATIONS PROCEDURES UNIT

```
{$s+}

UNIT locs;

  INTERFACE

    USES  applestuff,
          {$usk1.code} advdata,
          {$uprobs.code} probs,
          {$ucmds3.code} cmds3,
          {$ucmds2.code} cmds2,
          {$ucmds1.code} cmds1;

{ Location procedures: p<xxx> are declared in this }
```

```
{ interface. A location procedure only needs to    }
{ exist if a given location has special handling   }
{ that cannot be implemented in other ways.        }
{ See Adventure 2 and Adventure 3 for examples.  }

  IMPLEMENTATION

{ Put code for the location procedures: p<xxx> here}

BEGIN
END.
```

SKELETON COMMANDS UNIT 1

```
{---------------------------}
{ Source File: cmds1.text }
{---------------------------}

{-----------------------------------------------------}
{                                                     }
{   c  m  d  s  1      u  n  i  t                     }
{                                                     }
{ This unit contains all command processing           }
{ support procedures and functions.  Each             }
{ command in the adventure is carried out by a        }
{ procedure called p<cmd>, where <cmd> stands         }
{ for the name of the command, as typed by the        }
{ player: e.g. pcarry <===> carry command.            }
{ Some of the p<cmd> procedures are located in        }
{ this unit, the others are in cmds2 and cmds3.       }
{ Procedures and functions like travel, noway,        }
{ docommand, listen, and cmdlookup which are          }
{ invoked in order to recognize the command are       }
{ all located in this unit.                           }
{                                                     }
{-----------------------------------------------------}

{$s+}
UNIT cmds1;

  INTERFACE

    USES  applestuff,
          {$usk1.code} advdata,
          {$uprobs.code} probs,
          {$ucmds2.code} cmds2,
          {$ucmds3.code} cmds3;
```

```
PROCEDURE travel (

            nloc,
            sloc,
            eloc,
            wloc,
            uloc,
            dloc:   rooms);

PROCEDURE pcarry;
PROCEDURE pdrop;
PROCEDURE pshout;
PROCEDURE popen;
PROCEDURE pwadda;

  IMPLEMENTATION

VAR

  dchars:       SET OF char;

{-----------------------------------------------------}
{     c   k   p   r   o   b   l   e   m   s         }
{                                                     }
{ See if the player has solved any problems           }
{ because of the command just executed.               }
{-----------------------------------------------------}

PROCEDURE ckproblems;
BEGIN

  { This procedure may be used to check        }
  { indirectly for the solution of some        }
  { problems.  Look at Adventure #3 for        }
  { some good examples.                        }

END { PROCEDURE ckproblems };

{-----------------------------------------------------}
{     c   m   d   l   o   o   k   u   p             }
{                                                     }
{ Determine which command the player has typed       }
{ and dissect the command string into 'head'         }
{ and 'tail' for command verbs with objects.         }
{ This is the generic command lookup function.       }
{ It assumes the existence of an enumerated          }
```

```
{ type called cmds and an array of strings      }
{ called cmdname, indexed by cmds.  The string }
{ cmdname[xyz] contains the string which the    }
{ player must type in order to execute         }
{ command xyz.                                  }
{                                               }
{-----------------------------------------------}

FUNCTION cmdlookup : cmds;
VAR
  p:     INTEGER;
  lcmd: cmds;
BEGIN

  writeln;
  write ('your wish is my command> ');
  readln (command);

  p := pos (' ', command);
  { check for verb-object }

  IF p = 0
  THEN
  BEGIN


    head := command;
    tail := '';

  END
  ELSE
  BEGIN

    head := copy (command, 1, p-1);
    tail := copy (command, p+1, length(command)-p);

  END { IF p = 0 };

  cmdname[nocmd] := head;
  lcmd           := carry;

  WHILE head <> cmdname[lcmd] DO
    lcmd := succ (lcmd)
  { END DO };

  cmdlookup := lcmd;
```

```
END { FUNCTION cmdlookup };

{------------------------------------------------------------------}
{           p    s    c    o    r    e                            }
{                                                                  }
{ Calculate the number of points scored by the                    }
{ player up to this point in the game.                            }
{------------------------------------------------------------------}

FUNCTION pscore : INTEGER;
VAR
  r:    rooms;
  keepscore:    INTEGER;

BEGIN

  keepscore := 0;

  FOR r := start TO wmm
  DO
    IF visited[r] > 0
    THEN
      keepscore := keepscore + 5;

  IF saidwadda
  THEN
    keepscore := keepscore +
                  (350 - ord (fountain) - 24);

  IF location = fountain
  THEN
    keepscore := keepscore + 25;

  pscore := keepscore;

END { FUNCTION score };

{------------------------------------------------------------------}
{             l    i    s    t    e    n                          }
{                                                                  }
{ Dispatch calls to the command execution                         }
{ procedures ( p<cmd> as described in the                         }
{ header comment for this unit.)                                  }
{------------------------------------------------------------------}

PROCEDURE listen;
```

```
VAR
  lcmd: cmds;

  PROCEDURE lscore;
  BEGIN
    writeln ('If you should quit now, your score would be ');
    writeln (pscore, ' points of a possible 350.');
  END { PROCEDURE lscore };

  PROCEDURE lquit;
  VAR
    ch:   CHAR;
    {hold response for quit confirmation}
  BEGIN
    writeln ('are you sure you want to quit?');
    readln (ch);
    IF (ch = 'y') OR (ch = 'y')
    THEN
    BEGIN
      writeln ('you would have scored ', pscore, ' points.');
      exit (PROGRAM);
    END {IF (ch = 'y') ...};
  END { PROCEDURE lquit };

BEGIN

  REPEAT

    turns := turns + 1;
    lcmd  := cmdlookup;

    CASE lcmd OF

      take,
      carry:    pcarry;
      drop:     pdrop;
      help:     phelp;
      invent:   pinventory;
      score,
      tally:    lscore;
      look:     plook;
      quit:     lquit;
      nocmd:    ;

    END { CASE lcmd OF };
```

```
    ckproblems;
    { See if any problems were solved by the }
    { command issued by the player.          }

  UNTIL lcmd = nocmd;

END { PROCEDURE listen };

{-----------------------------------------------------}
{     d   o   c   o   m   m   a   n   d            }
{                                                     }
{ Call listen in a loop.  When the length of         }
{ head is greater than zero, the user has given}
{ a travel command so return the first letter  }
{ of 'head' to the caller.                        }
{-----------------------------------------------------}

FUNCTION docommand : CHAR;
BEGIN

  head   := '';
  tail   := '';
  chgloc := false;

  REPEAT

    listen;

  UNTIL length (head) > 0;
  docommand := head[1];

END { FUNCTION docommand };

{-----------------------------------------------------}
{       w   h   i   c   h   w   a   y              }
{                                                     }
{ Determine which way the player wishes to go. }
{-----------------------------------------------------}

FUNCTION whichway : directions;
VAR
  ch: CHAR;
  ww: directions;
BEGIN
  REPEAT
```

```
    ch        := docommand;
    whichway := x;

    CASE ch OF

      'n':       IF (head = 'n') OR (head = 'north')
                 THEN
                   whichway := n;

      's':       IF (head = 's') OR (head = 'south')
                 THEN
                   whichway := s;

      'e':       IF (head = 'e') OR (head = 'east')
                 THEN
                   whichway := e;

      'w':       IF (head = 'w') OR (head = 'west')
                 THEN
                   whichway := w;

      'u':       IF (head = 'u') OR (head = 'up')
                 THEN
                   whichway := u;

      'd':       IF (head = 'd') OR (head = 'down')
                 THEN
                   whichway := d;

      'q':       { empty for now };

    END { CASE ch OF };

  UNTIL ch IN dchars;

  writeln;

END { FUNCTION whichway };

{--------------------------------------------------}
{              n    o    w    a    y               }
{--------------------------------------------------}

PROCEDURE noway;
BEGIN
```

```
    writeln;
    writeln ('it is impossible to go in that direction.');
    chgloc := false;

  END { PROCEDURE noway };

  {-----------------------------------------------------}
  {              t    r    a    v    e    l             }
  {                                                     }
  { Handle travel to the next location.  The            }
  { possible destinations from the current room         }
  { or adventure location are passed to travel          }
  { parameters.  The value 'nowhere' means that         }
  { there is no way to go in the corresponding          }
  { direction.                                            }
  {-----------------------------------------------------}

  PROCEDURE travel;

    PROCEDURE newloc (loc:descs);
    BEGIN

      IF loc = nowhere
      THEN
        noway
      ELSE
      BEGIN
        location := loc;
        chgloc   := true;
      END { IF loc = nowhere };

    END { PROCEDURE newloc };

    PROCEDURE wingame;
    BEGIN

      show (fountain);
      writeln ('You scored a total of ', pscore);
      writeln (' points out of a possible 350.');
      exit (PROGRAM);

    END { PROCEDURE wingame };

  BEGIN      {***** t  r  a  v  e  l  ****}
```

```
  CASE whichway OF

    n:  newloc (nloc);
    s:  newloc (sloc);
    e:  newloc (eloc);
    w:  newloc (wloc);
    u:  newloc (uloc);
    d:  newloc (dloc)
    x:  BEGIN
          writeln ('I do not understand that.');
          writeln ('Please try another command');
        END;

  END { CASE whichway OF };

END { PROCEDURE travel };

{-----------------------------------------------}
{          p   c   a   r   r   y                }
{                                               }
{ Implement the carry command.  Call the        }
{ function 'objlookup' to determine which       }
{ object (if any) has been requested.  Then     }
{ call 'ckgoodies' to see if that object is     }
{ present in the current location.  If so, the  }
{ object is added to the set 'stash' and also   }
{ removed from the set 'whatshere[location]'.   }
{-----------------------------------------------}

PROCEDURE pcarry;
VAR
  it: goodies;
BEGIN

  it := objlookup;

  IF NOT ckgoodies (it)
  THEN
  BEGIN

    write ('I don''t see any ');
    write (tail);
    writeln (' here.');

  END
  ELSE
```

```
  BEGIN

    writeln ('Ok');

    stash := stash + [it];
    whatshere[location] :=
        whatshere[location] - [it];

  END { IF NOT it IN ... };

END { PROCEDURE pcarry };

{-----------------------------------------------------}
{           p   d   r   o   p                         }
{                                                     }
{ Implement the drop command.  similar in             }
{ action to the carry command (q.v.).                 }
{-----------------------------------------------------}

PROCEDURE pdrop;
VAR
  it: goodies;
BEGIN

  it := objlookup;

  IF NOT (it IN stash)
  THEN
  BEGIN

    write ('You are not carrying any ');
    writeln (tail);

  END
  ELSE
  BEGIN

    writeln ('Ok');
    stash := stash - [it];

END { PROCEDURE pdrop };

BEGIN

  dchars :=
```

```
    ['q', 'n', 's', 'e', 'w', 'u', 'd', 'x'];

END.
```

SKELETON COMMANDS UNIT 2

```
{-----------------------------------------------------------}
{                                                           }
{        c  m  d  s  2     u  n  i  t                       }
{                                                           }
{ This unit contains the procedure phelp.  The              }
{ help command needs no access to data in unit              }
{ 'advdata'.  It does use procedure 'show',                 }
{ however, and hence USES unit cmds3.                       }
{-----------------------------------------------------------}

{$s+}

UNIT cmds2;

  INTERFACE

    USES applestuff,
         {$usk1.code} advdata,
         {$ucmds3.code} cmds3;

PROCEDURE phelp;

  IMPLEMENTATION

VAR

  asked:          INTEGER;

PROCEDURE phelp;
BEGIN

  IF asked > 2
  THEN
    show (helpspiel)
  ELSE
  BEGIN

    writeln ('Help is on the way');
    asked := asked + 1;
```

```
  END;

END { PROCEDURE phelp };

BEGIN

  asked := 0;

END.
```

SKELETON COMMANDS UNIT 3

```
{----------------------------------------}
{ source file: cmds3.text               }
{----------------------------------------}

{-------------------------------------------------------}
{                                                       }
{  c  m  d  s  3      u  n  i  t                        }
{                                                       }
{ This unit contains procedures implementing            }
{ commands.  The particular commands implemented}
{ herein need access to the unit advdata, but           }
{ not to the unit 'probs'.                              }
{                                                       }
{-------------------------------------------------------}

{$s+}

UNIT cmds3;

  INTERFACE

    USES  applestuff,
          {$usk1.code} advdata;

TYPE

  directions     = (n,s,e,w,u,d,x);
  cmds           = (carry, drop, help, score, invent,
                    take, tally, look, quit, nocmd);

  pname          = STRING[40];
  storyline      = STRING[80];
  byte           = 0..255;
```

```
   whichsect       = (indexsection, descsection);

   placerec        =

     RECORD

       CASE section: whichsection OF

         indexsection:    (  tableentry:    INTEGER);
         descsection:     (  name:         pname;
                             id:           INTEGER;
                             dbegin:       INTEGER;
                             dend:         INTEGER;
                             link:         byte);
     END;

VAR

   xfile:          FILE OF placerec;
   narrate:        FILE OF storyline;

   places:         ARRAY [descs] OF placerec;

   command:        STRING;
   head:           STRING;
   tail:           STRING;

   cmdname:        ARRAY[cmds] OF STRING;

   chgloc:         BOOLEAN;
   { has player moved since last cmd? }

PROCEDURE pinventory;
PROCEDURE plook;
PROCEDURE show (where:descs);
PROCEDURE showgoodies;
FUNCTION  objlookup: goodies;
FUNCTION  ckgoodies (it: goodies) : BOOLEAN;

   IMPLEMENTATION

VAR

   r:              descs;
   plurals:        SET OF goodies;
   somes:          SET OF goodies;
```

```
  useans:         SET OF goodies;
  { for benefit of showgoodies }

{---------------------------------------------------------}
{               s    h    o    w                           }
{                                                          }
{ Retrieve descriptions from the database                 }
{ and display them on the player's console.               }
{ The argument to show is of type 'descs'                 }
{ which includes descriptions of situations               }
{ and spoken words as well as descriptions                }
{ of locations.  Show uses the ord function               }
{ to detect what kind of description is                   }
{ involved.  The description of locations                 }
{ suppressed if the player has not changed                }
{ locations or if the location has been                   }
{ visited recently.  If the player has not                }
{ changed location, then nothing happens.                 }
{ If the player has visited the same place                }
{ recently, then just the short description               }
{ is displayed.                                           }
{---------------------------------------------------------}

PROCEDURE show;
VAR
  i: INTEGER;
BEGIN

  IF (chgloc) OR
     (ord (where) > ord (nowhere))
  THEN
  BEGIN

    IF (visited[location] = 1) OR
       ((visited[location] MOD 4) = 0) OR
       (ord (where) > ord (nowhere))
    THEN
    BEGIN

      WITH places[where] DO
      BEGIN

        FOR i := dbegin TO dend DO
        BEGIN

          seek (narrate, i);
```

```
        get (narrate);
        write (narrate^);

      END { FOR i := ... };
    END { WITH places[where] };

  END
  ELSE
  BEGIN

    write ('You are ');
    writeln (places[where].name);

  END { IF visited[location] = 1 ... };

 END { IF chgloc };

 IF ord (where) < ord (nowhere)
 THEN
   showgoodies;

END { PROCEDURE show };

{-----------------------------------------------}
{      s  h  o  w  g  o  o  d  i  e  s         }
{                                               }
{ Print a list of the objects present at the}
{ current adventure game location.              }
{-----------------------------------------------}

PROCEDURE showgoodies;
VAR
  lobj: goodies;
BEGIN

  FOR lobj := nuggets TO noobj DO
    IF lobj IN whatshere[location]
    THEN
    BEGIN

      IF lobj IN plurals
      THEN
        write ('There are some ')
      ELSE
        IF lobj IN somes
        THEN
```

```
            write ('There is some ')
          ELSE
            IF lobj IN useans
            THEN
              write ('There is an ')
            ELSE
              write ('There is a ')
            { END IF lobj IN useans }
          { END IF lobj IN somes }
        { END IF lobj IN plurals };

        write (objname[lobj]);
        writeln (' here.');

      END { IF lobj IN whatshere... }
    { END FOR lobj := ... };

END { PROCEDURE showgoodies };

{--------------------------------------------------}
{      o    b    j    l    o    o    k    u    p   }
{                                                  }
{ Determine if the name typed by the player }
{ in a carry or drop command is the name of }
{ any object actually part of the game.  If }
{ so, return the internal value of the      }
{ object in question.                       }
{--------------------------------------------------}

FUNCTION objlookup;
VAR
  lobj: goodies;
BEGIN

  objname[noobj] := tail;
  lobj := nuggets;

  WHILE tail <> objname[lobj] DO
    lobj := succ (lobj);
  objlookup := lobj;

END { FUNCTION objlookup };

{--------------------------------------------------}
{      c    k    g    o    o    d    i    e    s   }
{                                                  }
```

```
{ See if an object is present.                     }
{--------------------------------------------------}

FUNCTION ckgoodies;
BEGIN

  IF it IN whatshere[location]
  THEN
    ckgoodies := true
  ELSE
    ckgoodies := false
  { END IF it IN ... };

END { FUNCTION ckobject };

{--------------------------------------------------}
{          p    l    o    o    k                   }
{                                                  }
{ Implement the look command.  This forces         }
{ out the full description of the current          }
{ location.  The variables chgloc and              }
{ visited[location] must be temporarily            }
{ reset in order to accomplish this goal.          }
{--------------------------------------------------}

PROCEDURE plook;
VAR
  savchg:         BOOLEAN;
  savisit:        INTEGER;
BEGIN

  savchg  := chgloc;
  chgloc  := true;
  savisit := visited[location];
  visited[location] := 1;

  show (location);

  visited[location] := savisit;
  chgloc            := savchg;

END { PROCEDURE plook };

{--------------------------------------------------}
{  p   i   n   v   e   n   t   o   r   y           }
{                                                  }
```

```
{ Implement the inventory command.  Print    }
{ the names of all objects carried by the    }
{ player.                                    }
{--------------------------------------------}

PROCEDURE pinventory;
VAR
  lobj: goodies;
BEGIN

  IF stash <> []
  THEN
  BEGIN
    writeln ('You currently hold: ');
    FOR lobj := nuggets TO noobj DO
    BEGIN

      IF lobj IN stash
      THEN
        writeln (objname[lobj])
      { END IF };

    END { FOR lobj := ... };
  END { IF stash <> [] };

END { PROCEDURE pinventory };

BEGIN

  plurals := [ { Put in objects whose names
                 are plurals. }];
  somes   := [ { Put in objects whose
                 descriptions should begin
                 with "some" : there is some
                 silver here. } ];
  useans  := [ { Put in objects whose names
                 begin with a vowel. } ];

  cmdname[carry]        := 'carry';
  cmdname[drop]         := 'drop';
  cmdname[help]         := 'help';
  cmdname[invent]       := 'inventory';
  cmdname[tally]        := 'tally';
  cmdname[take]         := 'take';
  cmdname[score]        := 'score';
  cmdname[look]         := 'look';
```

```
  cmdname[quit]          := 'quit';
  cmdname[nocmd]         := 'sentinel';

  reset (xfile, 'skel.x');
  reset (narrate, 'skel');
  r := start;
  seek (xfile, 31);
  get (xfile);
  places[r] := xfile^;

  REPEAT

    r := succ (r);
    get (xfile);
    places[r] := xfile^;

  UNTIL r = lastdesc;

  { lastdesc represents the last identifier in  }
  { the descs enumerated type.                  }

  close (xfile);
  chgloc := true;
  { Force out description of start }

END.
```

SKELETON PROBLEMS UNIT

```
{-----------------------------------------------------}
{                                                     }
{    p  r  o  b  s        u  n  i  t                  }
{                                                     }
{ this unit contains the single function:             }
{ solved.  solved is passed an argument of type       }
{ 'problems'.  the argument corresponds to one        }
{ of the boolean expressions used to detect the       }
{ solution of problems and components of              }
{ problems.  the rest of the adventure code           }
{ uses code like:                                     }
{                                                     }
{       IF NOT solved (luretrolls)                    }
{       THEN                                          }
{                                                     }
{ instead of using the complex expressions.           }
{ the details of the problem expressions are          }
```

```
{ contained here and may be changed without       }
{ forcing the rest of the adventure game code     }
{ change as well.                                 }
{                                                 }
{-------------------------------------------------}

{$s+}

UNIT probs;

  INTERFACE

    USES  applestuff,
          {$usk1.code} advdata;

TYPE

  {-----------------------------------------------}
  {                                               }
  { The problems enumerated type declares         }
  { identifiers that are used in representing     }
  { components of problems.  Each identifier      }
  { has a Boolean expression associated with it.}
  { When that expression needs to be evaluated    }
  { anywhere in the Pascal code of the game,      }
  { the function 'solved' in the INTERFACE of     }
  { this unit is called with the identifier of    }
  { that expression as its argument:              }
  {                                               }
  {      solved (probx)                           }
  {                                               }
  {-----------------------------------------------}

  problems = (prob1, prob2, prob3, prob4);

FUNCTION solved (which: problems) : BOOLEAN;

  IMPLEMENTATION

FUNCTION solved;
BEGIN

  solved := FALSE;

  CASE which OF
```

```
    { Each problem identifier has its boolean    }
    { expression inserted in the corresponding   }
    { CASE in this statement.                    }

    prob1,
    prob2,
    prob3,
    prob4:        solved := TRUE;

  END { CASE which OF };

END { FUNCTION solved };

BEGIN
END.
```

SKELETON ADVENTURE 3 DATA

```
{------------------------------}
{ source file: sk1.text        }
{------------------------------}

{-----------------------------------------------------}
{                                                     }
{  r  o  o  m  s          u  n  i  t                  }
{                                                     }
{  Types and variables used by all other units }
{  in skeleton  adventure.  This includes the  }
{  descs enumerated type, extended to account  }
{  for some descriptions that are not actual   }
{  game locations.  The goodies type accounts  }
{  for all objects in the adventure and the    }
{  objname array contains names for all of     }
{  them (for use in descriptions and in        }
{   commands).                                 }
{                                                     }
{-----------------------------------------------------}

{$s+}

UNIT advdata;

  INTERFACE

    USES applestuff;
```

```
TYPE

  descs = (start, nowhere, special, helpspiel);

  rooms = start..nowhere;

  goodies = (lamp, noobj);

  collection = SET OF goodies;

VAR

  location:     rooms;

  stash:        collection;

  whatshere:    ARRAY[rooms] OF collection;
  visited:      ARRAY[rooms] OF INTEGER;
  objname:      ARRAY[goodies] OF STRING[15];

  turns:        INTEGER;
  done:         BOOLEAN;

FUNCTION rand (low, high: INTEGER) : INTEGER;

  IMPLEMENTATION

VAR

  r:    rooms;
  { loop control for initialization }

FUNCTION rand;
VAR
  mx, c, d: INTEGER;
BEGIN
  rand := 0;
  IF low = high
  THEN
    rand := low
  ELSE
  BEGIN

    c := high - low + 1;
    mx := (maxint - high + low) DIV c + 1;
```

```
    mx := mx * (high - low) + (mx - 1);

    REPEAT
      d := random
    UNTIL d <= mx;
    rand := low + d MOD c;

  END { IF low = high };

END { FUNCTION rand };

BEGIN

  location := start;

  objname[lamp] := 'lamp';

  FOR r := start TO chasm DO
  BEGIN

    whatshere[r] := [];
    visited[r]   := 0;

  END { FOR r := start ... };

  whatshere[start] := [lamp];
  stash      := [];
  turns      := 0;
  done       := false;

END.
```

Appendix B
The Adventure 2 Database

In these final appendices I provide you with the source for the descriptions databases used in Adventures 2 and 3. This source is for use with the MAKEDESC program described in the text.

In order to make the text fit on the printed page, the long lines of description used in the MAKEDESC source have often been split into two parts. Every place this has been done, the end of the first line of the resulting two lines has been marked with a plus sign, +. Should you type this into your computer system, remove the + sign from the ends of such lines and "tack on" the following line to form a single line of close to 80 characters.

```
$START
You are standing by a hole in the ground.+
It looks big enough to climb
down.
$GRANDROOM
You are in a huge open room, with an immense+
expanse of ceiling.  A dark
passage leads west and a narrow crawl+
leads downward.
$VESTIBULE
You are in the entrance to a cave of passageways.+
There are halls leading
off to the north, south, and east.  Above you+
is a tunnel leading to the
surface.
```

```
$NARROW1
You are in a narrow passage that continues to+
the north.  It is extremely
narrow to the south.  A very tight crawl also+
leads east.  A curious odor
seeps through it.  I would think twice before+
trying to go that way.
$LAKESHORE
You are on the shore of a vast underground lake.+
Narrow passages wind away to
the east and south.  A small island is visible+
in the center of the lake to
the north.
$ISLAND
You are on a small island in the center of a+
huge underground lake.  Dark,
frigid waters surround you on all sides.+
You can barely make out the
shoreline to the south.  A message is scratched+
in the dirt here.  It says:
'The treasure may be found in the maze.'
$BRINK
You are on the brink of a steep incline.+
The bottom of a pit is over fifty
feet below you.  You could probably slide+
down safely, but I won't promise you
that you could climb back up.  To the west is a+
rubble-filled tunnel.  A
vampire bat just flew out of it shrieking.
$ICEROOM
You are in a room whose walls are formed from+
a deep blue crystalline ice.  To
the north a narrow tunnel opens.  From the other+
end of this tunnel an ominous
growling sound may be heard.  To the east a+
sparkling luminesence emanates
from a broad opening.  To the west a passage+
leads back to the vestibule.
$OGREROOM
You are in a low room whose walls are covered+
with grisly dark gouts of dried
blood.  The center of the room is dominated by+
a firepit, which contains
burned out coals and a long spit suspended over+
its center.  From one corner
emanates a horrible growling noise like that of+
```

```
some unspeakable monster
dreaming of rending you limb from limb+
and making you its dinner.
$NARROW2
You are in a very narrow east/west passage.+
To the west the passage opens
out by a lake shore.  To the east it becomes+
even tighter than it is here.
You might be able to squeeze through if you try+
real hard.  There is also a
strange looking alcove in the south wall that+
seems to open into a very dark
tunnel.
$PIT
You are at the bottom of a fifty foot pit.+
The walls are just a hair too
steep to climb.  The pit is empty except for a+
few old dried bones.  I can't
tell whether they are human or not!!  In the+
center of the pit is a narrow
shinny leading further downward.
$CRYSTAL
You are in a dazzling hall of crystal glass.+
It is intensely cold here, but
also chillingly beautiful.  There are glass+
formations rising from the floor
as if they had grown there, yet delicately+
sculptured with multi-faceted
sides.  A searing white light shines+
blindingly through the floor, itself
formed from fine mirror smooth lead crystal.+
The light sets off reflections
that corruscate through the room and make+
it virtually impossible to tell
where the room begins and where it ends.+
There might be an exit to the east,
although my eyes could be betraying me.
$BATSCAVE
You are in a steep cavern filled with+
shrieking vampire bats.  They swoop and
dive at you by the thousands.  I would+
suggest a hurried departure.  There are
openings to the west and north.
$STEAM
You have entered a room filled with a+
stifling steamy vapor.  There are
```

```
innumerable small geysers scattered about+
the floor of the room, each
contributing its own steam to the general mist.+
To the west is a dark opening
and another to the north.  Further out in the+
middle of the room an opening in
the floor is barely visible through the mist.+
Some of the vapor seems to ooze
through the opening as if it continued downward.
$DEADEND
This is a dead end.  There is a cryptic message+
etched in the stone of the
walls here.  It reads:+
'GOOD THINGS GO THROUGH SMALL PASSAGES.'
$LADDER
You are at the base of a huge ladder reaching up+
and out of sight.  It must
extend up at least 500 feet.  It will take+
someone very brave in heart to
scale it.  There are also passages here which+
lead to the north and down.
$MAZE
You are in a maze of featureless passages.
$STAIRS
You are on a steep stairway of rough-hewn+
granite blocks.  Your lamp only
penetrates the gloom for a few feet in either+
direction.  Above you is a
doorway leading to a large room.  Below is a+
dark and drafty continuation of
the stairway.
$ECHOES
You are in a vast underground cavern. The+
slightest sound seems to create a
resonating wave of echoes.  It is difficult to+
even hear yourself think.  To
the north an opening leads to a downward+
slanting corridor which quickly bends
out of sight.  In the center of the cavern,+
there is a set of rough stairs
leading downward.  Behind you a similar set+
of stairs leads upward.
$WARMROOM
You are in a confined space which is more like+
a widening of the corridor than
a room.  The corridor itself ends abruptly here,+
```

```
but a narrow shaft opens
downward.  There is a faint red glow to be seen+
if one peers into the shaft
and a warm draft of slightly sulfurous+
smelling air emanates from that open-
ing.  The corridor slants downward to the south.
$INCLINE
You are in a twisting, downward slanting corridor.+
The corridor forms a
Y-shaped intersection here with passages leading+
up, east, and west.
$HONEYCOMB
You are in a room with numerous honeycomb-like+
openings leading out.  The
largest of these appears to lead south.
$ROUNDROOM
You are in an almost spherically shaped room+
with exits to the west, north,
and down.
$MUDROOM
You are in a room filled with thick, knee-deep mud.+
Trickles of water flow in
from a narrow opening high above you on the+
west wall.  A passage leads up
from here and another down.
$DEEPPOOL
You are standing by a deep underground pool.+
The water is ice cold, but clear
as crystal.  There is nary a ripple on the surface.
$COLDROOM
You are at the bottom of an icy cold underground+
pool.  If you don't get out
quickly, you'll either drown or freeze to death+
or both.
$NARROW3
You are in a slanting N-S passage.
$NARROW4
You are in a sloping N-S passage.  A narrow slit+
opens downward, from which
emanates a warm, sulfurous draft.  A very faint+
red glow may also be seen
through the slit.
$RIVER
You are standing on the eastern shore of a swiftly+
running N-S underground
river.
```

```
$ROCKYROOM
You are in a room filled with irregularly shaped+
boulders.  To the east a low
opening below a huge boulder leads to an+
alcove of some sort, and to the south
the passage continues along the river bank.
$SILTROOM
You are near a large underground deposit of silt.+
A passage leads upward.
From it steadily oozes a flow of thick mud which+
must contribute to the
deposit.  Passages also lead north and west.
$ALCOVE
You are in a small nook off a large room+
filled with boulders.  The only exit
is to the east.  To the west you can see into+
the boulder room, but the exit
is blocked by a large, slippery boulder.+
A note here says: KEEP ON DIGGING!
$FLAMES
Unfortunately, you have fallen into an+
underground lava pocket.  It is the
source of the heat that produces the geysers+
in the steam room.  You have
been, to put it politely, 'toasted to a crisp!'
```

Appendix C
The Adventure 3 Database

```
$at the spectacular mountain view
You are in mountains.  To see all the snow-capped+
monsters hereabouts,
you would need to look up and turn in a full+
circle.  Near here is a
deserted monastery.  It is said that a sect of+
mountain worshippers once
lived there.  It is reputed that they have hidden+
various treasures in
these parts.  It is also said that somewhere in+
these mountains there
lives a wise seer who knows the secrets of life.+
Perhaps you will be
able to locate him.  Should you succeed in+
finding him and learning his
ways, you will receive many rewards.  Watch out+
for treacherous passages.
Do not necessarily believe all you see and hear.
$walking along a steep mountain trail
You are walking along a steep mountain trail.+
The footing is tricky
here.  Several snow-capped peaks are now visible+
```

```
in front of you.
$walking along a narrow mountain trail
You are walking along a narrow mountain trail.+
The footing is tricky
here.  Several snow-capped peaks are now visible+
in front of you.
$on a steep mountain trail
You are walking along a steep mountain trail.+
The footing is tricky
here.  Many snow-capped peaks are now visible+
in front of you.
$on a narrow mountain trail
You are walking along a narrow mountain trail.+
The footing is tricky
here.  Many snow-capped peaks are now visible+
in front of you.
$walking along a steep trail
You are walking along a steep mountain trail.+
The footing is very
tricky here.  You see snow-capped peaks in+
front of you.
$walking along a narrow trail
You are walking along a narrow mountain trail.+
The footing is very
tricky here.  You see snow-capped peaks in+
front of you.  I seem to
remember having been here before.
$scrambling through a rock-strewn col
You are scrambling through a rock-strewn col.+
Above and below you are
ledges that look safer than where you are now.+
Every now and then I
hear faint echoes of churlish voices.  It is+
difficult to tell from
which direction they come.
$in a tricky, rock-strewn col
You are trying very hard not to lose your+
footing.  This is a very
tricky, rock-strewn col.  Above and below you+
are faily secure looking
ledges.  They are quite a distance in either+
direction, but I think
you could make it to either one safely if you+
are careful.
$in a col with ledges above and below
You are scrambling through a rock-strewn col.+
```

```
Above and below you are
ledges that look safer than where you are now.+
Every now and then I
hear faint echoes of churlish voices.  It is+
difficult to tell which
direction they come from.
$in a rocky col
You are in a rocky col.  It is difficult to+
see anything from here as
you cling to the mountain.  The air is cold+
and the wind whistles as
it blows across the bare rock-scape.
$in a rubble filled hollow
This is a rubble filled hollow.  Talus from the+
higher points in the
surrounding terrain has accumulated here over+
the eons.  It is quite
difficult to maintain your footing in places.
$in a hollow filled with rubble
"
$at a grassy mound
You have surmounted a grassy mound.  There is+
a pleasant meadow here
filled with colorful wildflowers.  The+
fragrance is stimulating.  I
think I see an ancient looking building in the+
distance.  It is
partially hidden from view.
$at an ancient monastery
You have found the ancient monastery.  The+
building is partially
collapsed and all the entrances have been+
blocked with undergrowth or
boarded up with great hand-hewn planks of what+
looks like very hard
wood.  The tatters of what must once have been+
a flag flutter in the
light breeze from a high and pointed parapet.+
There is almost total
silence here apart from the sighing of the wind+
and the noise of birds
and small animals.  Yet there seems to be a+
ghostly echo of gongs,
cymbals, plaintive and monotonous chanting, and+
a rushing noise like
fire consuming an enormous pile of dead branches+
```

```
and leaves.  It leaves
an impression in the mind alone - the ears hear+
none of it.
The building leans into the sides of the steep+
mountain path.  Leading
to the now blocked front entrance is a set of+
broad wooden stairs.  Set
into the bottom of this staircase is a+
windowless wooden gate.  It is
hanging askew from its rotten hinges - I think+
you could squeeze by it
if you wished to.
$in a dank and musty cellar
You are in a dank and musty cellar.  It looks+
like it might have once
been a storeroom for the monastery.  There are+
empty barrels standing along
the back wall.  There are rows of dusty shelves,+
mostly empty save for an
accumulation of cobwebs.  In the floor are two+
trapdoors or hatches made
of the same rough-hewn planks seen outside.+
They both shut tightly.
$in an ancient catacomb
This is an ancient catacomb directly under the+
monastery.  The light is
extremely dim coming only from the cellar above+
down the steep stone
staircase.  The floor is littered with bones.+
Bits of what appears to
be dried flesh still cling to them in many cases.
$on a steep mountain slope
You are on a steep mountain slope.  There is no+
vegetation here, you
have passed beyond the treeline.  The bare+
granite peeks out here and
there from beneath the fresh dusting of snow.+
There are massive drifts
to either side.  Tread lightly, avalanches are+
easily caused here by
sudden noises.
$on a slope beyond the treeline
You are on a steep mountain slope.  There is no+
vegetation here, as you
have passed beyond the treeline.  You see bare+
granite here and
```

```
there from beneath the fresh dusting of snow.+
There are massive drifts
on either side.  Tread lightly, avalanches are+
easily caused here by
sudden noises.
$on a slope surrounded by drifts
You are on a steep mountain slope.  There is+
not any vegetation here.
You are past the treeline.  Bare granite peeks+
from beneath the fresh
snow.  There are also massive drifts to either+
side of the narrow trail.
I would be extremely careful about loud+
noises - avalanches have been
known to be caused by incautious travelers.
$on a slope bereft of vegetation
You are on a steep mountain slope.  There is+
not any vegetation here.
You are past the treeline.  Bare granite peeks+
from beneath the fresh
snow.  There are also massive drifts to either+
side of the narrow trail.
I would be extremely careful about loud+
noises - avalanches have been
known to be caused by incautious travelers.
$on a slope with granite underfoot
You are on a steep mountain slope.  There is+
not any vegetation here.
You are past the treeline.  Bare granite peeks+
from beneath the fresh
snow.  There are also massive drifts to either+
side of the narrow trail.
I would be extremely careful about loud+
noises - avalanches have been
known to be caused by incautious travelers.
$in a deep ravine
You are in a deep ravine.  All you can see is+
the tattered clouds
above.  They are racing along beneath the blue+
sky, carried by the
calamitous mountain gales.
$in a deep crevass
You are in a deep crevass.  There is a ridge+
above you - I think you
might be able to scramble back up with some effort.
$in a bitterly cold deep ravine
```

```
You are in a deep ravine.  All you can see is+
the tattered clouds
above.  They are racing along beneath the blue+
sky, carried by the
calamitous mountain gales.  Although the sun+
appears now and then
it is bitterly cold here.
$on a steep pitch
You are on a very steep pitch.  The bare rock+
beneath your feet is
treacherous in the extreme.  Any false moves+
here and you will not live
to tell your grandchildren about them.
$on an extremely steep pitch
"
$on a very steep pitch
"
$on a steep pitch with bare rock
"
$on a pitch with bare rock
"
$on a mountain peak
You have reached a magnificent mountain peak.+
All around you lies the
grandeur of the mountain range.  You can see+
several other peaks.  They
look so near you could almost reach out and+
touch them, yet they must
be several miles away, even as the crow flies.+
The wind here howls in
your ears, but does not diminish your pleasure+
in the vista.
$on a splendid peak
"
$on a magnificent peak
"
$on a grand mountain peak
"
$on a peak
"
$atop a saddle like formation
You are atop a saddle like formation.+
In some directions there are
dropoffs and in others the trail continues upward.
$on a saddle
"
```

```
$atop a saddle
"
$in a mountain cave
This is a mountain cave.  It continues on into+
the heart of the
mountain.  The passageway is very narrow and+
filled with debris.
There are pits in the floor of the cave.+
Some contain the remnants
of fires: charred wood and ashes.  Some of the+
wood is very strange
looking - sort of whiteish and quite long and narrow.
$deep in a cave
You are in a cave in the very root of the+
mountain.  It is pitch
black in here.  I wouldn't stay long - there are+
nameless things which
see in the dark.
$in a dimly lit mountain cave
This is a mountain cave.  The light here is dim,+
but further along
the passage there appears to be an opening from+
which it issues.
There is a draft coming from the darker side of+
the passageway.  It
whistles along and now and then seems to whisper.+
You can almost
make out faint words, but they make you shudder+
and want to turn
away.
$in a cave
This is a mountain cave.  The light here is dim,+
but further along
the passage there appears to be an opening from+
which it issues.
You feel a slight draft on your face.
$in a cave in pitch dark
You are in a cave in the very root of a mountain.+
It is intensely
dark here - you cannot see a hand held inches from+
your face.  As you
move, you brush against tendrils of a feathery+
substance.  It makes
your flesh crawl.
$in a cave with bones strewn about
This is a mountain cave.  There are remnants of+
```

```
cooking fires here.
There are old bones strewn on the floor.+
There are strange looking
runes or symbols of some sort carved into the walls.
$in a shallow gully
You are in a shallow gully.+
It seems to deepen further ahead.
$in a deepening gully
You are in a deepening gully.  In one+
direction it seems shallower.
I can't say for sure, but in the other direction+
there may be an
opening into the side of the mountain.
$on a barren hill
You have surmounted a barren hill.  There is the+
barest hint of foliage
here, but most has succumbed to the rigorous+
climate and the altitude.
$at a sheltered place
This is a sheltered place in the path.  It is a+
very deep cut in the
side of the mountain, not quite a cave, but much+
more than a mere
depression.
$on a narrow ridge
This is a narrow ridge.  The trail is only a foot+
or so wide here and
negotiating it will be quite a challenge.+
There are precipitous
dropoffs in some directions and the chasm yawns+
beneath you.
$on a very narrow ridge
This is a narrow ridge.  The trail is only a foot+
or so wide here and
negotiating it will be quite a challenge.+
There are precipitous
dropoffs in some directions and the chasm yawns+
beneath you.
$at the grandest peak
You have reached the grandest peak in the entire+
mountain range.  Here
there is almost an entire acre of flat from which+
to view the
surrounding peaks.  All of the other pinnacles+
are spread out beneath
the one you have reached.
```

```
On the far side of the small flat of the peak is+
a wizened old man.
He appears to have been here quite some time.+
Perhaps he can tell you
some interesting tales.
$chasm
You have fallen off the mountain side.+
The chasm that yawned beneath
you has claimed you for its own.  The drop of+
several thousand feet may
not have been enough to finish you off, but the+
sudden stop at the
bottom certainly was.
$nowhere
$cellardown
$at fountain of youth
You have located the fountain of youth.+
Never a wrinkle shall grace your
countenance.  Your quest is culminated.+
Congratulations.
$trtalk
There are several huge, ugly mountain trolls+
lolling nearby.
Unfortunately, they have spotted you.+
Quickly and rudely you are
surrounded and bound with rough thongs of+
ragged and grisly leather.  No
doubt the remains of the trolls last and+
(for them) meagre meal.  Now
they have you!!
With great gusto they truss you up to a+
gnarled and charred hardwood spit.
This, of course, is accompanied by flaying+
you and using the strips of your
flesh to make your bonds even more secure.+
They then slowly roast you to
a turn over their hastily built fire.+
You make a fine meal for these
famished, gluttonous villains.
The last sounds heard by your erstwhile,+
but discretely hidden, guide are
those of vast troll contentment.  Snores,+
great rude belches, slavering over
the last remnants of roasted flesh on what+
were your bones, and other more
unspeakable sounds.  I beat a hasty+
```

```
retreat from this gruesome location and
bid you better luck in your next+
re-incarnation.
$wmmblab
The wise man of the mountain speaks:
'I am exceedingly pleased at your obeisance+
and your gifts.  In return
for your devotion, I offer you a word.+
That word is: wadda.  Use it well,
my son.'
$wmmharp
The wise man of the mountain lifts a deep+
hood covering his face.  He gazes
at the items arrayed before him and speaks:
'You give me great displeasure oh profligate+
servant.  Of silver and gold
I will have none.  Treasures of the earth+
are but transitory baubles to be
scorned and discarded.  Take them from my+
sight and bring me gifts of worth
to the spirit.  I would sooner have one molar+
from the jaw of a troll than all
these worldly goods.  If you seek my wisdom,+
you will heed this charge.'
$wmmhello
The garbed figure comes toward you.+
He speaks:
'Welcome, my child.  You have achieved much+
simply to reach my mountain peak.
If you bring to me the treasures that I seek,+
then you shall know the secret
of everlasting youth!  Go now and fulfill+
your quest.'
$wmmsp1
The wise man speaks:
'So you return, my child.  I have been+
exceedingly occupied by my efforts at
omphaloskepsis.  You will excuse me if I+
do not linger.'
$wmmsp2
The wise man speaks:
'A seer once told me that only those who+
persist succeed in finding the true
secrets of existence.  Do not despair, your+
quest has just begun.  You have
much to learn and much to gain.  I must+
```

```
now feed and tend my yak.'
$wmmsp3
The wise man speaks:
'Have you read any good scrolls+
lately my child?'
$wmmsp4
The wise man speaks:
'Contemplation is good for the soul, my+
child.  But music and prayer also heal
many wounds.'
$wmmsp5
The wise man speaks:
'All that is gold does not glitter,+
my child.  A little wine for the stomach's
sake.  A stitch in time saves nine.+
Don't take any wooden nickels.  A flush
beats two pair any day, but then I don't+
have indoor plumbing up here.  Am I
boring you?  Maybe I should go say my prayers.'
$tgablure
The trolls seem very excited.  I can't+
tell what they want more - you or
those bones you are carrying.
$tgabbones
The trolls seem to have lost interest+
in you - at least for the moment.
They are gathered around the bones+
you have dropped.
Wait...  They are attacking the bones+
with great gusto.  There are crunching
noises and sounds of breaking teeth.+
I would take this opportunity to make
tracks.
$trhungry
Several huge, ugly, mountain trolls are+
lolling nearby.  Unfortunately,
they have spotted you.  They slaver and+
utter gutteral blasphemies.  They
gaze longingly at the bones you are+
carrying.  They rise.  They seem to
want to follow you.  I would find a good,+
out of the way place to ditch
those bones if I were you!
$trfollow
You are being shadowed by several huge,+
hairy, rude, and hungry mountain
```

trolls. They slaver and mumble in their+
gutteral speech. You can barely
understand, but the general idea is that+
they are famished and want bones
and flesh. Perhaps it is yours+
that they will get!

Index

Index

A

Adams, Scott, 1
Adventure, 1
Adventure code, 191
Adventure databases, structure of, 177
Adventure language, 191
Adventure on disk, 191
Adventure 1, 15
Adventure 1, data declarations for, 18
Adventure 1, functions and procedures, 18
Adventure 1, listing for, 23-53
Adventure 1, program code outline for, 17
Adventure 1, structure diagram, 21
Adventure 1, the map of, 55
Adventure 1, the maze map of, 56
Adventure 3, 192
Adventure 3, code outline of, 193-195
Adventure 3, database for, 250, 292
Adventure 3, extending, 254
Adventure 3, listing for, 203
Adventure 3, map of 197-201
Adventure 3, problems in, 245
Adventure 3, problems of, 201
Adventure 3, program outline of, 193
Adventure 3, relation of units for, 196
Adventure 3, summary map of, 196
Adventure 3, units in, 239
Adventure 2, 68
Adventure 2, database for, 286
Adventure 2, data declarations, 70
Adventure 2, listing for 78-114
Adventure 2, main program block, 73
Adventure 2, map for, 75, 76
Adventure 2, problems in, 130
Adventure 2, problems of, 77
Adventure 2, procedures and function, 71, 72
Adventure 2, program outline, 69
Adventure 2, structure diagram, 74
Adventures, systematic approach to writing, 256
Adventures, writer's checklist for, 256
AND, 131
Apple II, 12

B

Backup disks, 143
Beings, 1, 4, 6
Block structured, 63
Boolean expressions, 131
Boolean operators, 131
Boolean variable, 130
Browse, 145
Browse program, 175, 181

C

Case statements, 59
Clues, 8
Cmdlookup function, 116, 118
Code file, 241
Command dispatcher, 116
Command handling code, 116
Command processing, 115
Commands, 115
Continuation file instruction lines, 170
Controlling the game, 60, 115
Conversion of representations, 120
Conversion of values, 119
Crowther, Willie, viii

D

Database, 137, 177, 250, 286, 292
Database concepts, 145
Database index, 145
Database of descriptions, creating a, 166
Declarations, local, 63
Description lines, 168
Descriptions, 190
Descriptions index, 177
Dig command, 138
Direction, deciding on a, 61
Ditto lines, 169
Docommand procedure, 116, 118
Dungeons and Dragons, ix

E

Eat command, 138

Editor limitations, 139
Embellising the map, 6
Enumerated type, 54
Enumerated types, 118, 131
Escape key, 143
Events, 130
Exploration, 3

F

File creating program, 174
File managing, 139
File reading program, 174
File variables, 137
Files, loss of, 142-143
Files, random access, 173
Files, sequential, 173

H

Hash function, 184
Hashing, 182-183
Hash table, 185
Hash value, 183-184
Head string, 117, 120
Help command, 137

I

Index files, 177
Infocom, vii

K

K(runch command, 141

L

Lamp command, 137
Light command, 137
Linear search, 121
Linear searches, 183
Linked lists, 183
Linking, 198
Linking programs, 242
Listen procedure, 116, 118
Local procedures, 63-64
Location, the adventurer's, 60
Locations, 1, 2, 5
Locations, changing, 60-61
Logic, 9
Logical connectives, 131
Lookup techniques, 183

M

Main program, 240
Main program block, 17
Makedesc, 145, 167
Makedesc, running, 171
Make80 database generator listing, 147
Map, 254
Map layout, 6
Map organization, 6
Maps, 192
Menu-driven, 13
Microsoft, Inc. vii
Monsters, 1, 4, 6

N

Nested functions, 63
Nested procedures, 63
Nocmd, 123
NOT, 131

O

Objects, 1, 3, 6
Objlookup, 128
Ogre, 138
Operator procedure, 132
OR, 131

P

Parser, 115
Parsers, 116
Pascal, ix, 12
Pcarry, 127
Pcarry procedure, 128
Pdrop, 127
Pflames procedure, 67
Pisland procedure, 66
Placename, 168
Pladder procedure, 67
Pnarrow procedure, 67
Pogreroom procedure, 67
Postconditions, 132
Ppit procedure, 67
Preconditions, 132
Prefix #5, 141
Problem difficulty, 9
Problems, 2, 4, 6, 130
Pstart procedure, 67
Pvestibule procedure, 67

R

Random access, 175
Relational operators, 131
Repeatability, 9
Rooms, 1, 2, 5

S

Scanners, 116
Scoring, 137
Search, linear, 121
Searching, 121, 122, 183
Semantics, 240
Sentinels, 118, 123
Set, 125
Set relationships, 131
Set variables, 127
Sierra On-Line, ix
Skeleton, 66
Skeleton adventure, 256
Skeleton adventure, listing for, 261
Source file, 139, 140
Special conditions, 2
String comparison, 122
Structured design, 16
Surprise, 10
Swapping mode, 141
Symbol tables, 182
Syntax, 240

T

Tail string, 117, 120
Template, 66
Travel, 136
Travel, simplification of, 136
Travel indicators, 5
Travel procedure, 116
Treasures, 1, 3
Turns, counting of, 135

U

Unit, implementation part of, 241
Unit, interface part of, 241
Units, programming in, 239
USCD, ix, 13
USCD limitations, 252
Uses statement, 242

V

Values, external, 119
Values, internal, 119
Variables, file, 137

W

Whichway function, 116
Woods, Don, viii
Writer's checklist, 256

Z

ZORK, 1

Edited by Marilyn L. Johnson

Programming Your Own Adventure Games in Pascal

If you are intrigued with the possibilities of the program included in *Programming Your Own Adventure Games in Pascal* (TAB Book No. 1768), you should definitely consider having the ready-to-run tape containing the software applications. This software is guaranteed free of manufacturer's defects. (If you have any problems, return the disk within 30 days, and we'll send you a new one.) Not only will you save the time and effort of typing the programs, the disk eliminates the possibility of errors that can prevent the programs from functioning. Interested?

Available on disk for Apple II, II+ with 48K, Apple language card or other 16K RAM card, and Apple Pascal system; Apple *//e* with Apple Pascal system at $19.95 for each tape or disk plus $1.00 each shipping and handling.

I'm interested. Send me:

_______ disk for Apple II, II+, *//e* (requires Apple Pascal system) (6229S)

_______ TAB BOOKS catalog

_______ Check/Money Order enclosed for $19.95
plus $1.00 shipping and handling for each tape or disk ordered.

_______ VISA _______ MasterCard

Account No. _______________ Expires _______________

Name _______________

Address _______________

City _______________ State _______ Zip _______

Signature _______________

Mail to: **TAB BOOKS Inc.**
P.O. Box 40
Blue Ridge Summit, PA 17214

(Pa. add 6% sales tax. Orders outside U.S. must be prepaid with international money orders in U.S. dollars.)

TAB 1768